17/5/94

The Media Interview

Confession, Contest, Conversation

COMMUNICATION AND CULTURE SERIES

Series editor: Gunther Kress

Titles in the series

Communication and Culture edited by Gunther Kress
Radio in Australia by John Potts
Engendered Fiction : The Production and Reception of Texts
 by Anne Cranny-Francis
Textual Spaces: Aboriginality and Cultural Studies
 by Stephen Muecke
The Media Interview: Confession, Contest, Conversation
 by Philip Bell and Theo van Leeuwen

Forthcoming titles

Contemporary Television in Australia
 by Stewart Cunningham and Toby Miller

THE MEDIA INTERVIEW
Confession, Contest, Conversation

*Philip Bell and
Theo van Leeuwen*

*To our mothers, Rita Bell and Pien van Leeuwen-de Jong,
who taught us to seek answers and ask questions*

Published by
UNIVERSITY OF NEW SOUTH WALES PRESS
Kensington NSW Australia 2052
Phone (02) 398 8900
Fax (02) 398 3408

© 1994 Philip Bell and Theo van Leeuwen

First published in 1994

This book is copyright. Apart from any fair
dealing for the purpose of private study,
research, criticism or review, as permitted under
the Copyright Act, no part may be reproduced by
any process without written permission.
Inquiries should by addressed to the publisher.

National Library of Australia
Cataloguing-in-Publication entry:

Bell, Philip.
The media interview: confession, contest, conversation.

   Bibliography.
   Includes index.
   ISBN 0 86840 389 X.

   1. Interviewing in radio. 2. Interviewing in television.
   I. Van Leeuwen, Theo. II. Title.

302.234

Available in North America through:
S.B.S. Inc.
5804 N.E. Hassalo Street
Portland Oregon 97213–3644
Tel: (503) 287 3093
Fax: (503) 280 8832

Typeset in 11/12.5 pt Garamond by
Graphic Partners, Parramatta NSW
Printed by Southwood Press, Marrickville NSW

Contents

ACKNOWLEDGMENTS   vii

CHAPTER 1:   Questions in society   1

Questions and answers • The advantages of the interviewer • Interviews in their social context • Media interviews •

CHAPTER 2:   A short history of the modern media interview   28

Interviews as evidence and entertainment • Documentary impulses — reality, subjectivity and 'depth' • The interview as a documentary scenario — Oriana Fallaci. •

CHAPTER 3:   Caroline Jones and the search for meaning   60

Caroline Jones interviews Margot Cairnes on ABC Radio • The confessional interview • The revelatory genre • From confession to reflection • Closure: the revelation of meaning • Non-verbal aspects • Private religion on the public medium • An interview with Caroline Jones •

CHAPTER 4:   Political interviews: the adversarial genre   124

Paul Lyneham interviews Andrew Peacock • The political interviewer as 'honest broker' • The adversarial genre • Questions and answers in the adversarial interview • The political interview as television spectacle • Corporatist governments and non-partisan parties • An interview with Paul Lyneham •

CHAPTER 5:   Aspel and Co: the talkshow interview   178

Michael Aspel interviews Norman Tebbit • The exceptional and the ordinary • The conversational interview • The real and the role • Television and talk in the nineties • An interview with Michael Aspel •

CHAPTER 6:   Interviewing: the first word or the last word   222

Curiosity and power in the media interview • Marcel: an interview with Godard • Power and publicity • Ethics, interviewing and the future •

ENDNOTES	246
NAME INDEX	252
SUBJECT INDEX	255

Acknowledgments

We wish to thank several people whose hard work and co-operation made this book possible.

Jan Knapman has patiently and skilfully typed and re-typed versions of the manuscript, unflustered by our frequent revisions and inconsistencies. Marco Milic assisted with research and transcription. David Clark-Duff helped with technical aspects of our work. To them our sincere thanks.

This project was supported by a Macquarie University Research Grant.

Caroline Jones, Paul Lyneham and Michael Aspel gave generously of their time, allowing us to interview them and to reproduce their interviews. Their willingness to reflect on their own professional roles is greatly appreciated. Not all media professionals are as open to criticism.

Gunther Kress, the editor of this series, has consistently encouraged us in our attempts to investigate the semiotics of interviews. To him and to Julia Collingwood at New South Wales University Press, who facilitated the project by accepting that it was not too esoteric, our thanks. Our students and colleagues at Macquarie University have also stimulated us to think about media interviews in the way we have, and we hope that they will find our book of interest.

We with to thank the following for permission to reproduce excerpts of published or broadcast material:

ABC Enterprises for Caroline Jones' interview;

London Weekend Television for Michael Aspel's interview;

The British Film Institute for excerpts from the Godard/Miéville interview from *Sur et Sous la Communication;*

Cambridge University Press for except from E.M. Goody, *Questions and Politeness;*

Routledge (Methuen) for excerpt from J. Curran in M. Gurevitch *et al* (eds), *Culture Society and the Media.*

Pam Macmillan for excerpt from the *Great Shark Hunt* by Hunter S. Thompson.

Jean Rouch (Argos Films) *Chronique d'un Eté* by Edgar Morin.

Every effort has been made to trace the sources of material contained in this book. Where the effort has been unsuccessful, the publisher would be pleased to hear from copyright holders to rectify any errors or omissions.

1
Questions in Society

The interview has become a dominant mode of conveying information in the broadcasting media. Much of our news and current affairs show us, not what happened, but what people say about what happened (or might have happened, or will happen), and makes us eye- (and ear-) witnesses, not of events that would have occurred if no microphones and cameras had been present, but of events specially created for the purpose of being reported, such as press conferences and interviews.

These events always take the form of question and answer exchanges. Politicians now prefer being interviewed to giving speeches, because they believe that the public sees interviews as more reliable and truthful than other modes of address — in interviews they can be seen to speak 'spontaneously' and 'intimately' to the public, and the 'spontaneous' is generally seen as more truthful than the premeditated and the posed. People are continually interviewed in the streets of our cities and asked their reactions to the affairs of the day. Their impromptu answers are taken as representative of the feelings of the public, and used to legitimate or undermine the actions of those in power. Stars of stage and screen and other celebrities chat amicably and intimately with interviewers about their private lives, and so can become role models for the public, at once close to us and remaining at an Olympian distance. And these are only some of the many ways in which interviews are used in the media.

It is, then, both surprising and not-so-surprising that interviews have received relatively little attention in the now abundant critical literature on the mass media: surprising in view of the importance of interviews as a form of communication and a form of culture; not-so-surprising, perhaps, because interviews are now seen as the most natural and obvious way of gathering and disseminating information. They are taken for granted, as much by the mass media themselves as by the disciplines from which studies about the mass media tend to come — after all, these disciplines also place great trust in the information derived from interviews and questionnaires.

In this book we will not take interviewing for granted, but investigate it critically, examining the beliefs on which it rests. We will try to show that interviewing, as practised in the mass media, is not natural and universal, but a recent and culturally specific invention. And, above all, we will look in detail at how interviews work, for only this can provide answers to such critical questions as, when are interviews merely instruments for the production and reproduction of ideological consensus? When are they genuine, open, public, exchanges of knowledge and experience? When are they techniques of power rather than tools for radical questioning?

Questions and Answers

Question-and-answer exchanges in which one person asks the questions and another gives the answers play an important role in contemporary Western society. It is through the asking of questions that our notion of democracy is realised, with elected representatives of the people asking questions of government ministers or, more recently, with governments setting up 'hotlines' to allow citizens to ask questions. In police investigations and courtroom procedures, interrogations play a key role in establishing the facts on which judgment will be based, and although stories of 'false confessions' surface from time to time, such methods are rarely questioned. In schools and universities questioning is the dominant mode of teaching — though not of learning. In the social sciences, knowledge is constantly produced through the asking of questions, in questionnaires, 'field' interviews, etc. Employers often place crucial reliance on the way job applicants 'perform' in interviews. Doctors, psychiatrists, counsellors and social workers all use the interview to find out what they need to know about their clients. Churches have rituals in which their members are asked questions, in public (baptisms, weddings, confirmations) and in private (confessions), and the catechism, too, is in question-and-answer form. And, last but not least, the media have their interviews in which politicians, experts, celebrities, so-called 'ordinary people' and others must, at the behest of interviewers, answer their questions in front of an invisible public of many thousands.

All these social institutions trust interviews to provide the truths they need to function legitimately. In other societies and other periods such truths may derive from divine revelation, or from experience and experiment, or they may be deduced from the forms of the natural world by diviners or astrologists. In our society they are established in social interaction. They are the product of consensus-forming question-and-answer dialogues between social actors playing their different (and often unequal) roles in social institutions — the roles of parents and children, teachers and pupils, doctors and patients, governments and citizens. The difference between a truth established in interaction and a truth established in experience is strikingly illustrated by an experiment of Stephen Harris.[1] A teacher would say to a class: 'All wallabies are yellow. I saw a wallaby. What colour?' White children would answer 'Yellow', Aboriginal children 'Brown'. White children, according to Harris, accepted a truth established in interaction, Aboriginal children trusted their experience. And whether such social truths are obtained through verbal violence, as in certain kinds of interrogation, through clever manipulation, as in many opinion polls, or through more-or-less fair and equal negotiation, as in the best political interviews, they always need two parties to come about. They always need verbal interaction to be valid.

The pervasive role of question-and-answer exchanges is more or less taken for granted in Western society. Asking questions is seen as something positive, a way of revealing curiosity, concern, interest. Answering questions is an obligation: there is, in our society, 'freedom of information', 'the right to know'. In other societies this is not always the case. Australian Aborigines, for example, frown on too much curiosity and see too many questions as an invasion of privacy. 'Stop asking so many questions. You're not white kids,' says the Aboriginal teacher.[2] And there is not the same obligation to answer — certainly not until a relation has been formed between those who ask the questions and those who provide the answers. This is often misunderstood by white people. According to M.J. Christie, white researchers

> go to a community and ask 'Can anyone here speak the language?' or 'Does anyone know the story of what happened at such-and-such?' and people say 'I don't know', or 'Couldn't say'. The white person often misinterprets that to mean 'There is no one here with any knowledge on that topic'. Whereas what the Aborigines mean is 'We can't give you that information — we don't know what you'll do with the information, etc.'[3]

Needless to say, this attitude to the asking and answering of questions can cause Aborigines serious problems when they have to deal, for example, with teachers who fail to understand that teaching with questions and answers does not work; or who interpret the embarrassment and silence of Aboriginal pupils as backwardness, laziness or shyness, or with law enforcers who see these same embarrassments and silences as so many admissions of guilt. In short, these problems arise when Aborigines have to deal with all those professional questioners who never question their own questioning practices.

Different cultures have different rules for who can ask which questions, from whom and in which circumstances. In Western cultures, teaching is done by means of questions and answers, in others by means of imitation or of story-telling. In some cultures guilt is established by means of interrogations and confessions, in others by means of the 'judgment of God'. Our culture, too, has rules of this kind. Guests at a cocktail party may ask you 'Where do you live?', 'Where are you from?', 'What do you do?', but not 'How old are you?' or 'How many times have you had sex during the past week?' Researchers, however, may ask all these questions of total strangers, provided they can establish their status as researchers. The subjects of their research may refuse to answer, but they usually do so politely, without challenging the researcher's right to ask the questions. If they do, they either do not know the rules of the culture, or do not accept them, and may place themselves radically outside it, as rebels or dissidents.

Why is the question-and-answer exchange so effective as a vehicle for producing social truths? Are not questions in the first place vehicles for 'getting information'? They are, in a sense, designed for this very purpose. They can be seen as incomplete statements — statements from which some information is lacking, be it the 'who', the 'what', the 'when', the 'why' or something else. And it is that missing information which is to be supplied in the answer.

But questions do something else as well. When I ask, 'Why didn't John tell me?', I am not only asking for information, I am also giving information. I am stating that John didn't tell me. And this statement is not itself in question; it is assumed to be already agreed upon. All that is in question is the reason why John did not tell me. In fact the question states even more. It also implies that there is a reason. It says: 'John did not tell me for a reason. Please tell me that reason.' And if you answer, then you signal your agreement with my statement by the very fact of answering, even if, inwardly, you disagree: what you think, but do not express in word or deed, will not become part of social reality. You may of course hedge, and so express your unwillingness to answer. Or you may openly disagree, and challenge the premises of my question — 'But John did tell you' — in which case you are treating my question as a statement. This is more easily done when the questioner is your equal or lower in status than when the questioner has, for example, the power to pass or fail you in an exam, or to give you a job or withhold it from you.

However, not all questions contain the same amount of information. 'WH-questions' — also called 'open questions' and 'content questions'; the kind of questions which use interrogatives such as 'why', 'what', 'when', 'where', and 'how' — provide less information than yes/no questions, from which only the polarity, the 'yes' or 'no', is lacking. Among WH-questions, some lack a major element of the statement (the 'who' or the 'what'), others only an attendant circumstance (for example, the 'when' or the 'where'). In each case the form of the question itself encodes what information is to be provided in the answer. The question instructs the answerer to give a particular kind of answer, to complete the statement in a particular way.

This means that question and answer together form one statement — one statement produced by two people. It is not one person saying one thing and the other another thing, as would be the case if the answerer had expressed disagreement instead of answering; it is two people saying one thing together. This is at the root of the creative potential of the question, its ability to open up new ideas, but it is also at the root of its manipulative power, its ability to make people say what they might not otherwise have chosen to say and to enforce consensus. Questioners always have four distinct advantages over answerers: (a) they can choose the topic; (b) they can determine what will be treated as 'already agreed upon', as taken-for-granted; (c) they can direct the answerer towards certain kinds of answer; and (d) they can compel the answerer to answer (at least in all but a very few situations).

They can compel the interviewee to answer because questions are more than incomplete statements. They also embody a demand. They say: 'tell me where' or 'tell me why' or 'tell me who'. And this demand goes hand in hand with the assumption that the answerer knows the answer. The question says: 'John didn't tell me for a reason. Please tell me that reason, because I am assuming that you know and I will be disappointed with you if you don't.' In our society, not to obey such a demand is difficult. Disclaimers ('Don't know', 'Haven't seen that movie') will disappoint the questioner and hamper the conversation or interview. A refusal to answer will be seen as uncooperative and unfriendly if the questioner and the answerer are each other's equals, as obstinate and rebellious if the questioner is in a position of power. This obligation to answer is instilled in us when we are young children. Interchanges like this one, between a mother and a child between 18 and 24 months old, are typical for our early socialisation, but do not occur in many other cultures[4]:

MOTHER:	*What did you have for tea?*
CHILD:	(silence)
MOTHER:	*What did you have for tea, darling?*
CHILD:	Tea.
MOTHER:	*Yes, what did you have for tea?*
CHILD:	(silence)
MOTHER:	*Did you have an egg?*

CHILD:	Egg.
MOTHER:	*And some toast?*
CHILD:	(silence)[5]

The reason for 'interviewing' the child like this is not only to find out what the child has eaten, or to teach it to say words, but also to teach it to answer . . . to teach it to engage in verbal exchange, in producing shared meanings together with its mother.

In each question, then, there are these two dimensions: the 'statement' dimension and the 'demand' dimension. The latter is, in some ways, primary. It encodes the obligation without which dialogue cannot exist, and thus enables the formation of shared statements, the moment of social semiosis. At the same time, however, questions will differ in the degree to which the 'demand' function overrides the 'statement' function, and this, in turn, will depend on the power relationship between the questioner and the answerer.

The Advantages of the Interviewer

We have discussed the advantages which rest with questioners: they can choose the topic; they can determine the premises; they can direct answerers to certain kinds of answer; and they can compel answerers to answer. The anthropologist E.N. Goody compared the question to the gift:

> The gift, like the question, demands a return. Both may be seen as social devices for compelling interaction, for forcing two people to enter into a social exchange. Malinowski and Mauss emphasised that the critical feature of gift exchange is the delay between gift and return gift, during which time a debt relationship binds the two partners in unequal bonds. The giver is socially in credit, while the recipient is socially a debtor. The time-scale of a question–answer sequence is, on the contrary, collapsed

into the briefest of conversational pauses . . . Thus questioning binds two people in *immediate* reciprocity.⁶

In conversation, the advantage of the question is shared out equally. Each participant is now questioner, now answerer, now creditor, now debtor. In interviews, however, this is not the case. Interviewers, and only interviewers, ask the questions; interviewees, and only interviewees, give the answers. Interviewers receive, interviewees give. If this rule is broken, friction inevitably results. For the interviewer to give an answer is a refusal of the gift, hence a refusal of the social bond. For the interviewee to ask a question is a denial of the debt. Here is an excerpt from an Israeli television program in which the rules are broken.

INTERVIEWER: *Are you saying, Minister, that someone in television is trying to prevent you from stating your case?*
MINISTER: Let me explain. You recorded me. You conducted an interview. On Friday I received a message that for some reason it was all unsuitable for showing. Seems odd to me.
INTERVIEWER: *More precisely, your spokesman was informed in the morning, not in the afternoon.*
MINISTER: Are we having an interview or an argument? You don't have to mix in. Just ask your questions.
INTERVIEWER: *Are you saying that television has it in for you?*
MINISTER: God forbid, Elisha, don't identify yourself with television.
INTERVIEWER: *Although you seem to want to tell me how an interviewer should do his job, I still want to ask you: is it correct that one ought to mention that the message was delivered at seven in the morning? Is it correct that you refused to be interviewed? Is it correct that you made a speech repeating things that had already been said?*
MINISTER: It is not correct. As for my refusal to be interviewed: I don't want to be interviewed on the steps. It isn't efficient. Not in a hurry. The public has a right to know.

INTERVIEWER: *Minister, this is an interview, not a private conversation.*[7]

From this division of labour follows a further advantage for interviewers: whereas interviewees do not know what questions they will be asked and must therefore think on their feet and improvise their answers, interviewers can, to some extent, plan their speech in advance. Hence they are likely to come across as the more fluent and articulate speakers, the better communicators, while the interviewees — especially if they have relatively little experience in being interviewed or have to talk about things they have not formulated before — are likely to come across as the more hesitant, casual, colloquial speakers. They may seem unable to communicate as effectively as the interviewers, and this can then be presented as the reason why they need interviewers and cannot address the audience directly.

Advance planning also gives interviewers the opportunity to plan a logical or narrative structure for the interview as a whole, to control the sequence of topics and their interconnections. Journalists are well aware of this and tell us that the interviewer must 'direct the interview's course intelligently and with unwavering purpose',[8] 'arrive with a plan in his head',[9] and that interviewees should be denied the advantages of advance planning: 'Never agree to set questions';[10] 'Spontaneity demands that the interviewee know only the general areas of discussion'.[11] Thus, in a curious mixture of public and private speech, the interviewee is to speak the 'natural', 'spontaneous' language of the armchair conversation, and the interviewer the more formal, planned language of the platform monologue. This comes out, for instance, in the following excerpt from an ABC interview with an expert on road safety:

INTERVIEWER: *There has been an increased incidence in the drink-riding rate of motorcyclists. Why is that?*
INTERVIEWEE: Yes, that's quite true ... er ... I don't know why it is. I imagine it's because ... er ... a lot of people

are turning from the car to the motorbike because it's cheaper to run, with lower . . . er . . . petrol prices . . . it's important to keep the cost of running it down and there's more and more use of it for social purposes at the weekends that involves drinking and so there's more and more use of alcohol with the motorcycle. And of course if it's difficult to drive a car after drinking it is obviously ten times more difficult to ride a motorbike.

Throughout this interview, the interviewer remains in the formal mode, speaking of 'motorcycles' rather than 'motorbikes' and using phrases like 'increased incidence' rather than 'more and more', etc. The interviewee also attempts a well-structured, formal mode of speech. He is, after all, interviewed as an expert, and no doubt would like to be seen as capable of articulate, formal speech. But having had no chance to prepare his answer, he slips in and out of the formal mode, speaks sometimes of 'motorcycles', sometimes of 'motorbikes' or 'bikes', sometimes of 'riding a bike after drinking', sometimes of 'use of alcohol with the motorcycle', and so on. And most strikingly, he is making up his answer as he goes along. In fact, he explicitly says 'I don't know', but is then nevertheless compelled to go on because of the interviewer's silence. Given some preparation, he would probably have been able to provide a more thoughtful and informative answer, and to give meaningful figures, rather than lending his answer a spurious air of precision by 'imagining' it to be 'ten times' more difficult to ride a bike after drinking than to drive a car.

In interviews most of the talking is done by the interviewees. But while answerers in conversation receive constant feedback from questioners, in the form of verbal and non-verbal assurances that their answers are understood and attentively listened to, media interviewees must do without such support. Elwyn Evans, a former head of the radio training section of the BBC, notes this, though without venturing an explanation: 'For some reason spoken expressions of interest — "really", "how extraordinary", "hm hm" and the like — sound silly in the mouth of an interviewer'.[12]

Once again, the interviewee must do all the giving. Or to put the point more strongly: the interviewer possesses the power to control the interview. (S)he is not being 'tested', is not contingent, but given. There is, then, considerable asymmetry between the roles of interviewer and interviewee. Interviewers not only have the advantages of their monopoly on the question, they also have the advantages of advance planning. Interviewees not only have the disadvantage of their role as answerers, they also have the disadvantage of not being able to plan in advance even when they are, in fact, addressing a large audience. They also lack the listener support one usually receives when thinking on one's feet in conversation. Further, the interviewer is often familiar to the audience, and is presented as having high professional prestige.

In emphasising this asymmetry between interviewer and interviewee, it should be remembered that it is the institutional context (in this case the modern-day mass-circulation media) that determines such relationships of power. Just as magistrates or priests gain their power from the institutional purpose which they serve, so too do radio and television interviewers. The interview is always conducted and presented within the context of a particular institution, in which power is implicit. This is not to imply that media interviews are very similar to legal interrogations or to confessions, but to emphasise that interviewers inhabit roles which are embedded in institutions. They are not merely talented or charismatic individuals whose skill determines their right to ask, rather than to answer, questions in public. Interviews involve more than the two parties who interact through language. They, at very least, involve an institutional context and particular classes of real or potential audiences (remember the origin of the word — those who listen). And these institutions and listeners, as we shall see throughout this book, are always present in subtle ways as the interaction between questioner and answerer unfolds. Indeed, when we later distinguish different genres of media interview, it will be in relation to particular institutional contexts and the audience that these imply.

Interviews in Their Social Context: Other Practices

Some kinds of interviewees — business leaders, politicians, union officials — now have access to media training or 'image making' training as it is often called in the U.S.A. The training is usually given by ex-journalists, and the fees may run into thousands of dollars a day. This training can make interviews into a more equal kind of contest. Other interviewees, however, do not have the advantage of this kind of training. Paradoxically, they may find themselves exposed to a captive audience of perhaps hundreds of thousands of people, yet denied access to the linguistic means required to address such an audience in their own right, without an intermediary, because interviewers reserve these means for themselves. However, the advantages of the interviewer should be seen in the context of two other questions: (a) Does the interviewer have the 'correct' answer already in mind? and (b) Does the interviewer have the power to materially affect the life of the interviewee? These two factors, taken together, make it possible to distinguish a number of different ways in which question and answer exchanges are used in contemporary Western society. Both, it need hardly be added, relate to the interviewer's institutionally derived power.

TESTS

The mother, in the example given earlier, has what she sees as the right answers already in mind. She in fact feeds them to the child. As E.N. Goody has observed, mothers 'seem to use the questioning exchange as a way of telling the child what it wants and what it means'.[13] She also has the power to affect the life of her child both psychologically and materially: she can withhold her affection, deny the child material luxuries or even necessities. Teachers, similarly, want specific answers from their students. They are not seeking information; they seek to control what their students want and mean, or at least what they say they want and mean. And they, too, can affect the lives of those they question: failing exams can restrict the student's access to material rewards and social status.

It might be more appropriate to call these 'interviews' by the name 'tests'. In all of them, questioners have the power not only to ask questions, but also to give or withhold rewards, and this power is based on their knowledge of the 'right' answers. The questioners are doubly advantaged: by their role as interviewers, and by their material power. They use questions as a means of control. On the other hand, the ostensible aim of the test is ultimately to remove the inequality between the two participants. There is a return gift. The mother's knowledge of the right answers rests on her status as an adult and, if all is well, she aims to bring up her child to become an adult and, hence, an equal. The employment interview, to use another example, is a kind of initiation in which passing the test results in the interviewee's admission to the group represented by the interviewer or interviewers (which may, of course, have its internal inequalities).

Tests of this kind have a long history and can be found in many cultures. The historian Johan Huizinga gives many examples, amongst them the riddles the kings of Ancient India posed to their wise men and the tricky questions the marriageable girls of Vietnam address to their suitors. And he stresses how such tests were often important and festive events, and how much pleasure people took in them, even in cases where the wrong answer could cost the answerer his life.[14] It is only when the reward of equality, the element of initiation, is not there, or not meaningful and desirable — when, for example, teachers no longer see their students as future equals, or when students no longer want to be like their teachers and no longer perceive the knowledge they are taught as relevant and desirable, or when education can no longer deliver the rewards it promises — that tests can become a meaningless ordeal and/or an exercise of naked power. This is, to some extent, the situation imposed on the Aboriginal children to whom we referred earlier.

Educational 'tests' on the media include the television quiz show. The quiz seems to have retained something of the playfulness, the pleasure and the sense of a special, festive occasion that school exams have lost. On the other hand, as John Fiske has pointed out, the knowledge they test is the knowledge of the consumer, rather than knowledge that gives access to the class that asks the questions and to the means of producing the answers.[15] The reward is commodities or money, not equality. In addition, mixed in with the test is an element of the lottery, which diminishes the achievement of the quiz participants. In quizzes, people's ability to take pleasure in tests is sidetracked to the dead end of the 'trivial pursuit'; their skill in answering questions does not lead to material or social benefits in the realm to which the ritual testing refers.

CONFESSIONS

Among the institutions licensed to allow professional interviews are psychiatry, social work, counselling and the social sciences. In contrast to the mother and the teacher, their questioners do not already know the answer when they ask their questions. On the other hand, they do have, or claim to have, knowledge which their interviewees do not share — expert professional knowledge about people, about their thoughts, their fears, their desires. Indeed, if the interviewees also had this knowledge, the proper conduct of such interviews would become impossible. Their conventions require inequality of expertise. They require that the interviewer, in the end, knows, better than the interviewees themselves, who they are, what they feel, what they want, what they need. This is so, not only when the interview takes place in the context of a social institution that deals with people as individuals (medical and psychiatric interviews, counselling sessions and so on), but also when it takes place in the context of a social institution that deals with people as groups (market interviews, research interviews, polls, etc.). Anthropologists, for example, may ask Aborigines questions in order to learn more about their cultures, but they claim, at the same time, an expert knowledge of culture in general which their interviewees do not have. And never will have, as far as the interviewer is concerned. Something must always be withheld from the subject interviewed.

We can describe the interviewer's greater knowledge in this way: it is the knowledge of the more general significance of the answers, of what the answers mean: the knowledge of the 'whys'. Doctors, psychiatrists and researchers have this in common: though they ask their subjects many questions, they do not ask 'why'. The 'why' question they will address only to themselves. From their patients, clients, subjects of investigation, they may want the 'who', the 'what', the 'when' and the 'where', perhaps the 'yes' and the 'no' that will confirm their hunches, but not the 'why'. If they do ask 'why' questions (for example, 'Why do people watch soap operas?') they will have formulated the possible answers in advance, so that the 'why' question has in fact been converted into a series of yes/no questions behind which another 'why' can then loom up. (For example, if 'most people' select the answer 'It takes my mind off things', the consequent question is: 'Why do most people seek escapist entertainment?')

The answers to these 'why' questions will then be used by the questioners, or by the agencies for whom they work (the sponsors of the poll, the bureaucracies that fund the research) as ground for actions which will directly affect the lives of the interviewees — as a rationale for choosing how to treat a disease, how to schedule the programs of a television channel, how to change legislation. There is, then, a return gift — in the form of an instruction, a prohibition, a restriction of available choices. But what it will be, how it connects to the answers and whether it will benefit or harm the interviewees is something the interviewees cannot know when they answer the questions, because the interpretations, the answers to the 'why' questions, are withheld from them.

Interviews of this kind do not lead to ultimate equality, to the possibility of self-help or to active participation in decision making. And interviewees cannot directly learn anything from them, for their interviewers will always protect the expert knowledge on which their status (and livelihood) is based.

In contrast to the test, this kind of interview is a modern Western phenomenon. Michel Foucault has discussed its development in the Counter-Reformation, when the Catholic Church began to ask sinners to *confess*, not just socially unacceptable deeds, but also socially unacceptable thoughts, feelings, intentions and impulses.[16] In the late nineteenth century the confession started to become secularised into its modern forms, such as the psychiatric interview and the counselling session. Increasingly it institutionalised the Romantic belief that what people say spontaneously is more truthful than what they say after preparation and planning. Through psychoanalysis, for example, the truth became identified with the irrational, the emotional, the immediate associations of the unconscious and at the same time it remained 'sinful' — the shameful emotion, the cruel impulse, the unreasonable dislike. To be truthful meant to bare all, to reveal everything. The confessor, on the other hand, continued to reveal nothing, to act as what Michel Foucault called 'the master of truth' who, alone, knows the significance of the confessee's revelations. This was so not only in social institutions dealing with people as individuals, but also in those dealing with people as groups.

For example, questionnaires often instruct us to answer large numbers of questions on quite complex issues in an exceptionally short time. Here, too, the impulsive, immediate answer is seen as more valuable and more truthful than the carefully thought-out answer — or rather, the giving of carefully thought-out answers is reserved for the select few, for the professional experts who have, in any case, already learnt to base their answers in the unreasoned impulses of 'the people' in private confessions, whether statistically aggregated or not. It is interesting, in this connection, that telephone and face-to-face interviews, with the interviewers themselves filling in the questionnaire forms, now tend to be favoured in such research: in them the immediate reciprocity of the question-and-answer dyad is more effectively guaranteed.

Seen in this light, the confession is a way of arriving at social truths that is not only fundamentally unequal, but also fundamentally un-moral, unconcerned with any principles of justice. It is concerned only with the 'truthful' confession of private impulses and desires in the sense that these are *revealed*; evidence of truths beyond themselves.

INTERROGATIONS

At least until the age of the mass media, confessions were always private, even when people were interviewed as members of a group rather than as individuals. Interrogations, on the other hand, were frequently also public. They differ from confessions in another important, and perhaps related, way: in interrogations people are treated, not as irrational beings, but as rational and responsible actors.

This is so for the interrogation of 'witnesses' as well as for the interrogation of 'suspects'. In both cases the truth sought is not the 'spontaneous' and the 'truthful' but, quite simply, the 'true' — the question of what actually happened. Of course, such truths are hard to come by, and the belief that they can be determined at all is endangered by the 'psychological' view of humans as irrational beings who see and hear only what they want to see and hear, and remember only what they want to remember. Question-and-answer exchanges, moreover, are social interactions by their very nature and interrogations are therefore more likely to lead to social truths, to consensually accepted views, than to 'the' truth. But that does not alter the fact that, in principle, what is sought is an objective, concrete truth, and that the field of the interrogation is that of concrete doings and happenings rather than the field of mental processes. If the belief that 'the' truth can never be arrived at is taken to its extreme, with respect to doings and happenings as well, then the possibility of justice is fundamentally undermined and interrogators would then only be confessors, 'masters of truth'.

Interrogators certainly have power over those they interrogate. However, this power is not based on knowing the answers beforehand or on special expertise of the 'field' of the interrogation. That field is constituted by specific events of which the interrogators are ignorant, and of which they in fact seek knowledge precisely by means of the interrogation. Power is based on the prerogative of the interrogator (or of the institution on behalf of which the interrogation takes place) to determine who or what is responsible for what happened. For the interrogation is always concerned with something that has gone wrong, with a disturbance of the order of things, and to regain a sense of order a cause must be found, and the disturbance contained or made meaningful in some way.

As in the case of the test, what is at stake for those interrogated is their status in society. Suspects will be restored to their former social status if they are judged not responsible. If they are judged responsible, action will be taken against them, and this will affect their status in society. Witnesses, by the very act of witnessing, demonstrate their interest in restoring this order and, in the process, they exonerate themselves. A refusal to witness is easily seen as an admission of guilt. Not to speak the truth in witnessing is itself a disturbance of the order of things rather than, as it would be in the case of the confession, a symptom of something else. Witnesses and suspects alike know what is at stake and, again in contrast to the confession, know what action could be taken against them.

The interrogation, then, is not necessarily unequal. However, interrogations take place in the social institutions. These have a stake in arriving at certain versions of the events, in finding certain causes or certain culprits, so the questioners and the answerers do not have the same beliefs as to what is right and wrong. Institutional power means that some people are not regarded as responsible actors, capable of speaking the truth, so interrogations may become an instrument of intimidation and coercion and equality can no longer be a meaningful concept. When such conditions prevail, the borderline between interrogation and confession can become blurred. This happens not only when dissidents are treated in psychiatric hospitals, as has been reported from the former Soviet Union, but also when interrogators adopt psychological ways of thinking, and when laws are changed on the basis, not of principles of justice, but of 'what most people do' (as established by research based on the private confession).

INTERPELLATIONS

Despite our analysis so far, in some question-and-answer exchanges it is not the questioner but the answerer who has the greater power, although the questioner may still be granted some of the privileges of the interviewing role. Such interviews, which are necessarily public, have the character of a verbal contest in which the legitimacy of the interviewees' power is at stake — the honesty of the politician, for example, or the bona fides of a businessman. If the interviewee wins the contest, his or her power is legitimised. If they lose, their power is challenged and they will have to take action that can be seen to be in the interest of those the interviewers represent in order to regain legitimacy. Projected legislation might have to be altered if it is to pass through parliament; interviewees might have to change the views they state publicly if they are to retain a positive public image; and so on.

In certain kinds of media interview, for example, the interviewer acts as what Krishan Kumar has called an 'honest broker' who must 'take the role of "us", as the "unrepresented", the "consumers", the "suffering public", the victims of planners and public servants of all kinds, as well as of large industrialists, selfish trade unions, property speculators and the like'.[17] Such 'interpellations', close as they may come to the public dispute, nevertheless take the form of question-and-answer exchanges, perhaps to preserve a certain amount of deference towards the power of the interviewee.

Of course, there is always the problem of the broker not being quite so honest, the problem of whether the interviewer truly represents the interests of the 'voters', the 'consumers', the 'audience' or whatever. This is particularly so if the interviewer is in fact a self-appointed representative, as is the case with media interviewers. It is not always easy to determine where exactly the allegiance of the media professional lies. In the case of the commercial media, for example, there has to be allegiance both to the sponsor and to the public, and this can give rise to a good deal of tension, compromise and covering-up of the contradictions involved. The media's independence from government is jeopardised by their reliance on government agencies for information, dispensed at regular, predictable times and in forms suitable for the requirements of journalists. There is always the danger of the interpellator becoming a public relations agent, and the questions being merely rhetorical ones connecting the parts of what is, in reality, a seamless monologue by the interviewee.

QUESTION-AND-ANSWER DIALOGUES

Are there interviews in which the parties are equal in power, and in which the interviewer neither knows the answers in advance, nor has special power in interpreting them? Maybe not: true equality would seem to imply that either party may ask the questions or give the answers. But there are different kinds of inequality. Inequality of knowledge and experience does not necessarily entail inequality of power. The traditional Jewish Yeshiva, for example, is an institution in which the students, rather than the masters, ask the questions, and in which learning is not associated with material betterment but pursued for its own sake (although it does, of course, bring prestige). It would seem that there are few if any instances in our society in which question-and-answer exchanges of this kind are institutionalised, although they occur all the time in a more informal way. But in that case the divisions of labour characteristic of the interview need no longer be strictly adhered to: the power equality itself removes the necessity for such rules.

At first sight 'Socratic' dialogues might seem to belong in this category also. Here questioners aim at eliciting contradictory answers from answerers, so trapping them into admitting the untenability of their position. But in Socratic dialogues the questioners do, most probably, know the answers in advance and only pretend not to know them. The Socratic dialogue is therefore perhaps more aptly seen as one of the techniques of the interpellatory interview.

Media Interviews

Media interviews cover all the categories we have just distinguished: interviewers talk to politicians in the voice of the interpellator; to experts in the voice of the student; to ordinary people in the voice of the social researcher or the counsellor; to children in the voice of the parent or teacher; to 'deviant' interviewees in the voice of the interrogator. In these interviews the public receives a model for all of these situations, and it is from these interviewers that they receive an indication of the answers that are regarded as cooperative or uncooperative in each of them. *Yet media interviews do not have the same purpose as the question-and-answer exchanges on which they are modelled.* The material consequences are absent.

The media 'interpellator' does not vote on the legislative proposals of the interviewed minister. The 'student' does not aspire to the knowledge of the master. The 'counsellor' has no advice to give the interviewee. The 'interrogator' does not judge or punish. What media interviews do, instead, is give the public a perspective on the *social actors interviewed* and/or the field of their expertise or experience — a perspective from which to judge what they do and what they have to say. This perspective is sometimes that of power, particularly when ordinary people are interviewed, and sometimes that of those at the receiving end of power, as in the case of 'honest broker' interviews with politicians or business leaders. But it is always the perspective of the interviewer that is reiterated night after night. In later chapters we will demonstrate in detail that it is for the purpose of establishing this perspective, rather than for their substantive content, that interviews are essentially used. The substantive content is more often found in the anchorman's introductions, the on-camera reports, the narrations and other 'links'. We will also discuss how the interviewer's perspective is realised in the form of the interviews — in the framing of shots, the positioning of interviewer and interviewee in the frame, the eyelines and the use of interviewer reaction shots.

Media interviewers have the advantage that the interview is encoded from their perspective — both literally and figuratively. They also have advantages over their interviewees besides those of the interviewer role as such. In the first place, although media interviewers do not know the answers beforehand, they do operate with a sense of the 'correct' answer: the 'correct' answers are those that *correspond to their definition of the interviewee as a social type*, and of what constitutes valid and relevant knowledge and experience for an interviewee of that type. If interviewees give 'incorrect' answers they risk being seen as out of touch with the audience, as irrelevant, marginal or even deviant. It is the special expertise of media professionals to know what is valid, relevant, interesting or entertaining in the eyes of the audience. Secondly, however much media interviews may give the impression of being private encounters between an interviewer and an interviewee, they are always *public*. The interviewee is in the hands of the interviewer in front of a very large public. Giving the 'wrong' answers may have consequences beyond the interviewer's ironically raised eyebrow. And finally, the media interviewer can change the meaning of the interviewee's answers, through *editing* and through the way they are introduced and linked.

CHAPTER 1

In an *Actionline* consumer affairs news item on Sydney's Channel 10, a company was accused of selling the public fake diamonds. The first interview in the item was with a woman, a 'consumer', filmed in what looked like the company's showroom. This is the interview as it was recorded, with the parts retained in the edited version underlined:

INTERVIEWER: *The Minister for Consumer Affairs, Sid Einfeld, is saying that they're not worth 25 cents. Would you be happy to pay $10 for them?*
INTERVIEWEE: Yes, I'd pay twen . . . ten dollars for them, yes.
INTERVIEWER: *You don't think that's exorbitant?*
INTERVIEWEE: No, I don't, I don't think, I don't know a lot about jewellery, but my daughter says, I'm listening to my daughter and she says they will not fade, they will not go yellow and the gold will not rub off, and I'll take all . . . she works in a jewellery shop and I'd listen to what she had to say. I wanted a pair of diamond earrings for $68 and she said: 'Mum, you'd be just as happy or happier with standard earrings for $60 and they look nice. You should go down and have a look at them.'
INTERVIEWER: *And you're not worried that the Minister is saying that they're not worth $10?*
INTERVIEWEE: No, no that wouldn't bother me, as long as they look good on me, that's all that matters.
INTERVIEWER: *Thank you very much.*

It is obvious that the interviewer has some difficulty in depicting the interviewee as a duped consumer. She rejects his criteria of value ('fair price', authenticity) in favour of her own criteria of attractiveness and durability ('they will not fade'; 'as long as they look good on me'). She also rejects the authority he invokes and places more faith in her daughter than in the minister who, according to Channel 10, has her interests as a consumer at heart. And where the interviewer would clearly like to depict her as *unhappy*, 'worried', she says she is perfectly happy and not 'bothered'.

In other words, the interviewer cannot get her to react according to type, according to the way duped consumers *should* react.

However, editing, and especially 'introducing' and 'linking', can make up for this. In the item as it was eventually broadcast, the facts are first of all established by the anchorman's introduction. The diamonds are fake, and that's that. With all the weight of his position as an 'institutional voice' behind him (neutral studio background, detached camera angle, formal style of dress, impartial newsreader's tone and delivery) the anchorman pronounces: 'Consumer Affairs Minister Sid Einfeld has repeated outside parliament warnings about mail-order diamond earrings.

Yesterday he savagely attacked Mailex International for selling 25 cent earrings for 10 dollars...' The interviewer (he also acts as reporter) is then heard off screen, in a matter-of-fact voice-over commentary, accompanied by images of the earrings, certificates of authenticity, and so on:

> This set of diamond earrings sells for $10. The stone comes from the United States. It's cut in India. 20,000 sets have been sold at a profit of a dollar fifty each. Another 40,000 are on the way. Or at least, that was the plan before Sid Einfeld stepped in. But is $10 a fair price?

Our interviewee comes into view next: 'Yes, I'd pay twen . . . ten dollars for them, yes'. In other words, the introductory question (*'Would you be happy to pay $10 for them?'*) is replaced by the (rhetorical) voice-over question (*'But is $10 a fair price?'*) This is common practice in television news and current affairs. It links the otherwise separate parts of the item. But it does more than linking. It also creates the impression that the interviewee spontaneously takes up the topic of the 'fair price', rather than following the agenda set by the interviewer. It obscures the fact that the question she now appears to answer is not the one she was originally asked: she was asked about her *feelings*, not about an objective issue. Now, however, she appears to answer an objectively formulated question in a personal, subjective way, and this, in the eyes of the public, could transform her into a woman unable to discuss issues other than subjectively and emotionally — someone who, unlike Channel 10, cannot see the issue in proper perspective.

As a result, the reference to her daughter is no longer an affirmation of her own values and her own support system, but a symptom of her ignorance, particularly as it follows the admission that she doesn't 'know a lot about jewellery'. And her strongest and most confident argument ('they look good on me') is deleted. Thus she becomes the type of the gullible consumer, easy prey for the shady practices of sharp businessmen, a weak creature in need of protection from the fatherly figure of the Consumer Affairs Minister who will have the final word in the item.

Editing has achieved what could not be achieved through questioning. And in the process the interviewer's role has been much attenuated. He is no longer seen to provoke her opening statement and her defensive, almost hostile reaction; no longer seen to insist on the answer he is after by asking twice what is essentially the same question. He now seems only to react to her questions, a listener rather than an initiator. And the 'reaction shot', the close-up of the listening, understanding interviewer, with his steady and sympathetic gaze, interacts with the close-up of the nervous, defensive interviewee, shot from a high angle and looking down for most of the interview. It should be noted that such 'reaction shots' are recorded after interviewing has been completed, as are 'reverse-angle questions' we actually see the interviewer asking. In fact location interviews use only one camera, and during the interview this camera is pointed at the interviewee, taking in, at most, only the interviewer's back. For this reason the performing of 'reaction shots' and 'reverse-angle questions' already belongs to the editing process: reactions can be altered and questions improved upon, or even rephrased.

In this chapter we have looked at the role of question and-answer exchanges in society generally, situating the media interview among them by taking a more-or-less systematic, sociological approach. In the next chapter we will outline a brief history of the media interview. For the media interview is not natural and universal, but a surprisingly recent and culturally specific invention.

2

A Short History of the Modern Media Interview

Interviews as Evidence and Entertainment. When interviews first appeared in the press of the mid-nineteenth century, many saw them as an invasion of privacy, and as too trivial to be given the dignity of print and wide dissemination. 'The interview,' said an American magazine editor in 1870s, 'is the most perfect contrivance yet devised to make journalism an offence, a thing of ill savour in all decent nostrils.'[1] But the critics of interviewing were fighting a rearguard action. The interview suited new conceptions of journalism, which were gaining ascendancy at the time, for quite specific historical reasons. It was there to stay.

At one time there had been no separation between the role of 'reporter' and that of 'editor'. Journalists saw themselves not just as reporters of what others said and did, but as authors in their own right, responsible for the social and political import of their writing. Gradually, however, the separation between 'fact' and 'comment' was to establish itself, and journalists started thinking of themselves as 'middlemen', 'channels' for the accurate transmission of information from one place to another, reporters whose job it was to pass on what they saw and heard without any contamination by their own thoughts or feelings. Interviews, written with the aid of the new tool of stenography, suited this ideal of reporting — of handing on, literally, what other people said, rather than rendering it in one's own words.

Interviews also related to genres other than reporting. Broadsheets with the 'true confessions' of notorious criminals about to be executed, and usually with a moralistic ending, had been more popular than books since the seventeenth century. In the early nineteenth century, for example, Jemmy Catnach's Seven Dials Press sold more than 1,100,000 copies of the 'Last Dying Speech and Confession' of the murderer of Maria Marten.[2] There were also affinities with the realist fiction of the day (which, in serialised form, would itself become an important element of newspaper content). Early interviews contained elaborate and, by today's standard, quite literary descriptions of the setting of the interview (almost always a private house) and the appearance of the interviewee. They were, in other words, quite 'visual'. Here is an excerpt from what many American historians of journalism consider the first newspaper interview, with President Martin Van Buren, conducted by James Gordon Bennett of the *New York Herald* and published in 1839. Note that the separation between fact and comment is not yet very advanced:

> When my turn came, I went up to His Excellency. He held out his hand. It was soft and oily. I took hold of it, gently, by the very hand, too, which has quizzed him most unmercifully during the last four years, in those annoying four-line paragraphs.

'How do you do, Mr Bennett?' said Mr Van Buren with a half smile.

To which Mr Bennett responded:

'Pretty well, I thank you', with another half smile.

> I looked into his face — his eyes wandered over the carpet, probably thinking at that moment of the meeting of Agamemnon and Achilles. I was almost on the verge of bursting into a horse laugh, at the vagaries of human nature, but being in the presence of the head of the Democratic party, I restrained myself. I sat down on the sofa, crossed my legs, and looked very knowingly into the fine hickory fire blazing on high.[3]

Another often-quoted early example even comments on the speech of the interviewee. It is an interview with Brigham Young, president of the Mormon Church. The main subject matter is slavery. The interviewer is Horace Greeley of the *Tribune*, the year 1859: 'He spoke readily, not always with grammatical accuracy, but with no appearance of hesitation or reserve, and with no apparent desire to conceal anything, nor did he repel any of my questions as impertinent'.[4] The questions and answers themselves are reported verbatim:

GREELEY:	*What is the position of your Church with respect to slavery?*
YOUNG:	We consider it of Divine institution, and not to be abolished until the curse pronounced on Ham shall have been removed from his descendants.
GREELEY:	*Are any slaves now held in this Territory?*
YOUNG:	There are.
GREELEY:	*Do your territorial laws uphold slavery?*
YOUNG:	Those laws are printed — you can read for yourself. If slaves are brought here by those who owned them in the State, we do not favor their escape from the service of those owners.[5]

Interviews, as normal journalistic practice, arose from a more lurid motive as well. In 1836 Bennett followed up a New York *Sun* report that the body of a young prostitute (Ellen) had been found in a 'house in Thomas Street'.[6] Writing in the *Herald*, Bennett included paraphrases of the comments by the madame (Townsend) in his sensationalistic, investigative piece, and on 16 April 1836 the *Herald* printed what some historians regard as the first formal question-and-answer media interview.

TOWNSEND: The house was locked up for the night at twelve o'clock P.M. — I returned to rest. — about three o'clock A.M. . . . I smelt smoke, and on going into the parlor I found the back door open, and Helen's [Ellen's] lamp standing on the marble side table, by the door — I went directly to Helen's room, and found the door shut — I opened it, and on so doing, the smoke rushed out and nearly suffocated me . . .

BENNETT: *How did you know that the lamp on the table belonged to Helen's room?*

TOWNSEND: There are but two lamps alike in the house, the one used by Helen and the other by myself.

BENNETT: *Did you hear no other noise previous to the knocking of the young man you let in?*

TOWNSEND: I think I heard a noise and said who's there, but received no answer.

BENNETT: *How did you know that the person you let in was Frank [the name Robinson (the accused) was said to have been using]?*

TOWNSEND: He gave his name.

BENNETT: *Did you see his face?*

TOWNSEND: No — his cloak was held up over his face, I saw nothing but his eyes as he passed me — he had on a hat and cloak . . .

One of Bennett's biographers, Oliver Carlson, credits him, probably overgenerously, with having invented the 'formal interview' by reprinting this conversation. (Bennett's competitors at the *Sun* accused him of having invented the conversation.) Assuming Bennett can be trusted — and he was never proved a fake — this was something more than a tour de force of observation. This was the journalist as opener of closed doors, as inquisitor, as detective.[7]

Stephens points out that, prior to this, reporters 'did not print quotes, unless statements were made in public; they may have made enquiries but they did not interview; they refrained from addressing the principals; they did not intrude; they did not investigate'.[8] It appears that until this comparatively recent date, investigation and sensationalistic reporting had not motivated any clear violation of the privacy of the witness in the press.

In the mid-nineteenth century, as industrialisation gained pace and 'science' came to include the natural and social as well as the physical sciences, the gaze of the educated and literate fell increasingly on the poor, illiterate, deviant or racially distinct. 'Anthropology' and 'psychology' (as they are now called) began to construct knowledges which were both empirical and moralistic about 'others' ('natives', 'the insane', 'the criminal'). Popular newspapers, in parallel with these scientific discourses, began to investigate empirically and to judge more 'scientifically' those in society (or those on the margins of middle-class society) who were 'deviant' enough to be newsworthy. Interviews were extended from the public and political personages to ordinary people — participants and witnesses, though seldom the 'experts' who are today the staple of news and current affairs programs.

The mid-nineteenth century examples of interviews can be seen to anticipate many of the features of their twentieth-century audio-visual counterparts. They are evidential yet voyeuristic; 'objective' yet incorporated into sensationalistic contexts. As in some of the most important contemporary naturalistic literature (for example, that of Emile Zola), they 'scientifically' explored 'low life', producing objects of fascination for readers who were assumed to be different from the illiterate 'criminal classes'. Like 'case-study', socially conscious literature (including, perhaps, detective novels from *The Moonstone* in 1868, or the work of Dickens), the interview evidence was set in specific, detailed descriptions of the witnesses' environments, yet linked with the sensationalist 'dying confession' genre. Why did this new genre develop? Why this fusion between the popular genre of the 'last dying speech', the descriptive excess of realist fiction, and the serious genre of political comment? Why this concern for accurately transcribing speech, complete with descriptions of tone of voice, amount of hesitation and eye contact, facial expression and posture, and of the appearance of the interviewee and the setting in which the interview took place? To answer these questions we need to look at what happened to the press during the early stages of the Industrial Revolution.

In this period radical newspapers came into existence, voicing the grievances of the new, urban working class — in Australia most often the grievances of the settlers and freed convicts against the colonial government. Governments tried to repress these papers by imposing impossibly high taxes, by confiscating equipment and by fining or imprisoning editors, but with remarkably little success. Towards the middle of the century, however, the radical newspapers, fighting for the abolition of the taxes, received unexpected support from enlightened members of the ruling class who reasoned that retaining the press taxes would mean that the lower classes would not be able to afford newspapers, which, in turn, would mean that 'men of education and capital' would miss out on a good opportunity to reach and influence them. A free press was needed so the labouring class could be addressed by 'men, two or three degrees their superior in class', as Hickson, a member of the British Stamp Abolition Committee, phrased it.[9] In this way a curious alliance of 'freedom' and social control came about, producing a press which, in the words of the editor of the first journalists' trade magazine in the early 1860s, would be 'an army of liberty with a rallying point in every town', 'a police of safety, and a sentinel of public morals'.¹⁰ This, coupled with the gradually rising cost of running a newspaper due to advances in print technology, and with the ever-increasing influence of advertisers, led to the demise of the radical newspapers. One after the other they were faced with three alternatives: closing down, becoming a marginal, 'specialist' newspaper, or commercialising. By the end of the century most of them had passed into the hands of entrepreneurs with access to large amounts of capital.

Entertainment — crime, scandal, romance, sport, etc. — had always been part of the content of the radical newspapers, next to independent political opinion. What disappeared when the radical newspapers ceased publication or became commercialised was not entertainment, but a particular combination of entertainment and outspoken political comment. Entertainment, in fact, established itself even more strongly as a staple of newspaper content, but it was now used to further the interest of those who saw the newspaper as a form of social control and as a way to make money — as bait. Popular newspapers were no longer 'of the people', but 'for the people' (the 'masses'). Cheap papers with 'objective', 'impartial' news, presented stories without explicit comment, as a series of disconnected facts, in short items and in simple standardised prose, under increasingly large headlines. They enjoyed immense circulations, display ads, photographs, crime reports, scandals and personal interviews. These were the ingredients of what Matthew Arnold called the 'new journalism':

> We have had opportunities of observing a new journalism, which a clever and energetic man [W. T. Stead] has recently invented. It has much to recommend it; it is full of ability, novelty, variety, sensation, sympathy, generous instincts; its one great fault is that it is *feather-brained*. It throws out assertions at venture because it wishes them true; does not correct either them or itself if they are false; and to get at the state of things as they truly are seems to feel no concern whatsoever.¹¹

It was again in the U.S., and in entertainment-oriented programs, that something resembling the interview could first be heard on radio. A Bernarr MacFadden, for example, bought time, every morning, from WOR, Newark, to promote the magazines he published (physical culture magazines and a gossip rag called *True Stories*). In his programs he developed the format of physical exercises to music, which soon became very popular. For the chorus girls he paid to come in and exercise with him, he wrote lines like: 'I am so happy to be here with Mr MacFadden. I do these exercises every morning and I am sure I keep my figure and keep in condition just through these exercises. Thank you (GASP OF RELIEF). My gawd, I'm glad that's over.'[12] Other radio personalities of the early 1920s, similarly combining the role of entertainer and salesman, used 'vox pops' (literally, the voice of the people). This, together with the related rise of public opinion research, was soon to make its influence felt in other countries.[13]

In Europe, radio was initially government-controlled — in most countries commercial radio was not introduced until after the Second World War. It was seen as a means to reach 'the people'. Music programs alternated with speeches by experts who sought to give listeners 'education for citizenship'. David Cardiff has documented how, in the BBC, the interview developed from such speeches. The leaders of the BBC Talks Department had become increasingly aware that the intrusion of such public instruction into people's private living rooms was a rather drastic and unprecedented step, and they were looking for ways to soften it. To this end they encouraged radio speakers to speak in a more low key, 'conversational' manner. Some speakers were more successful at this than others. An industrial relations specialist named John Hilton, for example, introduced deliberate hesitations and errors into his speech in order to sound more 'natural' — but all these inarticulacies were in fact scripted. When a newspaper praised his style, he said, on radio: 'Oh yes, I like that. For, of course, I read every word. If only I could pull it off every time — but you have to be at the top of your form.

Yes, of course, every word's on paper, even now — it's all here.'[14]

Thus a new form of public speech developed, a genre which retained the logical structure and advance planning of the formal public monologue speech, but mixed it with elements of informal, private conversation — in a planned and deliberate way, and in order to develop a new mode of social control. Here the media professional would have a key role to play. Speakers like Hilton became the first professional broadcasters. By 1939 Hilton had abandoned his specialism and ran a kind of agony column of the air, championing the cause of the 'ordinary man' against 'confidence tricksters'.[15] He had moved from a position of addressing the 'ordinary men' from above to one of speaking for them, of being their representative. How genuinely egalitarian was such a shift? It must not be forgotten that this is also the period in which President Franklin Roosevelt developed the format of the 'fireside chat' to address American citizens, and in which Joseph Goebbels urged German radio announcers to use more informal, colloquial speech and local dialect in order to 'sound like the listener's best friend'.[16]

For some time, two kinds of program existed side by side in the BBC — the informal, conversational programs addressed to the 'ordinary man', and the formal monologues aimed at the 'intelligent listener'. It was in the former that experiments continued to take place. Thus the vox pop was introduced — fully scripted by BBC personnel, but read by real 'ordinary people' with authentic regional accents. Such vox pops, it was felt, had to focus on the way 'people feel about subjects' rather than consist of 'potted scientific analysis'. In another experiment the BBC used a 'plain man' to mediate between the expert and the public. As Cardiff notes: 'The idea is to keep the expert at a low level so that he is intelligible to the inexpert listeners and also to add lightness and entertainment to a serious subject by adopting the dialogue form'.[17] The experiment was considered successful and soon the 'plain men' were encouraged to adopt a style of interviewing which involved the interjection of critical questions throughout the talk, in order to provide an immediate element of balance.[18] It was still called a 'talk' but it had, in fact, already become an interview.

In Australia similar developments took place. Dorothy Vautier, a popular presenter of women's programs on 2GB, felt that interviews were especially suitable for female audiences because they catered 'for their interests in the personality of the speaker rather than their ideas'.[19] The ABC began to use interviews for subjects considered 'controversial'. In these the interviewer 'was said to represent the listener and the "man-in-the-street".'[20] A program entitled *The Voice of the People*, on Melbourne's 3KZ, was devoted entirely to street interviews.[21]

The development of the media interview, then, was linked to at least four factors. First, it developed in programs for the 'ordinary man or woman'. Initially the purpose of such programs was quite openly seen as social control, exercised from above. But before long a rationalising shift had occurred. The same people construed programs on the same subjects for the same audiences, 'on behalf of the people', as embodying a voice which was 'representative of the people' themselves. Second, interviews began in the broadcasting context of entertainment programs. Their subsequent introduction into more serious programs was seen as adding 'an element of lightness and entertainment' or a 'human element'. In other words they were, in part, used as audience bait (as they had been by Bennett in 1839). Third, in each case a *genre of speech* was developed which mixed elements of the formal, public monologue (advance planning, even to the point of entire interviews being scripted, tight logical coherence and so on) with elements from informal, private conversation (a more restricted and less formal vocabulary, grammatical constructions which were thought to be like conversation, deliberate inarticulacies and so on). Fourth, there was a transitional stage in which the answers of the 'ordinary people' were fully scripted by people who were not themselves 'ordinary people' — as though future interviewees were to be given an opportunity to learn what kinds of answer were expected of them before they ever had a chance to give any answers. And these answers were of a specific kind: they were, so it was reiterated again and again, to represent 'feelings', not 'ideas' — they were to be what, in this book, we have called 'confessions'.

The more formal address survived alongside the new genres of broadcast speech as, to some extent, it still does on more 'highbrow' public radio programs. Even in the late 1960s there were still restrictions on the ways interviews could be used. For example, on the ABC, news had always been seen as a highly formal, highly serious genre. When television was first introduced, there had even been reluctance to show the newsreaders on screen, and it had seriously been considered showing a picture of Big Ben while the news was being read.[22] Interviews were not to be allowed on such a program. They belonged to the more 'showbusiness' approach of public-affairs journalism. Increasingly, however, the forms devised for the 'ordinary man' became dominant. To watch television was to be addressed as such an 'ordinary man' — for all of us. And to be a good interviewee, regardless of whether one was a prime minister or a 'man or woman in the street', was to become complicit with this form of address, coopted into discourse of the 'ordinary man'. Interviews traded on their conversational origins to address listeners as the equals of the interviewed and to render the public issues of the day in the private vernacular of consumers, not citizens. The voices in the corner of the living room began to sound 'like us', even as the forms of media interviews proliferated to serve various professionally defined purposes.

Documentary Impulses: Reality, Subjectivity and 'Depth'

The interview is linked to the documentary impulse which finds expression in empirical ethnographic analyses of 'foreign' and 'primitive' cultures as well as revelations about one's own society. They provide evidence of the condition or nature of the society or sub-culture in which they are set. It is not surprising, therefore, that in the late 1950s and early 1960s a new impetus was given to many fields of journalism and film production in which interviews were to become ubiquitous, if not universal, features. For it was during this period that the invention of portable lightweight film- and (especially) sound-recording devices (the now ubiquitous tape-recorder) helped to generate a renewed interest in ethnography in Europe and a 'new journalism' in the U.S.A. Although broadcast television was already established in Europe and America by this period, its talk was anchored to the studio. The new recording equipment allowed access to sources of interview and settings well beyond the studio.

In the postwar period, documentary film practices (*cinéma vérité* and *direct cinema*) became the focus of experimental, formal innovation (Jean Rouch, Edgar Morin and Chris Marker in France; Donn Pennebaker, the Maysles brothers and Fred Wiseman in the U.S.A.). By definition, 'documentary' film continually returns to the issue of *recording* or *documenting* 'reality'. In the early 1960s film and the synchronised sound recorder became the means of novel interview-based social exploration, such as *Chronique d'un Eté* (Rouch et al., 1961) and *Le Joli Mai* (Marker, 1963) which produced a new sense of social reality by *realising* (making visibly real and documenting) the general, historical significance of ordinary people's personal and social lives. These films, however, were not merely objective, invisibly edited 'fly on the wall' observational documentaries. Despite their French label (which means 'cinema truth') they sometimes foregrounded the practices of their makers, who were not hidden from view and who acknowledged their own active roles. The French documentarist Jean Rouch, for example, argued that 'the camera acts as a stimulant' causing people to reveal themselves in unusually open ways. 'There is a strong element of the confessional in Rouch's films', claims Ellis, who likens this to the psychodrama and to group psychotherapy (both, significantly, practised during the 1960s as part of American 'personal fulfilment' movements).[23]

In *Chronique d'un Eté*, Rouch and Morin foreground their role as film-makers in initiating various interactions between a random collection of Parisians who interview each other, as well as commenting on their own interviews in what looks rather like a 'group therapy' session at the end of the film. Sometimes the film-makers themselves conducted the conversational-style interviews. One of these was this dramatic interview with Marilou, who at several points during the interview comes close to crying:

INTERVIEWER: *You're twenty-seven, an Italian living in Paris. These three years are in total contrast to your life in Cremona in a middle-class home. Here you live in a maid's room. You're a foreigner. You know men. You've come to know Paris. You've made new friends. Is there anything left for you?*

MARILOU: You spoke of the change in my life. My maid's room has its uses. I spent several winters there. There was no heating. I'd never been cold or gone without. It was a sap to my conscience. I was glad to have a hard time. It was the first time I'd ever worked. I'd wake up at seven, exhausted, but almost glad of the rush hour crowd. I think I really felt I belonged. But that didn't last. Now I'm sick of my room and the cold. I'm sick of the tube in the rush hour. And I don't . . . I find human contact . . . I dislike it . . . it's pointless.

INTERVIEWER: *But you've some aim, a hope?*
MARILOU: To be honest, I don't know. Sometimes I'm happy to be in Paris. I feel I've made up for lost time. When I came here I felt stranded, I was shut up in myself, isolated. When I was in Italy, I'd exhausted my inner resources. I wanted to come up against reality. I wonder if this was the right way. For example I drink, you see. I . . . I wanted to get rid of alibis when I came to France. I wanted to live on my own terms. I've destroyed the false reasoning, only to find it in drink, men. To put it baldly, in trash.

INTERVIEWER: *But what do you mean by reality? Is it a job that interests you? Doing what you like? Or is it to live? A man you love? Not have affairs?*
MARILOU: I want a job that doesn't scare me. To live with someone, for an hour, two hours, a month, two weeks even. Just to be with him, without any ghosts to stop me loving him. To get outside myself, to die even. Provided I'm in touch with something, instead of being forced back on myself. I've not even the right to kill myself. It would be an act.

INTERVIEWER: *[Pause] Why are you forced back on yourself?*
MARILOU: If only I knew . . .

MARILOU A FEW WEEKS LATER

INTERVIEWER: *Well, Marilou, it's a month since we had our discussion. It's August now, and there's one thing that struck me. Two nights ago walking along I told you about a question I'd put in this film. I asked Jacques and his wife: 'Are you happy?' They answered: 'More or less'. You said you'd give the same answer. Yet when I saw you a fortnight ago you were very depressed, and feeling none too well. Yet you can answer, more or less?*

MARILOU: Once again, I don't know what's happening to me. It's like 14 July all over again. The faces of all the people I'd known were pressing in on me. I didn't know what to do. I thought I was done for. I think things came to a head that night. Afterwards there were two days of emptiness. And then quite suddenly things fell into place. People became real again. I left my fantasy world. Everything became straightforward.

INTERVIEWER: *Did it happen suddenly? On its own?*

MARILOU: [Pause] From the moment I began to see the people around me, to feel part of life, I became ready . . . ready for anything. For . . . I don't know . . . friendship . . . and for love.

INTERVIEWER: *And that changed everything?*

MARILOU: [Pause] Yes, but one thing's strongest of all. Fear. Despite everything, fear! The same thing may happen as before. I'll find myself alone again. Cut off.

INTERVIEWER: *You won't again.*

MARILOU: What do you expect me to say? I can't talk about it.

Rouch links Marilou's social position (as a 'foreigner'), her sexuality and her employment to what, in retrospect, is a very 'existentialist' question — *'Is there anything left for you?'* Marilou's revelations are deeply personal and inconsistent. Yet they are accepted and discussed by the interviewer without pity or condescension. They are thereby 'documented' as symptomatic of French life during that period, not seen principally as symptoms of a psychological illness or maladjustment. Rouch interviews Marilou without the assumption that she is sick or deviant. Hence her 'depth' produces a form of ethnographic data, not a pretext for sensationalism or moralism.

Such interviews have become relatively common in 'ethnographic' documentary since then: The very popular *35-Up* (Michael Apted, 1990) and its predecessors (*28-Up*, *21-Up*) all sought to reveal the social totality in their class-located interviewees. Like *Chronique*, they emphasise the particular reality of people who are shown to exist beyond their presence in the film. By explicitly addressing the 'meaning' and 'purpose' of people's lives (including the prospect of suicide in the interview with the homeless Neil in *35-Up*), they develop an existential dimension. *Cinéma vérité*, therefore, is one obvious precursor to the modes of interviewing found in documentary genres in all media during the last thirty years. In the next chapter we will discuss in detail a contemporary radio example, Caroline Jones' interview program *The Search for Meaning*. The tape-recorder allowed the ethnographic and political discourses of postwar European culture to be realised in what the media called the 'in-depth' interview. However mannered and predictable most documentary interviews may have become, it is possible to see in examples such as *Chronique d'un Eté*, the radical potential of recorded questions and answers.

A second major factor in establishing interviews as credible or authentic media phenomena is the movement referred to as 'new journalism' (associated in the U.S.A. with names like Tom Wolfe, Hunter S. Thompson, Joan Didion and Norman Mailer). This movement is usually thought of as subjectivist and personal, overthrowing the canons of 'objective' journalism in literary, interpretive, ironic and innovative styles of writing. Hardly journalism at all! Yet it relates closely both to the impulses behind the nineteenth-century press interviews and to the ethnographic documentary spirit.

Tom Wolfe cites Balzac and Dickens in describing 'comprehensive reporting — that enables one to portray scenes, extensive dialogue, status life and emotional life, in addition to the usual data of the essay narrative'.[24] Proof of the journalist's ability as a writer guarantees the objectivity (what Wolfe calls the 'egotistical objectivity') of the reporting:

> The basic reporting unit is no longer the datum, the piece of information, but the scene . . .

> Therefore, your main problem as a reporter is, simply, managing to stay with whomever you are writing about long enough for the scenes to take place before your own eyes. There are no secrets of reporting that will help a man pull this off; it is completely a test of his personality.[25]

Wolfe advocated writing 'accurate non-fiction with techniques usually associated with novels and short stories'.[26] This literary impulse, originating outside the institutional norms of the journalism of its time, but close to the spirit of nineteenth-century journalism (compare with the Bennett interview) and in many respects as 'ethnographic' as the French documentary movement, turned to an involvement between what sociologists would call 'participant observers' and their subjects. The 'scenes' of the new journalism often centred on the comic incongruity of the interviewer–writer coming into contact with his or her prey. When Hunter S. Thompson found Muhammad Ali in Las Vegas (at midnight), Dr (*sic*) Thompson made *himself* rather than Ali the subject of the subsequent report on the encounter. His interview with the boxer was presented in the context of Thompson's own drug-or-alcohol-induced, paranoid self-consciousness. Here is a taste of the new ('gonzo') journalist's scene-setting introduction to the Ali interview:

> 'You *scared* me,' Ali was saying. 'You looked like some kind of a bum — or a hippie.'

> 'What?' I almost shouted. '*A bum? A hippie?*' I lit another cigarette or maybe two, not realising or even thinking about the gross transgression I was committing by smoking *and* drinking in the presence of the Champ. (Conrad told me later that *nobody* smokes or drinks in the same room with Muhammad Ali — and Jesus Christ! Not — of all places — in the sacred privacy of *his own bedroom at midnight*, where I had no business being in the first place.) ... But I was mercifully and obviously ignorant of what I was doing. Smoking and drinking and tossing off crude

bursts of language are not *second* nature to me, but *first* — and my mood, at that point, was still so mean and jangled that it took me about ten minutes of foulmouthed raving before I began to get a grip on myself.

Everybody else in the room was obviously relaxed and getting a wonderful boot out of this bizarre spectacle — which was *me*; and when the adrenalin finally burned off I realized that I'd backed so far away from the bed and into the bureau that I was actually *sitting* on the goddamn thing, with my legs crossed in front of me like some kind of wild-eyed, dope-addled budda (Bhuddah? Buddah? Budda? . . . Ah, fuck these wretched idols with unspellable names — let's use *Budda*, and to hell with Edwin Newman) . . . and suddenly I felt just fine.

And why not?

I was, after all, the undisputed heavyweight gonzo champion of the world — and this giggling yoyo in the bed across the room from me was no longer the champion of *anything*, or at least nothing he could get a notary public to vouch for . . . So I sat back on the bureau with my head against the mirror and I thought, 'Well, shit — here I am, and it's definitely a weird place to be; but not *really*, and not half as weird as a lot of other places I've been . . . Nice view, decent company, and no real worries at all in this tight group of friends who were obviously having a good time with each other as the conversation recovered from my flaky entrance and got back on the fast-break, bum-and-run track they were used to. [27]

A few pages later, Thompson did report the interview, which centred on Ali's loss to Leon Spinks. Thompson self-consciously and informally engaged Ali in analysing his own tactics and ability. But he allowed Ali the last word, and perhaps it is a comment on the self-confessed 'professional weirdo' interviewer when Ali says: 'Oh yeah, I like the pressure, need the pressure . . . the world likes . . .

people like to see miracles . . . people like to be there when history is made'.[28]

The new American journalists made this history into a frantic, comic theatre of absurdity through their own self-conscious style. They incorporated interviews into scenes of sociological hyperbole and stories in the first person about the experiences of the interviewer/journalist as reflective of the critical condition of America at the time. Through new journalism, interviews lost their inhibitions and their self-important formality. But being themselves comic, absurd or subversive, they could not be parodied nor become easily conventionalised as mainstream genres of media interview. So the 'hallucinated vision' which the new journalists conveyed through the 1960s and 1970s always remained marginal to the major newspapers, magazines and television networks. Their use of interviews as part of documentary literature remains eccentric and significant for helping to free journalism generally from its cold-war frigidity rather than for producing models of interviewing to be imitated by their successors.

More generally, the new journalism had produced scenes and stories of subjective literary inventiveness based on real persons or sub-cultures. The people who provoked the pens of Tom Wolfe or Joan Didion were rendered strange by the detailed, allusive and ironic modes of writing employed by these self-conscious journalistic mavericks. The sub-cultures (such as Hippies and Hell's Angels) so eloquently animated by Hunter S. Thompson's manic prose came to represent the limits or extremes of American society. The very subjectivity of this promiscuous journalism emphasised the veracity of its sociologically extended vision of America. The marginal and the eccentric seemed to illuminate the centre and the conventional (as, two decades earlier, B-movies and *films noirs* had done). These writers needed only a tape-recorder and a room of their own; they were not institutionalised journalists, but freelance observers of the symptoms of a society which, in a decade of change and protest, reflected on itself more critically in the public media than at any time in its history.

The new journalists observed and wrote scenes about people and events which were anything but traditionally newsworthy, but they also interviewed, in passing, the rich, the powerful and the famous, and incorporated these interviews into their stories. In doing so they offered 'deep' interpretation, oblique, ironic commentary and incongruous and amusing re-contextualisations of their subjects. They described and interpreted in ways which showed they had been in contact with their subjects (the 'having-been-there effect' of the film documentary), but they produced 'literature' of new mixed genres which raised the writers (rather than the written-about) to the status of fame. More importantly, perhaps, they practised, in journalism, many of the principles of the contemporary (cinema) documentary-makers: the creation of 'real' scenes around participant observation or verbatim recordings of interviews and conversations between the socially significant, the ordinary and famous alike. While new journalism seemed to foreground subjective writerly interpretation, it also sought to describe the deep texture of society and to examine that society from multiple subjective perspectives. Like the direct cinema's engagement with the minutiae of social interaction, the literary scenes of the new journalism were juxtaposed to reveal, through contrast and accumulation of detail, how the totality 'worked'. The marginal and the eccentric, the foibles of the famous, the cults and the charlatans, the politicians and the artists of America were all to be found, revealed and reviled, in the interviews of the new journalists.

The Interview as Documentary Scenario: Oriana Fallaci

Independently, but parallel to the rise of America's new journalism, the Italian Oriana Fallaci developed a literary, non-objective style of interviewing the famous, those 'whose celebrity is so vast, so clamorous, so exasperating that it obsesses us, plagues us to the point where we exclaim: God, what bores!'[29] Fallaci, like Hunter S. Thompson, trusted her tape-recorder while rejecting objectivity:

> I don't believe in objectivity. Objectivity is hypocrisy, presumption, since it starts from the supposition that the person who is providing a piece of news or a profile has discovered Truth with a capital T. In fact, when one writes a profile, there exists, there can only exist, the honesty of the person who furnishes the piece.[30]

Each Fallaci interview offers a brief pen portrait of its famous subject, but then lets him/her speak, with minimal questions in the published interview transcripts. Despite, or because of this, each is highly interpretive and clearly authored by Fallaci, whose contextualisation and direct, insistent questioning produce historically located, complex knowledge of their subjects — knowledge which they might usually prefer to conceal and which the interview itself seems uniquely to produce. Like Tom Wolfe's 'scenes', Fallaci's 'profiles' depend on the reporter managing to 'stay with' the subject long enough for her 'egotistical objectivity' to reveal the subject's existence in its contradictory complexity. Fallaci's interviews, perhaps because of her persistence, perhaps because of her participation as the equal of her subjects, seem to reveal what the speakers do not understand about themselves. They are not, therefore, *evidence* of a social problem, but nor are they savage unmaskings of self-deluded egoists. Instead, the subjective is revealed through essentially descriptive accounts of people's lives, through Fallaci's candour and openness to her interviewees' surprising revelations — despite, not because of, what they say.

Fallaci put the glamorous in front of an unflattering mirror, seeing in it Robert Kennedy as an overgrown schoolboy; Federico Fellini as an irritating prima donna; Norman Mailer as pathetically obsessed with his own masculinity.

Fallaci's questions were insistent and personal, yet curiously ingenuous in that she seemed to be demanding of her subjects what they were unable to reveal about their own existence. Her interviews resemble short two-person dramas ('scenes', again) and, as in scripted stage drama, the subtext reveals by its relationship to the text. Hence, Sean Connery cannot think of any admirable women, only men, and rather than pursue such troublesome questions he chooses to 'go and have a beer'. (Of course, these *published* interviews are all edited and compressed versions of less structured tape-recordings.)

Sometimes, as in the example below, Fallaci managed to create a genuinely 'strange' (and therefore existentially revealing) portrait through her tape-recorded conversations. By recording her talk to the apparently inarticulate bullfighter Manuel, El Cordobes, she paints a scene in which a beast is slaughtered as the background to their conversation. The distance which renders the interview so compelling is maintained by Fallaci telling the young matador of the cow's death and removal, as though he is too innocent to confront his own actions, a theme which is echoed in the interview generally.

This interview moves through a series of interactions in which Fallaci acts in precise ways towards her subject. She begins with an open, ingenuous question, but then becomes, in effect, his protector against what his frank and innocent answers reveal. She moves towards the role of exasperated parent, then becomes again the motherly protector, creating a 'happy ending' to the story that she has told her 'innocent' child. The simple, concrete language of the young man is repeated in her questions and narration (about the sea, the bulls, the moon). We reproduce very heavily edited excerpts of this wonderful interview below, beginning with part of Fallaci's introduction:

> He was an ugly, starving, filthy child, without father or mother . . . His only amusement was on the bull farm, practising with the muleta; for which his guardians would beat him across the shoulders and the chest until he

fainted. He was the living symbol, in those days, of a despairing, illiterate, defeated Spain. Today he is the most famous, well-loved, venerated, adulated, exalted man you can meet there . . .

On the day he finally made up his mind to talk to me he subjected me rather by way of vendetta, to a wild gymkhana in a Land-Rover, from which I still thank God I survived . . . On horseback he set off to find a fighting cow, on horseback he took us to a clearing, to work the cow with the cape: for his own pleasure or for ours, either way my only safety lay in a tree behind which I could hide in difficult moments. He worked the cow for so long that the moment came when, exhausted, she fell forward on to her nose and broke both her jaws and became an atrocious, useless, fountain of blood: the very symbol of today's Spain. So the banderilleros tied her to the tree to kill her and he himself suddenly calmed down, like a child who has broken a plaything and is about to cry over it. '*Vámonos*', he said roughly, dejectedly. Our dialogue begins here.

FALLACI: *That poor creature tied to a tree like a man about to be shot. With her jaws broken, her nose streaming with blood. Listen, she's still crying. What a tragic job yours is, Manuel. What on earth makes anyone become a bullfighter? Money, ambition, what?*

MANUEL: When a man's poor he's hungry for everything: not only for bread . . . Look, it hurts me to see an animal die, I can't even kill a hen; once when I was hungry I stole a hen and I killed it but I was shaking all over as I killed it and as I killed it I turned my head away and I didn't feel hungry any more. Have they killed her?

FALLACI: *Yes, they've killed her. Now they're taking her away with the tractor.*

MANUEL: She was a good cow, she was, she fought well and I respected her and I still respect her because she died at her work, see, just like I might or the horse

	might. It's true, see, that we come into the world to work and to die, all of us, men, animals, and the bull too, when he enters the arena he realises he's come into the world to work and to die. I know when he realises it because he fights hard to defend himself and then I'm sorry to kill him, see, and I ask the public for permission to spare his life: yes, it's a tragic job, mine. But when you're fifteen years old and you've been working other folks' fields for ten years and dreaming of being somebody and owning a whole ham, that's tragic too, see? . . . Have they taken her away with the tractor?
FALLACI:	*Yes, they've taken her away. Now they're loading her onto the truck.*
MANUEL:	She was a brave cow, see, she didn't deserve to come to such a bad end . . . The bull is a wild animal and in a bullfight the man is pitting himself against the wild animal, the animal has strength but the man has brain: but a man is a man and how can anything pit itself against a man? . . . Have they loaded her onto the truck?
FALLACI:	*Yes, she's on. Now they're taking her away. Don't think about it any more, Manuel.*
MANUEL:	Because, you see, I never went to school, it's barely a year since I learned to read and write . . .
FALLACI:	*But you must tell me what the priest teaches you, apart from religion and numbers and spelling.*
MANUEL:	He explains things to me. For example I ask him about the things I like most and he explains them to me.
FALLACI:	*And what are the things you like most?*
MANUEL:	Well . . . it may sound silly . . . because, you see, they're things nobody ever talks about, nobody, I don't know why, but they're fantastic things, see, wonderful, more wonderful than bulls, than anything . . . they're . . . they're things about the sky, astronomical things. I mean, do you know that

the Earth turns around the Sun, and also around the sun other planets like Earth are turning and that we can go to them? Of course you know, you do, and you know about the Moon and how to get there, but not me and so I asked the priest and he explained to me about these sputniks that go and take photographs that they send straight down to us on Earth, and when there are enough photographs they'll send up a man. Isn't that fantastic, tell me? Look, I'll tell you something, I don't like danger for danger's sake; for example I don't understand people who do parachute jumps for the fun of it, if it was necessary for something, for someone, I'd jump too, but for nothing, like that, just for the sake of jumping, no, never. But to go up, you understand, right up, with those sputnik things, I'd go up myself at once, see, it's truly extraordinary, just think, to be put in a rocket and sent up to the Moon. What fellows! Is it true that you know them?

FALLACI: *Yes, it's true.*

MANUEL: Listen then, when you see them couldn't you ask if they need anyone, me, say? I don't know, if they needed someone for something difficult or dangerous that the others don't want to have a go at, couldn't you tell them: look there's my friend Manolo who's a bullfighter and he'd be glad to go? . . .

FALLACI: *All right. I'll tell them. But aren't you afraid, Manuel?*

MANUEL: Of course I'm afraid, I'm afraid like anyone else . . .

FALLACI: *What did you buy, Manuel, with the first money you made as a bullfighter?*

MANUEL: I bought a big ham . . .

FALLACI: *Listen, Manuel, what else do you like besides bulls and the Moon and ham?*

MANUEL: Girls. Women. Women are beautiful, they're beautiful even when they're ugly, I couldn't do

	without a woman, no, I always have to have a lady love.
FALLACI:	*So then why don't you start a family, Manuel?*
MAUEL:	Hombre! Because I watch out! Look, I was engaged one time, see, when I was young I was seventeen. And she was from Palma del Rio. And she left me. Because I didn't have money or work, etcetera and her parents used to say I'd be a good-for-nothing because I wanted to be a bullfighter, and so she left me . . .
The cinema is like the city, full of noise and you have to wear a tie, I feel strangled wearing a tie. I like the country because it's what I know and because there are trees and horses and cows and the air is clean and you don't have to wear a tie.
FALLACI:	*And the sea? Do you like the sea, Manuel?*
MAUEL:	Yes, no, no! In the sea there are sharks and I don't know how to defend myself against sharks, because they don't go for the muleta, they don't, they tear a piece out of you and they're off, and you never know where they're coming from or how or why, and they scare me just like your complicated difficult questions.
FALLACI:	*And do you like El Cordobes, Manuel?*
MANUEL:	Yes, I do. I like him for the way he fights, I like him for the way he throws money away, I like him because of how he used to be hungry, I like him for the way he laughs, I like him for the way he defends himself. He never stops defending himself. I know he always has to defend himself, always, from bulls, from women, from friends, from enemies, from the difficult questions of a dangerous woman. Ask if they've taken away my cow, whether the butcher's come and so on.
FALLACI:	*They must have taken her away and the butcher must have come; there's no one left in the yard, Manuel. There's only silence and it will soon be dark; you'd*

> *think they'd all died along with the cow. But perhaps she isn't dead, Manuel, and perhaps she'll live again.*
> (Near Cordova, April 1965)[31]

Of course, Fallaci has herself edited the tape-recorded transcript on which this interview is based, especially reducing the length of her own questions to allow El Cordobes' revelations to flow freely. As published, the interviewer's protective but insistent interrogation allows El Cordobes to create his own concrete story as his unselfconscious, unreflective replies reveal his contradictoriness. The meeting between the two is as unusual as it is revealing: Fallaci (like her self-conscious, new journalist colleagues) is as present in the written story as her subject is. Yet he chronicles his own life in response to her presence, and as he does so the reader senses that this is the very first time that he has ever reflected on his own existence (his own 'subject-hood'). Fallaci's concern for him, realised through her urgent questioning, gives the exchange a drama and tension seldom found in media interviews, precisely counterpointed by the slow demise of the beast in the background. Though published in written form, the interview is a documentary-like scenario, with the physical context and background action essential to the scene and its significance.

As if to stress the distinctiveness of her subjective involvement in interviews, even those she conducted through the 1970s with the powerful (Henry Kissinger, Indira Gandhi), American commentators have emphasised the 'trials of strength' through which Fallaci engages with her interviewees, as well as her self-proclaimed disdain for objectivity. S.A. Arico notes:

> Fallaci's originality is the emotional entanglement that takes place when she meets the other person. Her degree of involvement makes most exchanges seen on American television look tepid. Journalists in the United States appear far too objective and composed to rate a valid comparison. On CBS's *60 Minutes*, Fallaci, who has never

understood the American insistence that all reporters remain impartial, said to Mike Wallace: 'I hate objectivity, you know. I have told it many times, I do not believe in objectivity. I believe in what I see, what I hear and what I feel which is a kind of blasphemy . . . especially for the American press.'[32]

However, Arico also points out that Fallaci's interviews with 'villains' of the 1970s (William Colby, Director of the CIA; General Nguyen Van Thieu of South Vietnam) follow a clear linguistic structure, involving confrontation, presupposition, self-revelation and emotionality. But, unable to see Fallaci as other than just an eccentric in the context of American journalism (he quotes her as saying 'An interview is a love story for me. It's a fight. It's a coitus') he falls back on seeking her *motives*, not showing how her interviews violate the norms of mannered *60 Minutes* professionalism.

The interview genres we will discuss in subsequent chapters — the political interview, the celebrity interview and the confession — link specific modes of questioning, specific kinds of speech acts, to specific categories of interviewees. Politicians are challenged ('*But last week you said . . .*'), celebrities are invited to recount ('*You had a difficult childhood . . .*'), confessees to reveal their feelings and desires ('*You must have been very worried*'). Fallaci uses the same tools, the same kinds of speech acts — challenges ('*So then why don't you start a family, Manuel?*'), invitations to tell stories ('*What did you buy, Manuel, with the first money you made as a bullfighter?*') or to reveal feelings ('*But aren't you afraid, Manuel?*') or desires ('*And what are the things you like most?*'). But she does not relate them in easily predictable, routinised ways to specific categories of interviewee. She challenges the celebrity, asks the politician to tell the story of his unhappy childhood, the witness to reveal her feelings, and this in an order which runs counter to expectations (in the extract, for instance, she asks 'why' before she asks 'what'). This throws interviewees off balance, making it impossible for them to give pat answers or tell well-rehearsed stories. Unexpected, even poetic conjunctions may result: bullfights, the moon and ham, rather than bullfights, injuries, machismo and glamour, for instance. And, as in a free musical improvisation, Fallaci sometimes leads, sometimes follows, sometimes introduces new themes. She picks up cues from her partner in the conversation, rather than anticipating the next chord in a pre-arranged harmonic sequence. This puts her interviews into a class of their own, which is quite distinct from such institutionalised question-and-answer exchanges as the confession, the interrogation, the expert testimony and the political contest.

At the same time as Fallaci wrote her subjective literary interviews, American documentary film-makers were developing a radically objectivist cinema of non-fiction. Recall that we discussed the French movement towards self-conscious *cinéma vérité* (for example, Rouch), in which the film-maker acts as a catalyst to the interviews and interactions depicted. By contrast, in the U.S.A. the new lightweight sound recording devices were used to document such issues as a presidential primary contest, social institutions (mental hospital, high schools) or the detailed behaviour of door-to-door salesmen by film-makers who sought *direct* ('unmediated', observational) representation of their subjects. Hence, in the direct ('fly on the wall') styles of film-making, interviews were rare or absent. The director sought to 'capture reality' through the self-justifying practice of seeing and hearing what audiences would be expected to believe.

So the tape-recorder was incorporated into varied film-making and journalistic practices, from the radically subjective to the (apparently) empirically objective. In television, where staged interviews in airports, studios and politicians' residences had emerged through the late 1950s (see Chapter 4), the interview became an almost inevitable component of current affairs reporting. However, it evolved different ways of balancing the intervention of the interviewer against the illusion of unmediated observation of the interviewee's experience or point of view. These are considered in following chapters but, generally, we can anticipate these analyses by saying that the role of the professional interviewer was foregrounded as a guarantee of objectivity.[33] Unmediated speech (for example, direct to camera) came to be seen as biased or subjective because it lacked the balancing editorial intervention of the professional journalist. Therefore, through the decades after the experiments we have outlined in direct cinema, *cinéma vérité* and the new journalism, a conventionalised, 'mannered' style of media interview evolved. A narrow range of formats, with the journalist present as the mediator and guarantee of 'truth', reflects a general tendency towards what Dai Vaughan characterises as 'mannerism' in television documentary generally since the early- to mid-1970s. Here is his critical description of this style:

> It can scarcely be disputed that television is becalmed in a mannerist phase. Every editor knows exactly where he is expected to cut; and the convention grows that the first cutting point is the best one: for to allow such a point to pass without cutting may be interpreted as laxness. This principle applies not only to action footage but even to talking heads. The interviewee must not be seen to hesitate, grope for words, or add qualifying clauses that would disrupt the crisp pacing of the program. Commentary, which six years ago was considered something of an anachronism, has returned to favour and is being used, not simply to clarify points in the narrative that would not reveal their full significance without it, but to supply wall-to-wall reassurance for the audience, who are held, despite the example of the commercials, to find film language too demanding. The doctrine of 'signposting', initially seen as an irreproachable attempt to point up the architecture of a film and to minimise confusion, has now swollen into a grotesque insistence that everything should be explained. The viewer must be told what a talking head is about to say, for fear he may presume to draw his own inferences from what is said.[34]

If Vaughan has not overstated his case, and we don't think he has, then the various cinematic and journalistic experiments with subjective yet ethnographically oriented interviews, using the potential of the newly-developed portable sound-recording equipment, have failed to inspire similarly reflective and open conversations in the medium in which the interview is now most common. The short grab of interview as evidence; the 'man behind the mask' political interview; the expert in lab-coat or in front of his (usually his) bookshelves — these have emerged as the staple fare of television interview-based films or programs. As interviews have become more frequent, their potential to evoke more than mere 'information' about an issue or a personality has apparently declined. Marilou and El Cordobes appear as disturbing and as strange today as they did when first interviewed. This seems to be partly because both are represented in *active interaction* with, rather than merely passively recorded by, their interlocutors. Because they matter to their questioners, they matter to the audience. Mannerism, in Vaughan's sense, allows the content of the historically specific interaction between people to be displaced by the form of the media-general interview itself. Television has learned how to *produce interviews* to fit their predetermined contexts.

In this chapter we have tried to outline how the sociological, ethnographic and literary-subjectivist impulses of writers and film-makers were realised through the use of verbatim recording of interviews and the contextualisation of these conversations in 'scenes', 'profiles' and scenarios. We have emphasised that even the most highly mannered television documentary program balances the objectifying tendency of audio- and video-tape *recording* against the subjective *interpretation* of the persons who use it. We can see interviews and the ethics and politics of interviewing as being tied to these tensions, which are only ever resolved provisionally by one set of practices (choice of setting, questions, etc.) being preferred to another. However, as interviews have become the ingredients of relatively formulaic types of programs, identifiable, perhaps even rigidly predictable, so too have *genres* of interviewing become relatively rigid. In following chapters we will investigate some of these genres in detail. In the final chapter, however, we will return to the theme of this chapter. For if the interview was shaped by the impulses we have described here, then it must still bear within it the potential that makes the Marilou and El Cordobes interviews such engaging records of human encounter. They must still bear within them the seeds of performative art of enquiry into the human condition that goes well beyond the mannerism of current interviewing practice.

3

Caroline Jones and the Search for Meaning

Caroline Jones interviews Margot Cairnes on ABC Radio.

CAROLINE JONES: *In this conversation we explore questions like, 'How possible is it to tell each other the truth and still remain friends?', 'What do people who get angry with us have to teach us?', 'Why do we attract certain people?', 'If there's a split between the real self inside, and the self I show to the outside world, what's the consequence of that?', 'How safe is it to show people who I really am?', 'Why are some Australian managers killing themselves by leaving the real person at home and putting on a highly controlled mask at work?', 'How good are we at seeing things as they really are?'*

Margot Cairnes is one of an emerging breed in the Australian business world, a developing profession of 'corporate wizards' or 'company doctors' who come into an organisation to facilitate some real and concrete change, and often improve the communication climate at the same time.

There have been distinguished pioneers in this field. Margot Cairnes, in her mid-thirties, is among the younger ones proving to be very effective. Her degrees are in education and management. She has worked as an executive and today is the high-paid, high-powered principal of her own company.

Margot always aims to take her real self to her work and as she ranges over a spectrum of issues, we see an integration of the adult aware of the imprint of her childhood, the corporate whiz-kid, the single mother, the beautiful woman speculating on the passing of physical attraction, the playgirl and the career woman, spiritual being and hedonist.

Here is someone who enjoys her body, who also prays continually; a woman whose life has been touched by very real setbacks, who describes her way of life as making strength out of weakness; a woman who can say 'I enjoy failure' and who has devoted herself to becoming all that she can be.

As we read Margot Cairnes's story, bear in mind that this young woman has been called in to work alongside some of the top management people in this country as an agent of change, and that she is highly successful at what she does.

So she's speaking from a position of rich experience with often demanding executives (mostly men) and with her own growing children.

Margot's openness is engaging and her honesty challenging.

MARGOT CAIRNES: My childhood was a very rich mixture of horror and creativity. Our family was not a happy home, my parents were not happy in their marriage, and we had a lot of problems around alcohol and aggression.

But my parents were both very amazing people. My father was a successful businessman. His great love was music and, as a child, I have a lot of memories of being around my father sitting at the piano playing, singing, dancing. It was a bit like . . . I always thought it was like being on the set of a musical comedy: a little bit unreal, but very exciting. And Dad, in fact, produced a lot of musical comedies and made a lot of money for charity.

My mother was a very successful journalist. She had been a war correspondent during the war — she had been attached to General MacArthur's headquarters and when the men came back, there weren't so many good jobs for the women, and she became the social editor of the local paper. But her real love, again, was theatre and art and music — and she also wrote the music, drama and art column. So, our home was full of a lot of music, a lot of art, a lot of very interesting people.

And we did have amazing parties; my parents had incredible parties. As a child it was a bit confusing because the adults were behaving a lot like children. But they were all amazing people — they were intellectuals, academics, painters, artists, poets. But at the same time the richness of that, the richness of poetry and of the discussion . . . I remember once coming out of my bedroom early in the morning and falling over the entire cast of *Boys from the Band* who had been to the party the night before and couldn't quite make it home.

So, I guess it was a mixture of confusion (because it was very confusing you know, what was happening and why did adults behave this way?) and, again, excitement because this was a whole other world. And, certainly, my friends at school didn't have this kind of world going on in their homes. It was . . . their homes, I understood, were a lot drier and more stable but also a lot less exciting, a lot less interesting.

JONES: *So what sort of ideas were you forming about creativity, I wonder, and creative people?*

CAIRNES: Well, it seemed to me that there was a lot of fun and excitement in that creative world but also a lot of pain. So when I married, I actually went into a . . . almost a creative void for about fourteen years: I turned my back on all of that. I went off and studied science, initially simply to get away from the creativity, because my feeling was that all these creative people were all kind of crazy and I really didn't want to spend the rest of my life around that craziness.

JONES: *And how did that work, that moving over to the other side — the scientific, the calmer, the quieter, the drier, I think you were saying?*

CAIRNES: Yes, well . . . it was a bit boring really — and it was no less painful. So what I found out was that creativity isn't painful and that a lot of creative people . . . and if you look back through history (I mean, I've read a lot of the biographies of the very creative people), a lot of them do have a lot of drama in their lives, but they're not necessarily . . . they don't have to go together. So you can have the creativity and the fun and the excitement without having the drama and the pain.

JONES: *Well, I'd like to explore more with you how you've come to those conclusions, maybe through some of the events of your life which you feel have been points of*

CAIRNES: *new insight. What would you choose to tell us about?*
Well, I guess, when I left home I'd been so 'there' for my parents in my home — I was very much the homemaker — so when I left there was a kind of a freedom and a liberation around that. But I married very young, so I very quickly put myself back into that role.

But, I guess, getting married — I was nineteen when that happened — was very much about growing up very early and taking that responsibility. But within a few years of my marriage, I decided that I did want to go back and I wanted to go into a more creative atmosphere, and I went to university and studied education. And it was a real revelation to me because I'd turned my back on the intellectual world for such a long time, and going back and studying again was like a new world: all these ideas and thoughts and people. I did a lot of economics and a lot of politics. And I was particularly interested in childcare: how we as a society rear our children, and how we provide for them on an economic and a political basis, and where they fit into society, and how society operates on where we're going.

JONES: *Any insight into why that was your concern?*

CAIRNES: Well, I think, because of my own childhood being so confusing, I just had a fascination for that.

I think that's quite an interesting story: I was the first person in . . . I don't know, twenty or thirty years . . . to win the university medal and the Department of Education gave me a prize for being the best practical and theoretical teacher to graduate that year but I couldn't get a job. I was put on a list and I was told it was seven years before the department (who had put me through university) would employ me.

So, at that time I went off to Darwin and I ran an

organisation up there which was actually made up of I think, eleven different companies. I had a staff of about sixty-four, and we had a turnover in the millions of dollars each year, and I was involved in managing all these companies, which were non-profit organisations so we got some funding, but we also had to make ends meet (I think we were funded 30 per cent), so I ran both a business and a government organisation simultaneously. And doing that, I learnt a lot about getting on with people and a lot about politics. I used to fly to Canberra all the time to negotiate our funding and negotiate with the state ministers. I helped rewrite the Act and I reorganised the organisation. And so, I began to — through experience — discover a lot about how the world worked, which was also very confusing. That led me to go and do some more study, which again helped to clarify and then sent me out doing the work I do. So there was all that sort of positive experience happening.

On the other side — in the personal arena — my marriage failed, which was a very traumatic experience for me. I found that very painful. And for the first time in my life, I guess, I had to turn around and admit to the world that I had failed at something. And I found that very hard to do: for me, being a good student and a good child and a good wife were very important, so turning round and saying to the world, 'I'm sorry, I've messed this one up' was hard.

And I guess the most recent event that's really been a life-turning event for me was the near-death of my daughter, which happened two years ago. At 11.30 in the evening, when I'd just moved into a new home, my daughter stopped breathing for thirty minutes. I was alone at home and the telephone wasn't yet connected, so it was very traumatic . . . basically, I had to respirate her until the ambulance arrived. A friend luckily was there when she . . . just before she collapsed, and I asked him to race and ring the ambulance, and when she did collapse and the breath stopped, I respirated her until . . . until the ambulance came and put her on oxygen and gave her adrenalin. But that was a very . . . oh! . . . It was an exciting experience, because I felt very much how important the relationship was and how important love was and how important life was. And every second of that experience was so valuable to me and to her, and it's been a turning point for all of us.

JONES: *Have you seen the world a little differently since that night?*

CAIRNES: Very much, very much. I now see the flowers and I see the boats and I see the water and I see the trees and I hear the music. When you come that close to death, life becomes very important and every second takes on a value beyond that which it had before.

JONES: *What do you think now about apparent failure or weakness or vulnerability? You said that when you had the first experience of that after many successes, it knocked you.*

CAIRNES: Well, I actually relish it. I enjoy failure. That probably sounds a bit perverse, but what I find is that when I have a success, I tend to grab it and run away. When I have a failure, I sit and I sit with it and I learn from it. And that brings strength and it brings joy and it brings advancement.

When my daughter became very ill, again that felt to me like a failure: I wasn't the perfect mother, my child was very ill and needed a lot of help. What that meant for me and my two children was that we went on a voyage of self-discovery together. We

	went on a voyage of learning about each other and about the problems that we had in relating to each other and the problems that particularly my children had in expressing negativity. Because until that time I'd been so positive that they felt that to be anything but positive was not acceptable. And so, when they had a problem, they didn't know how to talk to me about it. So we had to learn that.
JONES:	*How?*
CAIRNES:	Oh, by sitting down and telling each other the truth — which was very painful.
	What I have found is that, as a self-defence mechanism I've learnt to tell people what I think they want to hear. And a lot of that is to protect me and a lot of that is to protect them: I don't want to upset them and I don't want to hurt them and I don't want to spoil the friendship. But that's actually not very honest, because what I'm doing is telling them either a partial truth or an untruth. And because I tend to be very positive and because I tend to be successful, people want to follow suit, so we end up in a web of 'not-truth'. And this is what I'd done with my children — we had to sit down and say to each other things like, 'I don't like it when you do that!' My daughter at that time was very demanding and I had to tell her that some days I didn't want to come home, because I didn't want those demands. Now, when you have a child that's nearly dying, that's not an easy thing to say. But they were the sorts of things that we learned to say to each other.
JONES:	*So you got into new habits in that way?*
CAIRNES:	We did: we learned to disagree and we learned to tell each other the truth.
JONES:	*Has it made a difference?*
CAIRNES:	It's made so much difference, Caroline, I can't

begin to tell you. We've gone from being three single people living in a home being polite to each other, to being a very happy, full and rich family who interact and adore each other. Before, we loved each other politely; now we're passionate about each other.

There's choice and there's reality. And what I find, particularly in my work (and everything that I see in my work I see in myself), is that we tend not to see the reality and we tend not to make the choices. I know that's a little confusing so I'll explain it.

Reality is what is actually happening. Very few of us see what is actually happening. As we grow, as children, we form a set of defence mechanisms, a way of looking at the world, which is our way of coping with our childhood. Now, whether our childhood is good or bad, it's never perfect, because we're all brought up by human beings. And human beings do their best, but it will always be imperfect because that's what being human is. So we all develop this way of looking at the world which is our way of coping. Unfortunately, once it's developed, we tend to think . . . we see the world through that, and we tend to think that that is reality. So, for example, if we have a belief that people dislike us, no matter what anybody does we'll think they dislike us. So the reality may be that, in fact, people do like us. Our feeling of the reality, or our sense of the reality, is that they don't. And this happens in every situation. I've seen groups of very erudite businessmen and government leaders act in the most absurd ways which, sitting on the outside looking in, make no sense — until you realise that they're seeing the world not as you see it (which is through your reality), but as they see it (which is through theirs). And because

	most of us don't know that we're seeing an illusion (because most of us think that the illusion we see is reality), we don't know how we're behaving and we don't know the effect that our behaviour has on the people around us.
JONES:	*And you see this in the work that you do?*
CAIRNES:	Oh, very much.
JONES:	*With senior businesspeople and public servants and so on?*
CAIRNES:	Very much. Most of the problems that I see are very easy to solve on a rational basis. The issues are not generally that hard. It's not that they're not complex — they are; they're complex and they're ambiguous and they're changing. But if you've got a very clear mind and your emotions are not getting in the way, the solution, generally, is not that difficult.
JONES:	*And yet they probably call you in to solve some sort of rational problem, don't they?*
CAIRNES:	Very much, very much.
JONES:	*How do you get past that?*
CAIRNES:	Well, that's what we do: we solve the rational problem. But in solving the rational problem, we have to work with the illusions that get in the way. And the illusions are the sorts of things that get people to stamp their feet and walk out of the room. The illusions are the things that get people to undermine each other, to get people to withhold the truth, that get people to lay traps for each other. So my job, largely, is to help people stop doing that to each other long enough that they can get their rational mind into play and actually solve the issue that they're there to solve which, once you get the illusion out of the way, is not difficult. The difficult part is getting the illusion out of the way. Probably the best example that sticks out most vividly in my mind is . . . I was called into an

organisation that was going through a very major restructure after a change of ownership. I was working with the top team. There were ten people in the top team, and I divided them into two groups of five and asked them to go away and list the top ten problems that they saw facing the organisation at the time. Then they came back and each group was to report to the other group what problems they saw. The group that didn't have the managing director in it got up and gave their top ten problems and the managing director stood up and said that this was untrue, that these problems did not exist. And everybody else in the room turned around and said, 'But they do! We're your top ten people, and we're dealing with them every day. And we've had two major consulting companies come in and review us in the last eighteen months and these are the problems that they list and these are our problems.' And the managing director said, 'No, they're not. I won't accept it.' Whereupon he got up and he left the room and he actually went and played bowls leaving nine totally stunned (actually, ten — because I was stunned, too) people sitting in the room.

So, what was happening for that man was that he was simply not able to face the problems, because if he faced them, he would have to have done something about them. And at that time, because of the stress of the change that was happening in the organisation, it was overwhelming for him. So he wasn't needing criticism or rebuke, but actually help to cope with the stress that he was facing, and to be brought around to see that help was available from these people in the room. They weren't criticising him, they weren't putting him down, they weren't making him wrong; they were simply saying, 'These are our problems. We're here to help you solve them.'

One of my friends told me the other day how she valued my friendship because I didn't walk away; that no matter what happened I'd always come back and challenge and face the issues and work them through. And it's become so much part of me that I don't even know that I do it, and yet I see that in most people's lives what we do is . . . because we're too frightened to tell each other the truth, because we're too frightened to confront each other with the reality, and we're too frightened to confront ourselves with the reality, it's easier to walk away. And I understand that. I understand that very deeply, because having confronted myself and the close people around me with reality, I know how painful and how uncomfortable it can be.

JONES: *What do you think are the consequences of a habit of walking away, again and again?*

CAIRNES: Loneliness . . . a loneliness from yourself. It's like . . . if you walk away, you don't only walk away from others, you walk away from life. And you walk away from who you really are, so you're a shell of the possible. Whereas if you stay and you work it through with the other, with yourself, with life, then you have a richness and a fullness that otherwise you rob yourself of.

JONES: *Okay, let's see . . . what happens when someone does something that makes you feel angry? How do you see that and what do you do with that?*

CAIRNES: Well, usually I get angry, but I find a way of expressing the anger — usually not to the other person but to myself. The anger for me is a charge, an energetic charge and I get it out. But then I sit down and I think, 'Well, what is it about that person that I don't like? I mean, what is it about them that's making me angry?' being fully aware that it's probably something about me I don't like.

Recently a friend suggested that I become, in his words, 'more worldly'. And I was very angry, very very angry. And then I sat down and I started to think about what he was saying, and I realised that there was a lot of truth in it. And I also realised that his confronting me was something about me that I have trouble coming to terms with. So, after having expressed the . . . it took me three weeks, I might say, to get through this . . . after having expressed the anger, after having looked at the truth in the situation and after having looked at him more or less as a mirror of me and parts of me that I was not comfortable with, I was very grateful to him and was able to turn round and say, 'Thank you for that', and to maintain a friendship that I would otherwise have lost.

JONES: *What was his response, by the way?*
CAIRNES: Delight, just delight . . . and amusement . . .
JONES: *Really?*
CAIRNES: . . . amusement that something that he'd said that wasn't of great importance to him had had such a major effect on me.
JONES: *What would that have been like if there had been some sort of real malice or challenge or aggression in the comment that he had made to you? Would you have worked through it in the same way?*
CAIRNES: Yes, I think so . . .
JONES: *Because there still might be a mirror-effect for you?*
CAIRNES: Definitely, definitely. Because all of us are positive and negative. And if I feel I've attracted people into my life that are in some way putting me down, then that's just reflecting very strongly something about myself.
JONES: *I think we'd like to hear some more about attracting people into our lives. Is that how you see it?*

CAIRNES: Well, I do. I very much see it that we attract people into our lives. How else do you . . . I mean, that's true for all of us.

JONES: *Yes.*

CAIRNES: I mean, there's the people at the shop that we deal with and the people at the school and our friends, our family's friends . . . I mean, for all of us there's this huge pool of people, so how is it that we pick the ones . . . ?

JONES: *We choose to engage with certain ones.*

CAIRNES: Very much.

JONES: *But are you suggesting that we choose sometimes to become involved with people because they are reflecting back to us something within that . . . what? . . . that we don't want to face up to or that we haven't faced up to?*

CAIRNES: Well, there's . . . I don't know if you've read it, but there's a book by John Cleese and Robin Skynner called *Families and How to Survive Them*. And in it he gives an example of an experiment they do with people that are going into counselling training. They put fifty or sixty people in a room who've never met each other before and never talked to each other, and they say, 'Go and find a person in the room that has a similar family background to yourself'. And then when they have couples, they say to that couple, 'Now go and find people in the room that have a similar family background to you', and when they've got the fours, they say, 'Okay, now each take a role of mother, father, brother, sister, or whatever (which they do) and then sit down and discuss your real family background'. And every time this experiment is played, they find that people that had an alcoholic in the family are in a group of four, all of whom had an alcoholic in the family. Or, if there was aggression in the family, they're in a group, all of whom had

	aggression in the family. Or if the mother died when they were two, they're in a group, all of whom had a mother die when they were in early childhood. And the research is just so consistent that it's hard to believe that somehow people can't 'pick up' the people that had a similar family background.
JONES:	*But why do they want to be in the group with that similar background?*
CAIRNES:	We tend to draw people that have the most to teach us. And the people that have the most to teach us are the people that are most like ourselves, because it's so much easier (and I see this all the time in my work in business), it's so much easier to see your faults in another person than it is to see them in yourself.
	So, if I'm feeling angry, it's much easier for me to reflect that onto you than it is to own it for myself. If I don't like something that's happening, it's much easier for me to blame you than it is to look at my part in it. If I'm unhappy or sad, it's much easier for me to blame you than it is for me to say, 'Well, what am I doing wrong?' And so what I see in my work is everyone blaming everybody else. I call it the responsibility-free world: nobody is responsible for anything, it's all everybody else. So there's really nothing to be done about it, apart from whinge and complain, because the alternative is to say, 'Well, what am I doing here? And what do I need to do? And how can I change?' And that's painful: looking at yourself and looking at your own problems and where you've fallen down and what you haven't done right, and your own neuroses (I find looking at my own neuroses terribly embarrassing.) It's not comfortable.
JONES:	*But you do it?*
CAIRNES:	I choose to do it. I choose to do it.

JONES:	*Sometimes when we're attracted to someone else, we think we've fallen in love with them . . . ?*
CAIRNES:	Yes . . . we do . . .
JONES:	*You're giving that illusion a bit of shaking here too, aren't you?*
CAIRNES:	Well, there's a wonderful book that I've just finished reading, by Dr Robert Johnson, called *We: The Psychology of Romantic Love*. And he makes this point very strongly: that we, in fact, don't fall in love with another person at all — we simply project what we'd like to be onto that other person and fall in love with ourselves. And then when the other person refuses to live up to our illusion, we get very angry with them and walk away.
JONES:	*It's a very challenging idea, that idea of Johnson's isn't it?*
CAIRNES:	It's very uncomfortable, particularly if you've done it.
JONES:	*But you find it a satisfying one?*
CAIRNES:	Well, I find it a very liberating one because I've noticed for myself — and certainly for my friends — that this idea of falling in love can be a bit like an addiction. And you end up acting in a way that is neither comfortable nor does it make you feel in charge. And when you realise that what you're doing is simply fooling yourself then all of a sudden you can make choices and live your life the way you want to, and free yourself of the addiction. So it's a very liberating idea to me.
JONES:	*You use theatre, among other things, in your work — how does that work?*
CAIRNES:	Well, theatre is a very powerful way of helping people see reality. I have found that if I talk to people about reality and illusion, they often don't understand. And if I talk to people about emotion, often people deny they have any, particularly in the business and government world — where we're not

supposed to be emotional beings, we're supposed to be rational and objective. So I can talk to people about how emotions get in the way and about how our illusions get in the way and people think I'm talking fantasy.

The actors can act it out and it becomes so obvious and it's so funny, that we can no longer run away from it. So it's a very powerful teaching tool.

JONES: *Well, what are some of the roles you might portray? And do you bring actors with you or do you invite people from the management group, say, to take certain roles?*

CAIRNES: I do both. I have a troupe of actors and we go along and they will act out someone resisting change . . . or there's this wonderful thing where people say, 'I've told them, I've told my staff what they want and they still won't do it!' So we actually get the actors to tell each other what to do and when you watch this thing in progress you can see why the staff won't do it: because the message that's coming out of the mouth is very different from the message that's coming out of their body language, tone of voice and eye movement. So what people think they're saying is very often different from what they are saying. And the actors are very good at getting this across in a way that has everyone rolling in the aisles and then realising why it is their staff aren't hearing what they're saying.

JONES: *Really? Even those who have that habit and do it that way?*

CAIRNES: Very much because it's not them, you see, it's the actors. So you can project your own failings onto the actors, see it, laugh about it, and then very slowly come round to thinking that, 'Well, maybe I do this just a little bit'. And that's all we need — it's the beginning, when people begin to realise 'Maybe my staff behaving in this peculiar way has got just a little bit to do with me'.

JONES: *What are some of the other roles that you find yourself classically reproducing?*

CAIRNES: There's a thing that we're doing (in a forthcoming workshop) around expectations: where we're using something quite out of the business world, actually, out of male–female relationships. We're showing how people's expectations often stop them getting what they want. Because what we find is that people will come along and say, 'Look, this is what we want to achieve . . .' and if they head off to achieve that and they achieve all sorts of better things along the way, they don't want the better things: they want what they're there to get. So, what we're trying to show is that if you have a very set view, if you are very . . . tunnel-visioned, I guess, you can miss all the wonder that happens around. So, what we're actually using there is a situation where a man goes to one of these dating agencies and gets a range of women, and the women are magnificent and beautiful and fantastic in every way, but they're not what he asked for . . . until he eventually gets what he asked for and he can't cope with it. So we've used a situation out of the business setting which is one of the things that we try and do quite a lot, too, just to get people to see reflections of business in their own personal lives.

JONES: *So what would you want to say about that split we seem to have made in our habit of thinking: between that which we are (our being) and how we value that; and our doing, all our performance, our work? There's a real split there, in our society?*

CAIRNES: Well, I can answer that, I guess, on two levels. One is for myself: if I operate from a doing level rather than a being level, I get exhausted; I find that I have a lot to do and it takes me a lot of time and I tend to get fairly exhausted at the end of the day. Whereas if I come from myself, from the fullness of myself, then I actually don't seem to have so much to do. I mean, I get to spend time with my children, I get to spend time with my clients and I get to think through some interesting issues and I get to negotiate some interesting topics and I get to read some interesting bits of information, and then at the end of the day I probably get to go to the theatre or to the ballet or . . . whatever. So, by the time that the end of the day has come, I really haven't done anything apart from being myself and enjoying myself in doing it.

And what I see so much in organisations is that people leave themselves at home and they take a set of skills to work. So what happens is that people in organisations are, in fact, killing themselves on a very real level, on a very base level. In that, if you try and detach who you are from what you do, then you're really splitting yourself in half and leaving probably the fullest, most juicy bit at home.

And another way I look at it . . . it's like, we have energy and we have power and we can have that in a positive way or we can have it in a negative way, but it won't go away. So if we don't bring it out and use it in a positive way, it will go underground and be negative and drag us down and drag our organisations down. And so many organisations I work with are bogged down in the politics, and they're bogged down in the interactions, and they're bogged down in the crises that are simply a response to people pushing down all those positive things or even the negative things, but at least not getting it on the table and dealing with it. So all the energy is going into suppression and to interplay and to politics rather than to actually getting the job done that people are there to do, as themselves . . . coming to work and just getting on with it.

JONES: *But if I bring my whole self to work, will they like me? If they see all the rough bits and the negative bits and the parts that I don't think are so beautiful — if I bring that to my work or to my relationships, it's a risk.*

CAIRNES: Yes, it's certainly a risk, and they may not like you.

JONES: *But I want to be liked, don't I . . . don't we?*

CAIRNES: Well, I guess that's the problem. And that's something that I've personally been working through quite a lot, because I've always wanted to be liked. What I've found is, as I care less about being liked, I am more liked. And I guess that what happens there is: while we're trying to please the other, they're trying to please us; and nobody is actually pleasing anybody. So, instead of me honestly saying 'This is who I am and this is what I want', and letting you see who I am so you know who you're dealing with and what you've got before you here, all your energy is going into sussing out what it is that you might do that might please me. And what is happening for me is I'm feeling, 'Well, where is this person? You know, all I've got is this sort of crazy investigating energy that's coming over towards me and no real person to deal with, so how can I like you when you're not really there? Because where you are is over here investigating me.' So there really isn't anything there to like.

So what happens is we play this polite investigative, mutual game which takes an awful lot of time and an awful lot of energy — and often backfires, because if I don't end up being what you think you want me to be or I don't do what I think you think I want . . . you know, it's so tortuous that the energy dissipates, the day disappears and we've got so little done. Whereas if you just go to work and be you and get on with what you have to do, and I just go to work and be me and get on with what I have to do, when you and I meet, we're meeting someone, we can know what we're dealing with, we can deal with it and get on with it. And our energy actually happens in being ourselves and getting our job done.

JONES: *So let's stay with the challenge of being myself and being honest and being in the open about that. What are some of the ways, Margot, that you need to be mindful of to keep on doing that, to maintain some sort of equilibrium or honesty? Are there some practices that are in your life that need to be there, to help you get on with this?*

CAIRNES: I spend a lot of time with myself. I meditate every day . . .

JONES: *What form does that take?*

CAIRNES: I use two forms of meditation. One is a mantra meditation that I do for twenty minutes every day, every morning. And I also use a form of meditation which is basically just sitting: I just sit with my eyes open and I try and merge with the sea or the trees or the flowers or my environment, and really just be very peaceful and do what I call 'coming home'. I just go into myself and get to know me, because there's no way anyone else can get to know me if I don't.

I've done this often with businesspeople and often, when they 'come home', the shock is that there's nobody there, and that there hasn't been anybody there for such a long time. Because the demands of business are such that we're out there all the time, dealing with the clients and the staff and the boss and the children . . . so everything is out there for everybody else. So the shock is that when we do 'come home', often the house is empty.

JONES: *Just before we move away from that, what's busyness all about then? I mean, people keep so incredibly busy, don't they . . . we? (I can include myself in this.)*

CAIRNES: Well, what it's about is dealing with the 'out there' issues. So, what we do is, rather than 'come home' and know who we are and operate from where we're going and what we want, we respond continuously to the 'out there', feeling very powerless around that.

It's very interesting (I've done this with a number of groups now) — when I get people to draw a picture of all the outside forces and put themselves in the picture and to 'come home', they feel paralysed. They feel quite paralysed. So from that point of paralysis people hit out and grab what little bit they can, and stay busy around doing that, rather than get on with the fullness of who they are and where they're going and what they want to do.

JONES: *But why would we want to avoid coming home . . . doing the inner work?*

CAIRNES: Well, it's a bit of a shock to come home and find that it's empty. It's like walking into a house that needs renovation . . . I mean, it's much easier to go out and rent a flat than it is to buy your own home and renovate it.

JONES: *It's less risky.*

CAIRNES: It's less risky, it's less hard work . . .

JONES: *. . . less commitment . . .*

CAIRNES: . . . it's less commitment, it's less painful, it's less uncomfortable. It also means that you're less in control of your own life. Because what it then means is that you're really like a piece of driftwood on the sea, and you'll go where the water pushes you. Learning to 'come home' and to get in touch with yourself and your own power and your own desire and your own humanity is like . . . you know, building a huge ship. And anything like that takes time, it takes effort; you don't just snap your fingers and there is a ship. You have to plan it and you have to get the resources and you have to go out and build it. It takes a lot of time, a lot of effort. And, you know, it may not work. The fear is that it may not work.

With my meditation I have a mantra which is three mumbo-jumbo words (I mean it could be 'Coca Cola', it could be anything), which I just repeat silently to myself. And that helps me to . . . I suppose, almost go into a trance state, which allows me to go down into my subconscious and come up with a lot of solutions to problems. I very rarely sit down and think through a problem. What I do is I meditate, and the answers just come. What that means is: I often have very lateral answers to problems, and things that I wouldn't have thought of if I'd sat down and thought it through logically. And the mantra — by going into that sort of trance-like state, I suppose — allows me to access parts of my subconscious that I can't get to in a logical way.

JONES: *So you're suggesting that there is an inner solver of problems below or beneath or beyond the workings of the rational mind, are you?*

CAIRNES: Yes. Well, that's certainly been my experience and, I believe, the experience of a lot of other people as well.

JONES: *So, do you pray?*

CAIRNES: I do. I pray quite a lot. I'm not exactly sure who or what God is. Some of my friends tell me that God is an outside force; and some of my friends tell me that God is your inner core; and my son tells me that he's a blue energy field that incorporates everybody; and I sort of think . . .

JONES: *That's a nice one, isn't it?*

CAIRNES: I think that's as good an explanation as any, particularly as he was six when he came up with this explanation. I thought 'Well, yes, that's very probably what it is'.

But I find it very reassuring to think that there is a

	power greater than myself. And I have ongoing conversations with this power.
JONES:	*Quietly or out loud?*
CAIRNES:	No, quite often audibly which my children find embarrassing; they tell me that other mothers don't do this. But I find it very reassuring. It's like going through life with a friend holding your hand.
JONES:	*Is it asking for advice or just sharing your experience?*
CAIRNES:	Oh, it's everything, it's everything. It's asking for solutions to problems, it's asking for advice . . . sometimes someone to get angry with — 'How dare you do this to me!' And, knowing that whatever I say or whatever I do is totally acceptable to this unknown energy, it's very reassuring to me.
JONES:	*So there's a feeling of being loved and accepted . . .*
CAIRNES:	. . . and accepted totally.
JONES:	*. . . whatever you do.*
CAIRNES:	Yes, very much; total love and total acceptance. So I can say and do and be anything I want, with this energy field.
JONES:	*So, that's also what you think love should be, ideally, between human beings: people being themselves and accepting each other as themselves.*
CAIRNES:	Yes, I guess that's true. When you say that, I'm very mindful that I'm not an enlightened being, that I'm a very human being, and when other people are around me and they do and say and be things that I don't feel comfortable with, I have terrible trouble 'loving' them. I have terrible trouble accepting them totally as they are.
JONES:	*But that is your aspiration?*
CAIRNES:	That is definitely my aspiration.
JONES:	*Margot, in talking about an attempt to be ourselves, is there a risk of being selfish in that?*
CAIRNES:	Well, that's usually the excuse people put up for not doing it. The fear is 'I will become very selfish'. And what I've noticed is that when people start to

do this kind of work, they do appear selfish; because, like any new skill, when you start to look in and you start to observe yourself, it takes time and it takes effort, and it does take you away. And, also, if you've been playing a whole series of games with people ('I'll be there for you if you be there for me', 'If you be what I want, I'll be what you want'), when we pull away from that, we can't really expect the other person to like it. So, initially, the fear is that we will be selfish and we will ruffle the status quo — and, in fact, that's true. But what I've seen is that, over time, people that live this way become much fuller, much more expansive, much more able to give selflessly to other people; because, simply, they have more to give, there is more of them. So sharing it . . . it's a bit like the Magic Pudding — you know, the more you eat of the Magic Pudding, the more comes back, both for you to eat and for you to share. (In fact, there's a lovely part in Norman Lindsay's *The Magic Pudding* where he says he loves to be shared around.)

JONES: *Yes. So, although you suggest that sometimes we draw . . . attract towards us people from whom we need to learn something about ourselves, there can be the seeds in that, of a more wholesome relationship with another individual being him or herself.*

CAIRNES: Well, what I've noticed is that as I change, my relationships change. This has very much happened with my children, for example. As I've grown and learnt more about myself, I just feel so much more loving towards them. The things they used to do that annoyed me, no longer annoy me; and the things that used to exhaust me, now invigorate me. So, simply by coming back to me and being more selfish and being more myself, I'm much more able to be there for them.

In fact, I have a rule, as a single mother, that my happiness and my well-being are paramount. And, although that sounds remarkably selfish, the reason I've done it is that, if I'm not well and if I'm not happy, I can't be there for my children, and I can't go to work and earn the money, and I can't be there for my clients, and I can't be there for my friends, and I can't be there for my parents. So, if I'm not feeling well and happy and bright and expansive and able to give out, then all the people around me who rely on me simply would be let down.

JONES: *But, I guess, in the close relationships of family there needs to be some sort of agreement that this is the way we're all going to approach life . . .*

CAIRNES: Very much.

JONES: *. . . or you could have terrific conflict.*

CAIRNES: Well, what I notice is that as I change, the people around me change; so as my children see me do that, that's their role model. And I've noticed that my children are much more articulate now about their needs and what they want and what their limits are and what's important to them. Whereas once, when we were all being polite, they never told me. Now I'm very aware.

JONES: *Being a single mother and keeping yourself fit . . . what are some of the things you encounter there, some of the things you have to really be mindful of?*

CAIRNES: Well, I'm very pleased to be, as I call it, 'in a body'. I find that a lot of people that are searching for answers tend to do it in what I call 'an out-of-the-body' way — they spend a lot of their time, almost in another world. For me, I'm very pleased to be in this world with both my feet firmly on the ground. So I spend a lot of time doing that: I spend a lot of time walking on the beach, in the bush, swimming . . . the closer I can get to the ground and earth and nature, and actually doing something physical around that, the happier I am.

I also have a rebounder, which I use for all sorts of reasons — ostensibly to get fit, and I get up every morning and bounce — but I think that a lot of that is just a way of charging me up for the day ahead and really feeling the power in my human form. And also to help me express some emotions: if I'm feeling angry, I can bounce angrily; if I'm feeling happy I can skip or I can dance. And I also use it as a form of self-expression . . . so it's very much about being a very human person in a very human form.

JONES: *In a high-powered job as you have, do you find that you have to fight off against being anxious about your planning or worried about what you mightn't have done quite well enough yesterday or something? How do you deal with that? Because it's not an easy job, is it, that you have? It's a very responsible one.*

CAIRNES: Well, I guess it is, but I tend not to think about that so much as what I'm doing right now. If I sat and thought about where I was going and what I was doing and what might happen, I don't think I'd actually do anything. So what I do is: I do what I'm doing right now . . . like, right now, I'm sitting here talking to you — I'm not planning the workshop that I'm running tomorrow. So I try to do what I do when I'm doing it, and do it as much from myself and who I am as possible, and enjoy it. So I relax into it and be just here. Most of us spend our time worrying about what we did do and didn't do well, or what we will do and what we might do, and feeling guilty about what we didn't do. And all of that removes our energy from actually being where we are and getting on with what we're doing.

JONES: *And can you take that approach to your mothering?*

CAIRNES: I do. In fact, I had to learn to do that when my daughter was so very ill; because for quite a long time there, it was very touch-and-go — and if I had spent my life worrying about what might've happened, I wouldn't have enjoyed what time we had. As it was, she recovered and she's now a very healthy little girl, but for a long time we didn't know what it was, and the choice was: will I fret about what might happen or will I enjoy what I have? And we chose to enjoy what we had.

JONES: *What are your feelings about the ageing of beauty? For yourself?*

CAIRNES: That used to worry me a lot. I'd won a number of prizes for my beauty and it seemed to me that that was a very big part of me — I guess, the public face that I showed. And the fear was that, as I got older, obviously this would fade and I'd be less of who I was or have less attention from the world or be less of a person, and it was a real worry for me. But, as I have grown older, I feel so much more content with myself and so much happier with myself and so enriched by an inner beauty, that I feel that I don't really care what other people see, so much as the way that I relate to them and the richness of the relationships that we have and the love that passes between us. And whether they look at me and see a pretty face or not, seems of decreasing importance.

JONES: *You've had one very close experience with death — your daughter's death. Have there been other experiences that have given you some thoughts about death?*

CAIRNES: Yes. When I was a baby I came very close to death. I was, in fact, an experiment: I was the first baby in Australia, I think, to have an intravenous drip. It was very much a life-and-death situation and, although it seems a bit like fantasy, I can remember it, there is a flavour of it in my memory. And, also, with my daughter's near-death . . . it was a very peaceful experience and the flavour of the memory I have is of a very peaceful experience, so I've never really feared death. I've feared being maimed, I've feared being incapacitated, but not death because it was . . . the brushes were so peaceful and so reassuring almost, that there was a peaceful haven, and one was really passing from this present experience to another experience. But even . . . I've noticed that as I feel more content with myself even being incapacitated doesn't hold a fear anymore, because it's just being different, it's just a new lot of learning experiences, it's another way to go. And although it may be uncomfortable and painful — as other things have been — it is just another way.

Often when I'm feeling blue, I write down all the things that I have — the list goes on for pages and pages: I have my children's laughter, I have their smiles, cuddles and love; I have the sky and the water and the boats; I have the trees and the flowers; I have Mozart and Haydn and Rodrigo and Sting; I have Barbra Streisand, Placido Domingo and Whitney Houston; I have ballet and dance, theatre and film; I have exercise and the beach; I have my friends — their laughter, their trust, their love and their news; I have books and newspapers; I have my work and my clients; I have my poetry and my writing; I have skiing and swimming and bouncing on the mini-bouncer; I have sex and jokes and beautiful clothes; I have a home and a luxury car; I have my education, my excellence, my intelligence, my creativity — I have life.

The Confessional Interview

Caroline Jones is one of Australia's most well-known and accomplished interviewers. She was the first female reporter on the current affairs television program *This Day Tonight*, hailed as a trailblazer for women in the media, and quickly gained a reputation for her cool, incisive interviewing and reporting. Later she simultaneously presented the current affairs television program *Four Corners* and *City Extra*, a radio program broadcast every weekday morning on Radio 2BL. Her retirement from current affairs radio and television, and the personal 'search for meaning' and conversion to Catholicism which followed, have been given wide publicity throughout the 1980s. She has been on the cover of weekend magazines, and her portrait adorns the published version of her new radio program *The Search for Meaning*. Her personality and biography form an important part of the meaning and audience appeal of this program, in which she has pioneered a new kind of in-depth personal interview, exploring, with and for the audience, how the exemplary and charismatic individuals she interviews have found meaning and fulfilment in life. The program has gained a wide following and elicits many responses from listeners, some of which are quoted in the first volume of the published interviews. A woman from Western Australia, for example, wrote:

> I never thought I would ever hear publicly such honesty and depth, coming from so many people, from so many different walks in life. It's almost like a meditation in a strange sort of way in that it gives me so much food for thought and so many clues about living to hang on to.[1]

And a woman from Melbourne: 'It is like a mist of spiritual tranquillity filtering into my life, to listen to the deep and honest experiences and beliefs of your guests'.[2]

The Search for Meaning is produced by the ABC's Religious Department, but it is not religious in a narrow sense. The meanings found by Caroline Jones' interviewees may stem from religious beliefs, but they may also stem from secular philosophies that offer a vision of hope for the future, from Aboriginal spirituality, from the sense of unity with nature experienced by the mountaineer or the surfer, from the pursuit of art, or from devoting one's life to helping the underprivileged or to fighting just causes. The central theme, however, is always the result of these beliefs, experiences and practices for the individual— the subjective, spiritual experience of finding peace, happiness or fulfilment in relation to some kind of higher value, be it one's true self or God, love or nature. In a foreword to the first volume of the published interviews, David Millikan, head of the ABC's Religious Department, defends this broad approach on theological grounds, quoting Calvin, according to whom there is a *sensis divinitatis*, a 'sense of the divine', in all people.[3] Many different beliefs, then, not all of them overtly religious, qualify as beliefs in the 'divine'. But not all. Not, for instance, what Caroline Jones calls 'modern belief': 'Modern belief in scientific, individual, materialistic, irreligious, mechanistic man: abbreviated man, diminished man, trussed in his own abstract arithmetic'.[4] And not 'religious fundamentalism' or 'atheistic materialism':

> We cannot expect vision for the future from either the religious fundamentalists who have a vested interest in Armageddon, or the ruling atheistic materialists who believe only in their own finite existence. We need other prophets and role models, and we are discovering them ... I believe that what they have to say lights the way forward for us all in wisdom as they take the risk of revealing their striving to be all that a human can be.[5]

In what follows we want to ask why and how this search for meaning is conducted by means of *interviews*. For although Caroline Jones often refers to her programs as 'conversations', they have all the basic characteristics of interviews: the interviewees do most of the talking while the interviewer confines herself to questions, promptings, brief reactions; the interviewees reveal much of themselves while the interviewer reveals comparatively little; and the interviewer, in the end, controls the flow of dialogue while the interviewees allow themselves to be guided by the interviewer.

We will try to describe the subtle ways in which Caroline Jones conducts her search and guides her guests through her interviews, comparing these to the therapeutic interview and the pastoral interview. We focus on the interview as a mode of interaction, on the way Caroline Jones *interacts* with her interviewees and with her listeners. But in the process we will also have things to say about the subject matter of the interactions, about the field of experience with which they deal, and about the way they make sense of that field. The two aspects are, in any case, closely related. Not every mode of interaction can be used for every kind of topic. Confessional interviews, for instance, deal with the field of the personal (life histories; problems, anxieties and traumas; failures, weaknesses and sins), but they are also characterised by specific modes of interaction. Adversarial political interviews, on the other hand, not only deal with different topics, but also have a different structure, and use different kinds of questions (as we shall see in Chapter 4).

The Revelatory Genre

As we have seen, Caroline Jones' interviews all testify to the discovery of meaning, be it in God or the self, in love or in nature, in art or in philosophy. Rather than being searches themselves, they provide evidence of searches. They go back over journeys successfully completed, and dispassionately review the tests or trials (illness, grieving, traumas) the interviewees lived through before finding meaning. Many of the interviews are like recollections of therapy or confessions of failure overcome through insight and acceptance of self. As these recollections proceed, the real biographical interviewees are transformed into meaningful exemplars, role models for the listeners. Although their lives are given different meanings, all interviewees are alike in being artists of life itself. Not just anyone can be called: only the reflexive, the articulate, the successful, the charismatic. These exemplary persons are not, as in social-problem documentaries, evidence of social, political, nor even of psychological problems beyond themselves — problems such as gender or class-related oppression. Rather, they are exemplary because, in this quasi-religious context, with its assumption of a fallen world, they have each achieved some acceptance of their place. They have transcended the mundane and the material, or at least appear to do so as the interview unfolds.

Thus each interview has the structure of a revelation, an elucidation of the process of discovery. But each interview is at the same time itself a search. This is what makes the interviewer necessary. While the interviewees have already completed their search, the interviewer is *now* searching for meaning on behalf of her listeners. She does not conduct abstract intellectual discussions of humanistic religious values with her interviewees, she is actively seeking and producing these values. Like therapeutic (counselling) interviews, Caroline Jones' explorations do not merely reveal the hidden, but actually *constitute* meaning through the revelatory process itself. The interviewees, the audience and the professional mediator might all be equally surprised by the results. For it is only in the act of being spoken that meanings materialise. Meanings do not lie dormant in some pre-linguistic state waiting to be expressed. They do not lie in the darkened basement of the mind waiting to be revealed by the torchlight of the professional psychologist, priest or radio personality. Interviews, like interrogations, narratives, poems or news items, are not simply contexts in which meanings are expressed, but contexts in which meanings are actually constituted or realised. So the genre of interview we are seeking to characterise here is important because, without it, the particular meanings it realises could not exist.[6]

Genres, in the sense in which we use the term here, are types of interactive processes realised in and by language. They can be described in terms of the things one can do with language to or for people, in terms of the communicative functions that language can fulfil — functions such as narrating, confessing, revealing, challenging, prompting, reacting. A genre is a typical sequence of such communicative functions which, as a kind of schema, underlies and structures the texts that realise it. Genre is therefore relatively independent of field, of the subject matter of the text, although, as we have already noted, certain genres tend to combine with certain fields, in alignments which are subject to change under the influence of social and historical factors. This view of genre entails that the *interactional* aspect is most strongly responsible for the structure of texts, for their 'beginning–middle–end' forms. Genres can be characterised as means to achieve certain communicative, interactional ends, in this case, the searching for and revelation of meaning.

The revelatory genre that structures Caroline Jones' interviews can be described as going through four major stages, in this order: (a) the introduction, (b) the confession, (c) the reflection, and (d) the testimony.

THE INTRODUCTION
The introduction, a monologue by the interviewer, sets the agenda of each search for meaning. In the case of the interview with Margot Cairnes this centres on the question of identity, of the self: how can I overcome 'the split between the real self inside, and the self I show to the outside world'? Margot Cairnes is then introduced as a person who can show us how, as one who has transcended this split, who 'always takes her real self to work' and who has overcome the trauma of alienation.

The introduction, then, already gives us the outcome of the search. It poses an existential problem and tells us that the solution of this problem lies in 'overcoming the split between the real self and the self I show the outside world'.

It is like the opening of a detective story that tells us of the outcome of a long chain of events (for example, a body found murdered) to then begin to unravel how this murder happened. The outcome of the search is given. But the most important questions (How did it happen?; How did this outcome come about?) are not given and the answers to these questions are the real objects of the search. It provides the suspense, the thread that guides the listener's attention through the interview: how did Margot Cairnes overcome that split, and how can I, the listener, follow her example and come to feel at one with myself?

THE CONFESSION
After Caroline Jones has set the stage, the dialogue begins, and the interviewees are asked to reveal significant episodes from their lives. As in therapeutic interviews, the interviewees are invited to narrate the traumas and conflicts they lived through as a child (or, if they had a happy childhood, in their early adult years), and to confess the failures, weaknesses and uncertainties they experienced (in Margot Cairnes' case, for example, the failure of her marriage).

Caroline Jones plays a mostly supportive role here, prompting the interviewee to reveal her past ('*So what sort of ideas were you forming about creativity, I wonder*'), to confess ('*You said that when you had the first experience of [failure] after many successes, it knocked you*'), and inviting her to answer by narrating the story of her life ('*maybe through some of the events of your life . . .*'). The interviewee does most of the talking.

In the interview with Margot Cairnes this part of the interview ends when Caroline Jones concludes 'So you got into new habits', and then asks 'Has it made a difference?' From that point on she no longer seeks to find out 'what happened', but predominantly asks questions like 'How do you see that?' and 'What do you think of . . .?'

The Reflection

Having revealed suffering, traumas and conflicts, having confessed to failures and weaknesses, interviewees are now asked to stand back and interpret their early experiences and feelings in more general terms.

Caroline Jones elicits this kind of reflection in her questions (*'What do you think now about apparent failure or weakness or vulnerability?'*) and begins to take a more active part in the proceedings. There is more give and take in this 'reflection' stage. The interview becomes a little more like a discussion, although the interviewee still does most of the talking, and the reflections remain very personal (the typical question is not 'What is failure?', but 'What do you think about failure?'). In the interview with Margot Cairnes this section ends when Caroline Jones begins to sum up (*'So you're suggesting that there is an inner solver of problems below or beneath or beyond the workings of the rational mind'*) and to inquire about the way in which Margot Cairnes achieves and maintains her equilibrium in daily life.

The Testimony

Finally the interviewees are asked to distil from these reflections the central theme of the interview, the meaning of their lives; to reveal how they actualise that meaning in their life; and to testify to the value of their approach.

Caroline Jones' questions now begin to seek conclusions (*'So, that's what you think love should be, ideally, between human beings: people being themselves and accepting each other as themselves'*) and to tease out how the meanings arrived at may be actualised in the practices of everyday life (*'So do you pray?'*). This move from what the interviewees think to what they do is crucial, because, although only indirectly, it provides the listeners with 'clues about living', suggestions on how they might achieve in their own lives what the interviewees have accomplished in theirs. In the interview with Margot Cairnes, for example, such practices include meditation, prayer, walking, swimming and exercising on a rebounder. The interview then closes on the reply to Jones' request for 'thoughts about death', with the interviewee's testimonial catalogue of her virtues and possessions, including 'life' itself.

The revelatory genre, then, moves from childhood, conflict and uncertainty to the adult proclamation of having negotiated successfully the problems of love, family and profession, through insight, work, prayer and commitment. At least in the retrospect constructed though the radio interview, meaning has been found by the exemplary interviewee. As a schema, the revelatory genre can accommodate the stories of many different interviewees. Not all interviews follow it exactly and the boundaries between the stages are not always clearcut. There may, for instance, be a brief return to reflection in the testimony stage. And there may be embeddings of other genres, as when Caroline Jones asks Margot Cairnes a number of matter-of-fact information questions about her work. But each interviewee does act in each of the ways we have described. As a media genre the revelatory genre is, we believe, an innovation by Caroline Jones. Many interviews follow patterns that are not of the interviewer's making — tried and proven schemas, formulas. Caroline Jones, however, has invented a new pattern, a new genre. In the area of literature study, 'genre' literature has often been unfavourably compared with 'high' or 'artistic' literature, seen as trite and conventional where 'high' literature is seen as original and creative. (More recently, in a postmodern reversal, genre literature has sometimes been elevated above high literature). But the distinction between following established genre patterns (and often there is no need for inventing new ones) and creating new patterns can be applied to every form of communication. And genre, in the sense in which we have defined it here, plays a role in both cases. Inventing a new genre is creating a new pattern out of existing patterns, a new genre out of existing genres, a new selection from and sequencing of the communicative functions that language can realise. We will return to this aspect of the revelatory genre in the final section of this chapter.

From Confession to Reflection

To show precisely how Caroline Jones steers the interview through the stages of the revelatory genre, we now look in more detail at the linguistic strategies she employs, concentrating on the stages of confession, the reflection and the testimony.

Confessions are stories in which the narrators reveal mistakes, weaknesses, wrongs they have committed, or feelings and opinions that are risky to declare because they might be prejudicial to them. Key elements in the language of the confession are therefore: (a) the first person (confessors must declare themselves, must always say 'I'); and (b) active verbs (confessors must clearly reveal themselves as responsible for their actions and feelings, must say 'I did this', 'I felt this way'). The verbs (c) are usually in the past tense, although the present tense may be used if feelings or thoughts are confessed; and (d) must denote something that the listener might judge negatively, something that puts the confessor at risk for being honest, for revealing secrets.

Caroline Jones reacts to the confessions of her interviewees with sympathetic concern, sometimes with surprise or delight (as in the interview with Barbara Blackman: '*What an extraordinary thing to suddenly know at that age, Barbara!*'). As confessee, she takes the role of a sympathetic listener: 'My approach to the radio interviews in '*The Search for Meaning*' has been that of a listener, not of one who had definite ideas to present herself as well'.[7] Nevertheless, her reactions do not leave the interviewees' confessions completely unaffected. In subtle ways they transform the interviewees' subjective, personal confessions into more abstract and general reflections.

NOMINALISATION

One of the strategies by means of which Caroline Jones achieves this transformation is nominalisation, the transformation of verbs into nouns. In the following quote she carefully connects her question to the preceding answer, through words like 'insight', and 'concern' about 'that'

(that is, childcare), all of which tie in with what Margot Cairnes has been speaking about. But what, in Cairnes' answer, was formulated as an active verbal process, realising Margot Cairnes' agency ('I was interested') becomes, in Caroline Jones' question, an abstract noun ('concern'):

CAIRNES: I was particularly interested in childcare: how we as a society rear our children, and how we provide for them on an economic and a political basis, and where they fit into society, and how society operates on where we're going.
JONES: *Any insight into why that was your concern?*

Other examples are not difficult to find. Cairnes' 'I turned my back' and 'I went off' become, in Jones' rephrasing, 'that moving away'. Cairnes' 'my marriage failed' is turned into 'marriage failure', her 'I found that painful' is reformulated as 'weakness'. In short, personal and active verbal formulation, the language of 'I did', 'I thought', 'I felt' and 'I liked', is transformed into impersonal and objective nominal formulation, into the language of abstract issues and objective reflection.

ABSTRACTION

A similar effect is achieved by means of abstraction. Cairnes' 'I studied science', for example, becomes, in Jones' next question, 'the scientific side'; her reference to 'creative people' is reformulated as a reference to 'creativity'. Concrete events and people are transformed into abstract qualities.

GENERALISATION

Jones also generalises the particular incidents recounted by her interviewees. When Margot Cairnes has told her 'I've attracted people into my life that are in some way putting me down', Jones asks her to say more about 'attracting people into our lives'. The reference is not only nominalised but also widened from the particular case of Margot

Cairnes to people in general ('we', 'our lives'), a reformulation which Cairnes then accepts in her reply:

JONES: *I think we'd like to hear some more about attracting people into our lives. Is that how you see it?*
CAIRNES: Well, I do, very much.

OBJECTIVATION

While her interviewees talk about things they did and things that happened to them, and of things they thought and things they felt, Jones frequently reformulates these in terms of more impersonal, objective propositions. After Cairnes has told her 'I meditate and the answers just come', for example, Jones says '*You're suggesting there is an inner solver of problems . . . are you?*', thus rephrasing actions ('I meditate') and events ('answers just come') in terms of what the linguist Halliday has called 'existential processes',)[8] that is, sentences which state the objective existence of things, and which typically begin with 'there is a . . .' or 'there exists a . . .'. Tags such as 'are you?' or 'isn't it?' then quietly urge the interviewee to agree with the reformulation.

QUESTIONS INVITING REFLECTION

More than a third of the questions in the interview with Margot Cairnes invite her to reply in terms of what we have called reflection. The key linguistic features of such questions are: (a) they are WH-questions, typically using the WH-word 'what', and therefore leaving the interviewee a great deal of scope as to how to answer; (b) they use the second person ('you') coupled with a so-called cognitive mental process verb,[9] that is, a verb such as 'think' (or 'feel' or 'see' as metaphors for 'think'); (c) they contain a nominalisation, abstraction or generalisation (for example, 'failure', 'weakness', 'creativity') as the object of this cognitive mental process. Some examples:

What do you think now about apparent failure or weakness or vulnerability?

> *So what sort of ideas were you forming about creativity, I wonder, and creative people?*
>
> *What do you think are the consequences of a habit of walking away, again and again?*
>
> *What are your feelings about the ageing of beauty? For yourself?*

CHALLENGES

We already noted that, in the reflection stage, Caroline Jones' role becomes somewhat more active. She begins, for example, to challenge her interviewees. Unlike interrogations, cooperative interviews like those in *The Search for Meaning*, do not frequently challenge or confront. They may, however, ask a slightly incredulous 'Really?' or suggest the 'risk of being selfish'. Or they may test the validity of the interviewee's approach to life by confronting her with a hypothetical situation:

> *What happens when someone does something that makes you feel angry? . . . What do you do with that?*

More direct challenges take the form of polar questions, the kind of questions which can be answered with a mere 'yes' or 'no' and seek confirmation or denial rather than information.

> *Margot, in talking about an attempt to be ourselves, is there a risk of being selfish?*

Even more direct challenges are linguistically realised as statements, preceded by 'but', to indicate that they are objections to what was said in the preceding answers:

> *But, I guess, in the close relationships of family there needs to be some sort of agreement that this is the way we're all going to approach life . . . or you could have terrific conflict.*

In all these instances the meanings offered by the interviewee are challenged, put to the test, and the interviewee is invited to defend her point of view and argue her case.

EXTENSIONS

Jones' more active role also comes out in the way she occasionally finishes the interviewee's answers for her:

> *Because there might still be a mirror-effect for you?*
>
> *But you find it a satisfying one?*
>
> *But that is your aspiration?*

And in the way she extends topics to new areas, not previously mentioned by the interviewee:

> *And you see this in the work that you do? . . . With senior businesspeople and public servants and so on?*
>
> *And yet they probably call on you to solve some sort of rational problem, don't they?*

Such extensions are hardly questions at all, though they do evoke a further response. They demonstrate also how intimately acquainted with the interviewee, or how well researched, is the interviewer. She shows her professional preparation and her psychological insight by means of such questions which arise out of the information she herself provides.

Closure: The Revelation of Meaning

We have seen that interviews are dynamic, involving relations of linguistic, indeed more generally ideological, control. Even Caroline Jones' quiet conversations involve mediated interactions directed through language towards quite definite, bounded meanings. We will now investigate the linguistic strategies Jones uses to ensure that the interview achieves closure in the testimony stage.

CONCEPTUAL FUSION

In the testimony stage, Jones begins to introduce new terms as synonyms for those the interviewee has used. Still taking her cues from what the interviewee has said, she does not substitute different terms for those of the interviewee, but simply puts her own terms beside them. In this way new overtones of meaning are added. Jones' meanings and those of the interviewee are fused into broader concepts. When Margot Cairnes says 'honesty', for example, Caroline Jones paraphrases 'honesty or equilibrium'. When Margot Cairnes says 'it's much easier . . .', Jones adds 'less risky . . . less commitment . . .'. Cairnes then repeats these terms, incorporating them in her own conceptualisation of the meanings for which the program is searching. The key revelations of *The Search for Meaning*, then, do not come from the interviewee without mediation. They are, in the end, the result of negotiation between interviewer and interviewee.

INTRODUCING TOPICS

Although Caroline Jones always takes great care to tie her questions in with what the interviewee has said, she does occasionally introduce topics herself, especially in the testimony stage. The subject of prayer, for example, is first mentioned by Jones. We cannot be sure that it would have been mentioned spontaneously by the interviewee. In further questions about prayer ('how questions', see below) Jones introduces quite specific alternatives — on the subject of prayer she is 'one who has definite ideas to present herself as well':

> *Quietly or out loud?*
>
> *Is it asking for advice or just sharing your experience?*

CONNECTING TOPICS

Towards the end of the interview, Caroline Jones also tries to draw together the various threads of the interview into a coherent whole. Earlier, Margot Cairnes had said that 'falling in love can be a bit like an addiction' and that, in reality, 'we fall in love with ourselves'. Later she describes the effect of prayer as 'being totally accepted for what you are'. At this point Jones skilfully draws the threads together, adding, in the process, an emphasis of her own: *'So, that's also what you think love should be, ideally, between human beings: people being themselves and accepting each other as themselves',* she says and, a moment later: *'So, although you suggest that sometimes we draw . . . attract towards us people from whom we need to learn something about ourselves, there can be the seeds in that of a more wholesome relationship with another individual being him or herself.'* Clearly she does not want to leave the earlier, somewhat negative view of love unresolved, and seeks to balance the value of 'being yourself' with an emphasis on love and on giving to others. The interviewee accepts this: 'by . . . being more myself, I'm much more able to be there for them' (that is, her children). Again, the meanings towards which the interview converges are the result of negotiation, and the interviewer has a definite role in formulating them.

How Questions

We have seen that the interviews in *The Search for Meaning* also seek to provide listeners with 'clues for living', oblique advice on how to behave. As the interviewee is a 'role model' it follows that she has exemplary skills (interpersonal, professional, or both). These are elicited through 'how questions'. Jones' 'how questions', however, are indeed oblique. Instead of 'How do you keep fit?', for example, Caroline Jones asks:

> *Being a single mother and keeping yourself fit . . . what are some of the things you encounter there, some of the things you have to really be mindful of?*

Instead of 'How do you maintain your equilibrium?', she asks:

> *What are some of the ways, Margot, that you need to be mindful of to keep on doing that, to maintain some sort of equilibrium or honesty? Are there some practices that are in your life that need to be there, to help you get on with this?*

Jones' 'how questions', then, are given a surface of 'questions inviting reflection' ('what do you need to be *mindful of*'), even though they in fact inquire about practices, as if reflection must constantly be in the foreground, and practices only alluded to, except in the case of prayer. The questions are nevertheless understood by the interviewee as 'how questions' and in her response Margot Cairnes explains in some detail how she keeps fit, and how she meditates.

CONCLUSIONS
The conclusion is perhaps the key strategy for eliciting testimony and achieving closure. By the time Jones begins to draw conclusions (always preceded by 'so', to indicate their nature as conclusions), information is no longer sought. The interviewee is asked only to confirm and perhaps fine-tune Jones' summaries. Some of Jones' conclusions are tentatively formulated, as polar questions, for instance, or as statements with a tag, or with a rising inflection at the end of the sentence (here indicated by a question mark). Others are quite definite statements, ending in a falling intonation (here indicated by a full stop):

> *So you're suggesting that there is an inner solver of problems below or beneath or beyond the workings of the rational mind, are you?*
>
> *So there's a feeling of being loved and accepted . . .*
>
> *So, that's also what you think love should be, ideally, between human beings: people being themselves and accepting each other as themselves.*

These moves clearly bring the interview to its conclusion in terms, if not actually proposed by the interviewer, then at least selected by her from the options raised in the answers.

'Search' implies a goal, and this interview genre has a clearly defined end, in both senses of the word. Doubt, anger, rebellion, conflict or disharmony cannot be expressed as ends, only as problems to be overcome. They cannot, therefore, remain, to leave the interview open. This would contradict the implicit goal of the interview. The interview must have the *closure* appropriate to meaning being discovered through life's experiences, because its structure rests on the promise of success in the search for meaning. And this closure is not just a matter of what is discussed or asserted, but also of how it is rendered exclusive of alternative interpretations and how it is signalled as the end to which the linguistic processes of the preceding interview were moving.

Non-verbal Aspects

We have discussed the role of the interviewer and the way it is realised linguistically, and we have seen how this role changes as the interview moves through its various stages. Other aspects of the relation between interviewer and interviewee, however, remain relatively stable throughout the interview and lend it its overall quality of an intimate, cooperative, explorative conversation. We would like to draw attention to two aspects of language that play an important role in realising this: modality and non-verbal communication.

MODALITY

The term 'modality' refers to the ways in which speakers can convey how certain (or uncertain) they are of what they are saying. Caroline Jones' speech is characterised by many markers of low modality, of relative uncertainty. In this way she signifies the exploratory, non-assertive nature of her role — her listening attitude. Some of these markers of low modality are verbal — adverbs like 'probably', 'maybe', 'perhaps', auxiliaries like 'may' and 'might' and 'can' and 'could':

> *And yet they probably call you in to solve some sort of rational problem. Because there still might be a mirror effect for you.*

Others are non-verbal — tentative intonations or reformulations, deliberate hesitations to convey the sense of a search for the right word, hesitantly rising inflections or tags on the interviewer's statements, especially when these contain an element of challenge (Caroline Jones' challenges sound much less confrontational than they read):

> *They are reflecting back to us something within that . . . what? . . . that we don't want to face up to or that we haven't faced up to?*

Jones does not, of course, use low modality because she is uncertain in her role as interviewer. Nor do her hesitations and pauses suggest disfluency. These features of her speech quite deliberately seek to convey a non-assertive attitude and to signify the tentative, exploratory, 'search'-like nature of the genre.

COOPERATION AND CONTROL

Speech involves more than words. It includes voice quality, accent, pitch, tempo, pauses. Radio (and television) interviews are spoken, and listened to. We have already discussed the role of non-verbal communication in realising modality. We will now conclude with two other aspects of the interviewer's role that are also realised, at least in part, by non-verbal means: cooperation and control.

Interviewers have generally learned to suppress the feedback noises ('mm', 'I see', 'right', etc.) which occur every six seconds or so in normal face-to-face conversation. In *Radio: A Guide to Broadcasting Techniques*, Elwyn Evans, a former head of the radio training section of the BBC, says: 'For some reason spoken expressions of interest — "really", "how extraordinary", "hm hm" and the like — sound silly in the mouth of an interviewer.'[10] In Caroline Jones' interviews, however, such noises, though faded down, remain audible. Encouraging 'mms', a soft 'yes' on an intake of breath, almost like a sigh, the occasional 'right' of approbation and recognition all serve to maintain the positive, cooperative tone of the insight-seeking interview, and to express Jones' interest in and sympathy for her interviewees.

Despite the deliberate tentativeness that translates the search for meaning into the search for the right word,

Jones' tone of voice — soft, delicately paced and quietly pitched — attests to a continuous, quiet and unassuming authority. Even her occasional interruptions are positive (and always successful in being accepted by the interviewee). Control and direction are established in a non-assertive way, reassuring to the interviewee, and they are maintained by cooperation, by joining the interviewee in the quiet process of exposure and discovery.

THE INTIMATE VOICE OF RADIO

Radio would seem to be a particularly appropriate medium for *The Search for Meaning*. More than any other medium it can project a sense of intimacy and of interiority (and remember that, in religious confessions, the confessor traditionally does not see the confessee). The absence of exterior signs of social status can bring the guests closer to the listeners than might have been the case if they could also have seen how old the guests were, how they were dressed, where they lived — factors that can bring out the social distance between guest and listener. It therefore came as somewhat of a surprise when, in May 1991, *The Search for Meaning* began to be broadcast also on the ABC's Sunday night television program *Compass*. Without comparing the radio and television versions in detail, we noticed that, in the television version, Jones' role became more that of a presenter and less that of a conversation partner. We see her introduce the guest, locate him or her in an appropriate place for the interview and, as we see contextualising images of the guest's work or social life, we hear her link the parts of the program with abstract, interpretative comment. By contrast, her role in the actual interview becomes less visible, as many of her questions are edited out. In the television interview with Maina Gielgud, Jones' role was reduced to a few reaction shots in which we see her listen earnestly to her interviewee, though in other programs, for instance the interview with Rene Rivkin, her part in the interview was more prominently featured.

It seems to us that *The Search for Meaning* is most engaging when it is mediated aurally, as private verbal testimony, rather than displayed to the more public gaze of the camera. On television, the search becomes less of a journey, less of a struggle, and the meaning of the program derives more from the process of editing and from the way the presenter elaborates and encapsulates that meaning, than from the unfolding of an interactional *process*. Thus the program acquires the status of evidence for Jones' interpretation, rather than allowing the listener to witness an interactional process as it is happening, and it loses something of the intimacy and the sense of interiority it has on radio.

Summarising our discussion in this and the two preceding sections, we can say that the linguistic realisation of the interview is structured as follows:

1. Concrete events and mental processes are abstracted and generalised by the interviewer. This involves nominalisation and objectivation, and an emphasis on reflection rather than on description.
2. The subjective, personal, behavioural answers of the interviewee are used to illustrate general, objective rules of behaviour and observations concerning meaningful practices and beliefs.
3. Jones' non-verbal behaviour controls the direction and tenor of the confessional and testimonial aspects of the conversation. Challenges and confrontations are downplayed. Cooperation and support help to elicit self-revelation.
4. Questions perform various functions, principally those of inviting reflection, and of reformulating and extending the discussion of topics chosen from the narrative of the interviewee.
5. The genre involves closure, signified by a negotiated agreement between the two participants about the significance of the interviewee's life as exemplary when abstracted through the interviewer's discourse.

Intertextual Connections

Caroline Jones' interviewing strategies resemble those of psychotherapeutic interviews, especially those based on the 1960s' humanistic psychology of Carl Rogers and Abraham Maslow, two theorists who saw 'self-actualisation' as the principal goal of psychological health and adjustment. R. Nelson-Jones summarises their goals and the qualities they valorise in the person counselled[11]:

Looking down the list of qualities on page 110, one is struck by their congruence with the explicit verbal controls and summations Caroline Jones uses to orchestrate the interview we have analysed. Acceptance of self — of self-responsibility, liberated thought, insight and openness — lead to a 'yearning for the spiritual', much as in Jones' interviews:

> *People being themselves and accepting each other as themselves.*

> *A feeling of being loved and accepted . . .*

Or, in another interview, with Paolo Totaro:

> *So what are . . . the moments in which you feel most real, most yourself, most authentic?*

The humanistic self-centred (or client-centred) therapeutic interview characteristically invites clients to reflect on and to clarify the conflicts and feelings of low self-worth they volunteer. Neurosis, it is argued, stems from lack of congruence between self-concept and psychological environment. The gap is bridged through counselling. Therapists bring their clients to an awareness of this disharmony. Clients then accept this as a motivation for self-actualising adjustments. Therapists must be communicative, empathetic, non-directive and non-judgmental. Above all, they must listen. This fundamental acceptance of the client allows the latter to achieve an insight which is given expression in the conscious formulation of striving for authenticity and self-acceptance, sometimes formulated as harmony with the spiritual, sometimes as the actualisation of selfhood.

Rogers' and Maslow's goals for counselling and for living

Rogers	Maslow	Rogers
Overall goal: the fully functioning (mature) person	Overall goal: the self-actualising (psychologically healthy) person	Overall goal: the person of tomorrow
Qualities	*Qualities*	*Qualities*
Open to experience and able to perceive realistically	Superior perception of reality	Openness to the inner and outer
Rational and not defensive	Increased acceptance of self, of others and of nature	Desire for authenticity
Engaged in existential process of living	Increased spontaneity, simplicity and naturalness	Scepticism regardarding science and technology
Trusts in organismic valuing process	Increase in problem-centring	Desire for wholeness as a human being
Construes experience in extensional manner	Increased detachment and desire for privacy	The wish for intimacy
Accepts responsibility for being different from others	Increased autonomy and resistance to enculturation	Process persons Caring for others Attitude of closeness towards nature
Accepts responsibility for own behaviour	Greater freshness of appreciation	Anti-institutional Trust of the authority within
Relates creatively to the environment	More frequent peak experiences	Material things unimportant
Accepts others as unique individuals	Increased identification with human species	A yearning for the spiritual
Prizes himself	Deeper, more profound inter-personal relations	
Prizes others	More democratic character structure	
Relates openly and freely on the basis of immediate experiencing	Greatly increased creativeness	
Communicates rich self-awareness when desired	Superior ability to discriminate ethical values	

Unlike their psychotherapeutic counterparts media interviews are not, of course, dyadic — there is always a third party involved, the audience. And media interviews aim to engage, entertain and inform their audience, not to intervene therapeutically in the lives of interviewees who have, in any case, already negotiated the difficulties of life. That is why they are of public (that is, mass-media) interest. So Jones' interviews are structured to reveal *to the listener* the *possibility* of self-actualisation, spiritual fulfilment and meaning, not to change the self-perceptions or values of the interviewee. If any self-perceptions are to be changed, they are those of the listeners who are, so to speak, Jones' 'clients'. But as we have seen, this can only be done obliquely in media interviews. In short, Jones' interviews are not identical to the humanistic self-realising counselling interviews on which they are partially modelled. But they do bring to the public domain many of the values (one might say the ideology) of the self-insight, new age, humanistic psychology of the 1960s–70s: they are *intertextually* related to the counselling interview.

Media interviews do not arise solely from within the medium on which they are made public. They are elaborations or transformations of pre-existing genres; among them, in this case, the genre of the psychotherapeutic interview.

The psychotherapeutic interview, however, is not the only intertextual connection. As we have seen in the first section of this chapter, there are also connections with religious genres, for instance with the testimonies of renewed or newly found faith which form part of the ritual of certain Protestant denominations. Like radio interviews, they occur in public, but unlike radio interviews, they are monologic rather than dialogic. They are also similar to pastoral counselling interviews. Pastoral counselling predates Freud, but more recently it has been profoundly influenced by the theories and techniques of the psychotherapeutic interview.[12]

Many Christian counsellors, however, are worried about this development and point at irreducible contradictions between the values that underlie psychotherapeutic counselling and the teachings of the Bible, between the role models of psychology and the *imitatio Christi*, the adoption of Christ as the one and only 'role model'. P.C. Vitz observes that:

> The relentless and single-minded search for a glorification of the self is at direct cross-purposes with the Christian injunction to lose the self. Certainly Jesus Christ neither lived nor advocated a life that would qualify by today's standards as 'self-actualised'. For the Christian the self is the problem, not the potential paradise . . . Correcting this condition requires the practice of such un-self-actualised states as contrition and penitence, humility, obedience and trust in God.[13]

We have seen that self-actualisation is positively valued in *The Search for Meaning*. But we have also seen that Caroline Jones tries to steer Margot Cairnes away from too one-sided an emphasis on self-actualisation towards more altruistic concepts of love ('more wholesome relationships'), and that it is precisely at those points that Jones becomes in her own words a little less 'non-directive' and 'non-judgmental' and has 'definite ideas to present herself as well'. It is striking that the conclusion of the interview realises in secularised form what G.R. Collins sees as another 'distinctive of Christian counselling', namely 'the promise of life eternal in Heaven after death'.[14] Jones asks Margot Cairnes for 'thoughts about death' in relation to the near-death of her daughter, who was revived after having stopped breathing for thirty minutes. Not only does Margot Cairnes respond to this question with a strong affirmation of life; it also turns out that she herself had been near death as a baby. About these two brushes with death, she then says:

'The brushes were so peaceful and so reassuring almost, that there was a peaceful haven, and one was really passing from this present experience to another experience'.

Jones' emphasis on prayer and meditation finally adds another element which writers on Christian counselling find lacking in the psychotherapeutic interview. According to Vitz:

> Selfism is an example of a horizontal heresy, with its emphasis only on the present, and on self-centred ethic . . . What is excluded is the spiritual life of prayer, meditation and worship — the essential vertical dimension of Christianity, the relation to God.[15]

The Search for Meaning, then, attempts a synthesis between the public media interview, with its aims of engaging, entertaining and informing the audience, the intimate and personal psychotherapeutic interview, with its aims of healing and enabling insight and self-actualisation; and, in somewhat secularised form, the religious dimension, with its emphasis on more altruistic values, on prayer and on salvation. For this no ready-made genre exists. A new genre must be developed from existing genres which each achieve part of what *The Search for Meaning* attempts to realise. The genre of the psychotherapeutic interview provides a model for intimate and explorative interaction, for the non-assertive and empathetic mode of interviewing, and for the movement from confession to insight. The genre of the media interview provides a model for the 'search-like' structure in which the outcome is given in advance, and which can therefore hold the listener's attention in the same way as do other types of 'search' narratives, such as the detective novel; and for the use of exemplary, charismatic people who can become 'role models' and give the audience 'clues for living'. Religious genres, finally, provide the element of testimony and the necessity to intervene more directively when the meanings offered by the interviewee are not sufficiently consonant with the meanings and values the program ultimately wishes to communicate.

Private Religion on the Public Medium

The fusion between self-actualisation and religious or quasi-religious spiritualism that characterises the meanings searched for in Jones' interviews is not, of course, unique to her radio program. Ever since the late eighteenth century, when barriers began to be erected between the private and public spheres of life, mainstream Western Christianity has become more and more a private matter, a matter of one's personal relation to God rather than of doing God's work in the world. Non-Christian forms of spirituality, many of which find public expression in *The Search for Meaning*, exhibit the same feature. The sociologist and theologian A.C. Zijderveld has called such forms of spirituality 'gnostic', after the Hellenistic sects which similarly sought salvation in 'the road inward': 'Like Hellenistic man, many a modern individual thirsts for the meaning that overrationalised abstract society denies him. He is in search of charismatic experiences and believes that these can be found in his "deepest" subjectivity.'[16]

Zijderveld sees this as a very understandable reaction of protest against a society in which public life is increasingly rationalised, governed by bureaucratic routines and principles of efficiency and profitability that leave no room for moral responsibility and can create a profound sense of alienation. But he also sees dangers. One of these he relates to the concept of 'charisma', a term he uses in the sense Max Weber gave to it. Weber contrasted the power of rationalised social institutions to the personalised power of charismatic individuals. Such charismatic power, he argued, is, in the end, fickle. Charisma cannot last, and Zijderveld observes:

> During the evolution of Western civilisation, charismatic movements have emerged regularly. The prophets in ancient Israel, protesting against a routinised priestly religion, the gnostics in the days of the early Christian Church, searching for meaning, reality and freedom in the

alienating chaos of the Hellenistic era, the monastic orders and various sects in the Medieval Church, the Marxists and the hippies in industrial society, are examples of human attempts to escape from the petrification process of institutionalisation and rationalisation. But they all share a common tragic fate: the charismatic movement they instigate is doomed to wind up in institutional structures with a rational organisation, that is if it does not disappear altogether. Sooner or later all charisma is doomed either to turn into its opposite or to fade away.[17]

Zijderveld's second objection relates to the one-sidedness of 'the road inward':

During their many ages of development, the civilisations of Occident and Orient have both explored various ways to escape from routinisation and its inherent coercion. Among several, the 'road inward' has always been prominent. Despite his constitutional dependence on exteriority, man [sic] has always tried to withdraw from the outer world of nature and culture into his own subjectivity; he has always been attracted by the irrational abodes of his emotional nature where he remains irresponsive to social rights and duties — in a sense 'socially dead'. The Indian nirvana is a perfect example of such a 'social death'.[18]

It should be noted that Zijderveld acknowledges that the boundaries between gnosticism and activism, another form of social protest he recognises, are not always clearcut. Activists, too, may have 'gnostic traits'. Yet:

Although protesters may share many gnostic traits, they do not revolt primarily against rationalisation and routinisation, but against the existing authority and power relations of the established adult world . . . They aim at the renewal of reality, meaning and freedom within the framework of socio-political reality.[19]

It cannot be said that *The Search for Meaning* is wholly on the side of the 'road inward'. Caroline Jones often interviews people whose charisma derives from their active pursuits in political society (Phillip Adams, Helen Caldicott, Marcus Einfeld, to mention just a few). In her introduction to the interview with Margot Cairnes she stresses quite strongly that Margot Cairnes 'aims to take her real self to work' and that overcoming 'the split between the real self inside and the self I show to the outside world' will be a key theme of the program. Indeed, Cairnes herself makes the meanings she has found in her own personal search for meaning socially productive. Yet, on balance, the values towards which most of the radio interviews converge construct meaning as something personal and subjective. Of course, it may be important that such meanings are given public attention. We are, as Zijderveld also recognises, 'double beings', 'unique individuals with our own mode of existence, our own thoughts and emotions, our own experiences of love, anxiety and loneliness' as well as 'social beings', who must 'act and feel according to the rules and patterns of our society'.[20] And if we are to seek meaning in life, it must, perhaps, be sought on both these levels.

An interview with Caroline Jones

After completing this chapter, we showed it to Caroline Jones and invited her to comment on our analysis. This led to the following conversation between Caroline Jones and Theo van Leeuwen.

CAROLINE JONES:	You say 'The interview must have the closure appropriate to meaning being discovered through life's experience because its structure rests on the premise of success in *The Search for Meaning*. I want to discuss that point with you, because it

seems to me that, yes, it's mostly true, but not always. I am absolutely open to someone telling me 'There is no meaning' or 'I have been unsuccessful' or 'I can see very little'. The interview with René Rivkin is an example. He says: 'There is no meaning in life, and the only recipe I can find is the minimisation of pain and the maximisation of pleasure'. You see, I don't have any difficulty in accepting that. I find myself as interested in that as in all the various explorations of finding meaning.

THEO VAN LEEUWEN: *But you yourself are still searching for meaning in that interview...*

JONES: With him.

VAN LEEUWEN: *With him. And then in the end you more or less give up. The interview doesn't lead to the kind of answers you might have...*

JONES: No, it's not that I give up, it's that I accept him. I accept what he's saying. I don't feel defeated or disappointed.

VAN LEEUWEN: *But what about the audience? Wouldn't they expect the program to find meaning, to express values?*

JONES: Well, I don't know the answer to that, but I must tell you that of the whole television series this program had the biggest response in terms of numbers of letters and phone calls. And what people were attracted by was his honesty. One man, a very senior man in this community, and a very powerful man, said to me: 'The man's soul was open. I found myself liking him more and disliking him more than I had previously. I can't imagine that I would be able to make such a revelation myself.' It really touched something with him.

VAN LEEUWEN: *So maybe the program did express a value after all. The audience was hearing someone who sees things clearly, including himself, which not many people do.*

JONES: While we're on that subject, you also say: 'Not just anyone can be called, only the reflexive, the articulate, the successful, the charismatic'. I would have thought the field was broader than that. Many of the people who have spoken in the program are not publicly known at all and not terribly articulate in the accepted sense of the word. There was for example a canecutter with very little education. And I also wanted to comment on that word 'successful'. What we've tried to do in these programs is to redefine success. There is a prevailing view of success in this materialistic society which has to do with money, position, status, notoriety, celebrity. I think we are redefining it. I hope we are. We are suggesting that it is the holding of values that might define a successful life, or lead to a successful life. And that might be something as unfashionable as service to people, or having suffered and made some sense of it and being able to talk about it. And I would want to say the same thing about charisma. Sometimes we run the risk of inviting people to speak on the program who are not particularly charismatic. You hear people talk about the pain of having cerebral palsy and you hear them struggle through a speech impediment to speak of their deepest thoughts. That's very hard to listen to, sometimes. But it's important. We need to hear that. Now such people cannot be said to be charismatic. So I'm not looking for the star performer. Many of the people are not star performers. You're saying very definitely 'Not just anyone can be called'. I'm saying: 'Almost anyone can be called.'

VAN LEEUWEN: Except the dogmatic.

JONES: Yes, well, maybe I'm saying that. With people who are very certain through a dogma you hear a great fluency and a great certainty, but you're not sure on what level you're corresponding with them. You should change it. I'm simply saying to you, it doesn't look or sound or feel dispassionate. It sometimes brings tears! I cannot accept an objective, dispassionate mode of interviewing. I cannot regard people as an object or specimen. And I would think largely the media does. People are objects to be written about, sometimes ridiculed. I don't find that very satisfying as a listener or reader and I don't ever want to do it myself. I have of course been an easy target for people who are much happier to stay in an objective, dispassionate mode of interviewing. And people have been confused, because I come out of that mode myself. It was my training in current affairs.

VAN LEEUWEN: *So do you edit mostly in the first part of the interview, the confession, as we called it?*

JONES: Yes.

VAN LEEUWEN: *And when the interviewees begin to reflect on their story you allow yourself a more active role.*

JONES: Yes, I agree with all that, although I hadn't seen it before.

VAN LEEUWEN: *Do your interviewees have a say in the editing?*

JONES: Yes, there is always consultation at the end of the interview: Do you feel happy about it? Did you say anything you would rather not have broadcast? Sometimes people ring and say, just leave such-and-such out. Often it's something that to me is not particularly intimate, but it might hurt a member of the family. That's easy. We always do it. It's a cooperative, collaborative process.

VAN LEEUWEN: *When does the cooperation start? How much goes on between you and the interviewee before you start recording?*

JONES: Very little, by design. I send them a list of questions and suggestions I have, about four pages. It's a framework of guidelines. It's left very open. It's intended to begin a train of thought.

VAN LEEUWEN: *The same thing for every interviewee? A general thing?*

JONES: Yes, it's very general. And Louise, my colleague and researcher, will often have a biographical conversation with them, usually on the telephone. Sometimes people respond to the four-page thing that goes out. They send some notes back, and that's very helpful to me. It helps me to find the really meaningful turning points, so that I know to concentrate there. But once I get together with the person the story begins, and it might as well happen in the studio, while we're recording.

VAN LEEUWEN: *Do you formulate questions in advance?*

JONES: I've got the story in mind, or as much of it as I have been told. I know where there might be highlights, but I try to keep it pretty open. Sometimes I have things written down, just to remind myself, but my main preparation is to be clear to myself, so that I can put myself aside, and be there with the person. It's almost a state of mind, a presence, a being.

VAN LEEUWEN: *I am asking that question because I think that there is always a degree of inequality in interviews. The interviewee is not used to the interview situation, doesn't know what is going to happen, and must talk spontaneously. The interviewer is used to the situation and has a chance to prepare and might therefore well sound more fluent and articulate. And, added to that, the interviewer doesn't have to give so much of him or herself while the interviewee has to bare all, so to speak.*

JONES: I agree. I try to redress it as best as I can, with verbal reassurance and with taking plenty of time, because I want them to be as comfortable and as confident and I suppose safe as they can, not just for the sake of getting a good interview, but because if anybody would end up hurt by one of these interviews that would be the worst thing that could happen to me. Now that's a very unfashionable thing to say. Journalists are not supposed to say that. But to me it matters. It has to be handled delicately, with sensitivity, and with plenty of opportunity for the person to have their say. And whenever I've been asked to leave anything out I've always done it. There's never been any argument.

VAN LEEUWEN: *We made some comments on the differences between the radio and the television versions of* The Search for Meaning. *How do you react to that?*

JONES: I'm inclined to agree with what you say, but I want to keep exploring the visual medium, to find ways of revealing that search for meaning. I have a very strong commitment to radio, but television is there, I would like to try and find a way to use it. And there's also print. Our predominant mode of learning is still print, so we want it reinforced in print, and I think that's why the books sell in such an extraordinary way. It's a record of it, in print. So I suppose the answer is, I'm interested in doing this sort of work in whatever medium will take it.

VAN LEEUWEN: *There is a bit of a paradox about* The Search for Meaning *in that it is on the one hand a religious program, but on the other hand made for a secular audience, or at least for an audience that cannot be supposed to be religious. Do you find that difficult to negotiate?*

JONES: No, I like it. The more blurred it stays, the better. It's more inclusive in that way.

VAN LEEUWEN: *It reaches people who might be turned off by the language of religion.*

JONES: Yes, it's almost a search in language, to find ways of talking about this stuff, because many people apparently feel that the language of dogma has failed them or hurt them.

VAN LEEUWEN: *But often you are quite direct in asking about prayer and meditation.*

JONES: Yes, I found it so interesting that you picked up that I do have an agenda although I have said I don't. I was happy to have you pinpoint that. But I do want it to stay blurred. I love anything that crosses the disciplines. I am very anti compartmentalisation of knowledge because to me that's all part of mechanisation and utilitarianism, and I think it's dehumanising. See, one of my main guides would be the reactions I get from the people. I've always had that, my whole journalistic career. Somebody recently said to me: 'Why do you say at the end of the program "Peace be with you"? That makes the hairs rise on the back of my neck because it takes me back to the dogmatic Catholic Church of my childhood, and I think it's frightful. Why do you do it? Don't you understand that that turns off many people like me?' I'm really thinking about that now. I personally find it very pleasant and quite warm to have somebody wish me peace, but of course it has connotations. And if it's such a switch-off to people, I will have to think about it.

VAN LEEUWEN: *It's certainly different from the usual sign-off.*

JONES: A good thing that it comes at the end of the program! But does it mean that the person who's been offended will never listen again? In this case it didn't.

VAN LEEUWEN: *What did you think of our comment that the program mainly concentrates on the 'road inward'?*

JONES: I am very interested in the points you make there and I just want to point out what you have also pointed out a little later on, that we don't stay exclusively with the road inwards. There are many examples of that. Fred Hollows, Tom Uren, Ian Cohen, the environmentalist who demonstrates by hanging on to the prows of battleships and so on,

Ian Gawler who had to do the inner work in order to go out and work with other people who have cancer. It is generally my intention, even though I don't always realise that intention, to hear the fruits of the inward search. That comes out of my personal belief that contemplation is wonderful, but you've got to make it active, otherwise it would be very selfish, I suppose.

VAN LEEUWEN: *But it is the search or the story that is central.*

JONES: Yes. To me the hearing of the story is a sacred undertaking, a ritual. Do you know the interview with Magda Bozic?

VAN LEEUWEN: *Yes, though I only read it. In the first book.*

JONES: That's almost my favourite, I think. She just began and I really didn't have very much to say on the way through. I remember her describing how she left Warsaw, left her friends, a little knot of people on the platform of the railway station. There goes the train and gradually the group recedes, and she knew she was leaving everything, family, language, everything that was familiar. I just sat and cried. That was the only appropriate response. All I could be was an accompanist, another human being hearing reverently what she was telling. There is then a mood or momentum set up which cannot be interrupted and really only be accompanied, in silence, a deep listening. It is a mysterious and awe-inspiring process.

4

Political Interviews: The Adversarial Genre

Paul Lyneham interviews Andrew Peacock, Leader of the Opposition, on ABC Television's *7.30 Report*, 29 September 1989.

[Introduction: Trish Goddard in studio]

GODDARD: to the Opposition it's nothing but a desperate bid to win the next election. To the Government it's a trade-off. The banks get more interest back on the money they have to deposit with the Reserve Bank, and in return, interest rates on home mortgages won't be lifted above 17 per cent.
Opposition Leader Andrew Peacock is talking to Paul Lyneham about today's developments and other matters.

PAUL LYNEHAM:	*Mr Peacock, thanks for joining us. What do you think of Paul Keating's attempt to cap mortgage rates at 17 per cent?*
ANDREW PEACOCK:	Well, it really is just playing with the system. It puts more money into the system, and therefore there's more available, but, eh, it is in essence a cosmetic job. What Australians want are real reductions in interest rates, not tampering in a cosmetic way like this.
LYNEHAM:	*Could be popular with home-buyers though, couldn't it?*
PEACOCK:	Well, it's hardly going to reduce their interest rates. It's certainly going to have the effect of pegging them at the moment; but while the Government continues with a one-dimensional policy of just high interest rates, they're not going to have people tiptoeing through the tulips with joy.
LYNEHAM:	*Do you think it could send out the wrong signals and put a bit more heat back into the economy?*
PEACOCK:	Well, it's an easing of policy, of course, so, er, to that extent it will have that effect. The Government's been squeezing money supply and therefore forcing interest rates up. And this, of course, is a slight turn in the other direction.
LYNEHAM:	*Do you think it makes Dr Hewson's timetable of a December 2 Federal election more likely?*
PEACOCK:	Well, that could be. Ah, I mean I don't know and John is of that view and I've, I've certainly put it as one of the options that the Government has. I think they'd be altogether foolish to do it, but if they want to embark on some form of masochism for themselves, that's up to them.
LYNEHAM:	*And you'd be elected despite your 28 per cent approval rating?*
PEACOCK:	Ah, despite all sorts of things I think we'd probably, ah, be elected.
LYNEHAM:	*If you believe in market forces, Mr Peacock, and as a*

	conservative you presumably do, the market is not buying what you're selling.
PEACOCK:	Well, eh, I'll, you know, as far as I'm concerned there are polls and polls and polls. We seem to have more polls than you and I have breakfasts.
LYNEHAM:	*They all say the same thing, Mr Peacock.*
PEACOCK:	Well, they all say the same thing fairly critically and it is that we're in front.
LYNEHAM:	*Yes, but I mean state of the parties in the last Morgan Poll you're 2 per cent in front. With 17 per cent interest rates you should be streets ahead, surely.*
PEACOCK:	[Laughs] You know, one of the worries about Paul, polls Paul, when I'm being interviewed by fellas like you is that if we're behind you want to know why we're not in front, and when we're in front on all the polls, you want to know why we're not further in front. Now I can say to you that I'd like to be further in front and I believe, ah, when we release our expenditure savings and tax package in the next fortnight we will drive further in front. But the fact that we're in front would indicate to you if you ask me whether we would win the elections, that I can speak with some confidence and say yes, we would.
LYNEHAM:	*But, Mr Peacock, the basic fact is that since you replaced John Howard there has not been any decisive swing towards the conservatives.*
PEACOCK:	Well, I think that, er, the polls have fluctuated. There's no doubt about that, and on occasions we've been well ahead. Then we've even been at one point, I think, half to one per cent on one poll, behind. Eh, but we are ahead, and I believe that, as I've indicated to you, though eh, I think, eh, after the last of these policy documents is issued, and the real incentive is given to Australians, then we'll forge further ahead.
LYNEHAM:	*And last month's poll that said that 70 per cent of*

	coalition voters didn't have a clear understanding of your economic position?
PEACOCK:	Yeah, ah, that was worrying. I have to admit that to you, because whilst I would have liked to immediately have then put the last elements in the economic program out, which would certainly have turned that around, I am, in fact, forced to wait another fortnight. But that's okay.
LYNEHAM:	*How close are you to getting those new tax scales worked out?*
PEACOCK:	Ah, we'll be releasing that in the second week of October, which means as we're talking now, of course, the week after next.
LYNEHAM:	*Got a date yet?*
PEACOCK:	Well, I'll finalise that date. I mean, I'm look . . . trying to, ah, organise ah, the ah, around the 11th or 12th of October.
LYNEHAM:	*Is the two-tier system still very much on your agenda?*
PEACOCK:	Well, now that we're so close to releasing it, you can wait. I'm not going to release it on this program.
LYNEHAM:	*But I gather you've said it won't be just two tiers when it first comes out. You'll still be working towards that.*
PEACOCK:	Well, it's very difficult immediately to make the changes to introduce the two-tier system. Ah, ah, I've indicated to you that that's our aim, and you'll see the way it works out, eh, when we release it in two weeks.
LYNEHAM:	*Now, in June, after your Federal Council in Sydney, you said to me in an interview that you would get to this two-tier system within the first term. Is that . . . of your government . . . Is that still the case?*
PEACOCK:	Yes, that's what, that remains the policy. Ah. There's no doubt about that.
LYNEHAM:	*You also said in your speech in reply to the budget, 'We will ensure that the top rate for individuals is not higher than the company tax rate'. That still the go?*

PEACOCK: Yes, that's right. And I've, eh, found it very difficult to comprehend why the Government having advocated the same thing but not implemented, ah, sought to attack me on that. 'Cos time and again the Treasurer himself spoke of that as more than simply an aspiration, yet they've refused to do it.

LYNEHAM: *Also within your first term of government?*

PEACOCK: I, er, I don't retreat on anything I've said. But you'll see all the detail anyhow when we bring it out in a fortnight's time.

LYNEHAM: *Mr Peacock, is there any case for keeping the fringe benefits tax as it is now?*

PEACOCK: Well, it's part of our policy as you know, ah, that we will abolish the fringe benefits tax.

LYNEHAM: *Abolish it entirely?*

PEACOCK: That's been part of our policy since we released the shape of it in around about April of last year.

LYNEHAM: *And you've not had any second thoughts since then?*

PEACOCK: Well, you have second thoughts when you do reviews of all of them. But, ah, of course, you've got to weigh up all the interlocking factors but you'll see what we do with it in two weeks.

LYNEHAM: *Do you approve of Justice Maddern's intervention in the pilots' dispute?*

PEACOCK: Well I see nothing wrong in ah, in ah, Mr Justice Maddern calling the parties together, but, there's no real role in this obviously. I mean, everyone seems to indicate that the matter can be settled, eh, if there can be negotiation. We, in fact, eh, would have had it fixed weeks ago.

LYNEHAM: *On the other hand there are a lot of people who think the Opposition's had more positions on this than the Kama Sutra.*

PEACOCK: [Laughs] I'm sure you'd want to be advocating that view. Here's a reality where a government has simply given up governing, cannot solve the dispute, and you wanna talk about what the Opposition are

	doing. It wouldn't happen under us. But if we were in we'd have fixed it. Because I would have directed Australian Airlines to negotiate. We own it, the Government.
LYNEHAM:	*But I heard two different versions on one day last month — your version and John Howard's at the Press Club.*
PEACOCK:	No, the view of the Opposition is that you negotiate with the pilots either directly or through the federation.
LYNEHAM:	*And you're definitely going to be Prime Minister by this time next year?*
PEACOCK:	I would think earlier than that. Ah, I don't know whether it will be a December election or between February and May, but it will be some time there unless he wants to go as long as he can and have a half-Senate election before then. But on all the indication the Government is in very real strife and that's because, as I've said to you, they've given up governing.
LYNEHAM:	*Thank you for your time.*
PEACOCK:	Nice to be with you.

The Political Interviewer as 'Honest Broker'

In the early years of television, political interviews did not have the combative, adversarial tone to which we have now become so accustomed. Interviewers asked polite, deferential questions, often let their interviewees nominate the topics of discussion, and went through several rehearsals with them before the interview was actually broadcast. They saw themselves as facilitating the transmission of information, as a conduit between the country's leaders and the public. Compare, for instance, these questions, the first two from interviews with Clement Attlee and Anthony Eden, the third a bold, confrontational statement from a

1982 *Weekend World* interview with opposition leader Michael Foot:

> *Can you, now you're back, having cut short your lecture tour, tell us something of how you view the electoral prospects?*
>
> *I wonder if I may introduce a question which I'm sure will infuriate you, but since I'm here presumably for that reason . . . It has often been said in recent times that the Conservative Party is a war-mongering party. Isn't there a shred of truth in there or is there?*
>
> *Let me tell you what I think many members of the public would regard as an absurdity. It would be the height of absurdity, would it not, not to get any sort of firm and coherent guarantee (from the trade unions), then to form a government, then to have roaring inflation as happened last time, and start imposing things. Surely the time to get it right is now. Especially if you want to win the election.*

In Australia, ABC current affairs producers were not allowed to approach politicians for an interview without special permission from the general manager. The procedure was so time consuming that, until 1967, political interviews remained a relative rarity, except in election times, when they were subject to very strict rules. Such political interviews as were conducted tended to be filmed in the politicians' homes or offices, rather than the interviewees being called to the studio, the interviewer's home ground.

But things were not to stay this way. As Churchill had foreseen when he called television a 'robot organisation that threatens the supremacy of Parliament',[1] television was destined to change the nature of politics. In Britain it was the introduction of commercial television which brought a new style of interviewer and a new style of interviewing. When ITN began transmission in 1955, it promised to provide 'television's first popular newspaper' and featured 'deft flashbacks and live interviews with bystanders'.[2] For over five years the BBC had not even shown its newsreaders' faces, in an attempt to guarantee the impartiality and objectivity of the news. Now commercial television introduced 'personality' current affairs presenters and interviewers who related to political interviewees in new ways. Rather than allowing them rehearsals and the right to set the agenda for their interviews, they cornered politicians in airport lounges with aggressive questioning ('It is in airports that television chooses to lurk', said Harold Macmillan), and rather than visiting the politicians in their homes or offices, they summoned them to the studio, located close to Westminster. They also broke the rules that barred coverage of elections and discussion of issues currently debated in the House of Commons with impunity. F. Wheen discusses the rise of the celebrity interviewer on non-BBC television in the U.K.

> One of the most notable differences between the two channels was in the conduct of interviews. The BBC continued to be deferential in the extreme ('I wonder, Prime Minister, whether you would care to say a few words to the viewers') but ITN's style was more probing and combative.
>
> The BBC's remaining strength was that people were believed to turn to it at moments of crisis — a legacy of the importance of BBC radio during the Second World War. But by 1956 even this monopoly was endangered. When the Hungarian uprising was put down in October, only ITN managed to bring back news film from Budapest. During the Suez crisis, a month later, it was ITN that broadcast the first pictures of British and French troops landing at Port Said. ITN followed this success with another world exclusive in 1957, when Robin Day interviewed President Nasser in Cairo. Since diplomatic relations between Britain and Egypt were still severed, Nasser's comments generated enormous interest, especially as he expressed his willingness to resume Egypt's 'friendship' with Britain. For Day, too, the interview was a triumph, proving that the ITN style would be applied even to Heads of State. When Day asked whether Nasser

accepted Israel's right to exist, the President accused him of 'jumping to conclusions'. 'No', Day replied, 'I am asking a question.'

Day and his colleagues soon became celebrities, just like any other television performer. There was the glamorous young athlete, Christopher Chataway, who had held the world record for running the mile. There was Ludovic Kennedy, who attracted attention because of his marriage to Moira Shearer, the dancer. There was Reginald Bosanquet, who wore a toupee and slurred his speech; his cheeky smirk was said to drive female viewers wild with ecstasy.[3]

In Australia, on the other hand, the impetus for change came from the ABC, the state broadcaster. Although the commercial channels had featured more political interviews than the ABC, with programs such as Channel 7's *Meet the Press*, in which politicians were interviewed by a panel of journalists, and Channel 9's *Kevin Sanders Reports*, in which Sanders provided a 'stimulating personal slant on the political scene',[4] *Four Corners'* Michael Charlton became Australia's first celebrity current affairs presenter. A few years later, *This Day Tonight*'s first presenter, Bill Peach, was the first to see his face marketed on badges and his name featured on 'I like Bill' car stickers. It was on the latter program, which started in 1967, that politicians were, for the first time, 'interviewed regularly and at length on television',[5] and this 'with an unusual lack of deference, even with cheek'.[6] The program was not averse to 'creating events', 'confronting people with each other' in 'verbal punch-ups', and 'offering viewers the sensation of watching both news and a kind of sport'.[7] Key interviewers and presenters like Robert Moore, Mike Willesee, Gerald Stone, Richard Carleton and Paul Lyneham began their careers with the ABC and many formed their views of the role of the political interviewer while working on *TDT*. Commercial television was not to follow *TDT*'s lead until four years later, when Mike Willesee started *A Current Affair* on Channel[9], in 1971.

More than any other program, *TDT* taught Australian politicians to become conscious of their 'image', and finally to absorb the lesson of the first 'television election', the 1960 U.S. Presidential election which Richard Nixon is said to have lost because of his 'five o'clock shadow', and of which John Kennedy had said: 'We wouldn't have had a prayer without that gadget [that is, television]'.[8] An older school of politicians resisted. In 1970 New South Wales Premier Robert Askin vowed he would never appear on *TDT* again, and in the same year South Australian Premier Steele Hall banned all ABC staff from government offices after Clive Hale had announced, on air, that a minister had declined to appear, raising an eyebrow while doing so. But Gough Whitlam already handled his television appearances with more confidence than Robert Menzies and Harold Holt had done, just as in Britain Harold Wilson had been the first to adapt to the requirements of the age of television politics. For Macmillan, television had still been 'a twentieth-century torture chamber',[9] and Douglas-Home had blamed his 1964 electoral defeat on 'the way they make me look on television', but Wilson carefully fostered a 'common man image' and felt that 'what he said on television was less important than the impression he gave and what he looked like'.[10] Regular pilgrimages to the television studios became part of politicians' jobs, whether they liked it or not. Refusal to appear, frequently announced on air, was risky, tantamount to showing disdain for the viewers (who became increasingly synonymous with the electorate), or to an admission of having something to hide.

TDT's first executive producer, Allan Martin, who had previously worked for *This Week*, the commercial counterpart to the BBC's *Panorama*, had said, in 1968: 'A public affairs producer needs a bit of a crusading spirit. It is not his job to start a revolution, but he must have a sense of justice, of what is wrong, and what needs changing.'[11] *TDT* interviewers were not just to facilitate the transmission of information, not just to act as a conduit between the country's leaders and the public. They were to play a more active role, a role the sociologist Krishan Kumar characterised as that of an 'honest broker' of opinion. According to Kumar, broadcasters

> must not stand, certainly must not seem to stand, far Left or Right ... One marked expression of this position in recent years has been the way in which the professional broadcaster has taken to identifying with 'us' — that is, taking the role of 'us', 'the unrepresented', 'the consumers', 'the suffering public', the victims of planners and public servants of all kinds, as well as of large industrialists, selfish trade unions, property speculators and the like.[12]

In other words, 'honest brokers' remain *neutral* in that they allow equal access to the plurality of views that exist in modern society, but they are *partial* in that they take the side of the viewers, the 'ordinary people', the 'voters', the 'consumers', the 'citizens', and in doing so they take up a more active, more investigative and more interrogative role. This is done on behalf of the audience, for their interventions will always be legitimated by an appeal to the interests of the public, as mediated by opinion polls or justified by their own and other media professionals' (for example, newspaper journalists') knowledge of what the public thinks, needs and wants. This often results in a 'quizzical, amused, slightly sceptical' attitude towards politics and politicians, an attitude which, it is assumed, is shared by the public. The satirical sketches in David Frost's *That Was the Week that Was*, an early 1960s current affairs program, may have contributed to the formation of this attitude:

> On Monday, in *Panorama*, you may have seen a profile of a Prime Minister. At one point he crossed to a dispatch box, opened it up and revealed a copy of *Roget's Thesaurus*. What word could he have been going to look up? 'Politics', do you think? Section 702 of *Roget's Thesaurus*, Penguin edition, gives the following alternatives for that word: 'cunning', 'craftiness', 'sharp practice', 'manoeuvring', 'chicanery', 'jugglery', 'concealment', 'foul play', 'diplomacy', and furthermore 'dodge', 'artful dodge', 'white lie', 'tricks of the trade', 'imposture', 'deception', 'live by one's

wits', 'gerrymandering', 'stoop to conquer', 'steal a march upon' . . .

In a 1964 pre-election interview with Harold Wilson we already see the 'honest broker' stance emerging. The interviewer, Desmond Wilcox, invokes 'the people' and 'the electorate', even though his questions still mainly seek information and clarification:

> *You talk about a new Britain and about getting Britain on the move again, Mr Wilson. Are you asking people to accept a drastic change in their lives?*
>
> *Sir Alec Douglas-Home has called the Labour Party Manifesto a 'menu without prices'. How much is this plan going to cost the electorate?*

In Brian Walden's 1982 *Weekend World* interview with Michael Foot, all deference has disappeared. The interviewer now meets the interviewee as his equal. He comes armed with his own information and confronts the interviewee with facts and opinions, to which the interviewee is then obliged to react. And the scepticism of the public is explicitly invoked in Walden's introduction: 'His [that is, Foot's] task, if he is to make Labour an election winning party, is to begin to nudge it, bit by bit, towards a posture that will overcome the electorate's scepticism.' In later 'questions' Walden cites opinion polls and 'vulgar populist opinion' as expressed, for instance, in the press: 'It's the polls, you see. It isn't just me saying it, it's the people,' and later:

> *Well, the trouble with that answer — excellent, splendid though it is as an exposition of the [Labour] constitutional position — is that vulgar populists like myself and the newspapers and all that want to know who is going to be chucked out. For instance, in one of this morning's papers it said that Foot is in favour of throwing eighty people out. Now is this report correct?*

We are writing a decade later. Since at least 1980 in Australia, and 1983 in Britain, political discourse has become even more exclusively preoccupied with economistic managerialism, with leadership and personality, with public opinion polls, and with a general scepticism about politicians and about the value of the parliamentary process.[13] The key questions have become 'Which team is more competent to manage the economy?' and 'Which leader will appeal most to the voters?' The 'slightly sceptical' attitude of which Kumar spoke has hardened into a deeply ingrained cynicism about the powerful, as a result of which interviews have often become contests in credibility and sincerity. However, as we will argue in more detail in the final section of this chapter, the essential features of the 'honest broker' approach to the interviewer's role are still in evidence, and the Lyneham–Peacock interview on which we will focus stands directly in that tradition.

Paul Lyneham, the Canberra-based political interviewer of the ABC's *7.30 Report* (successor to *Nationwide* which, in turn, succeeded *This Day Tonight*, in 1978) is unburdened by timidity and humility as he faces his opponents in quick-witted, rapid-fire debate. He is an extremely well-informed investigative journalist, and a highly skilled exponent of the adversarial political interview. Just how his and others' adversarial interviews are structured and controlled, and what role these interviews play in Australian political life, we will examine in the remainder of this chapter.

The Adversarial Genre

Adversarial political interviews can be seen as similar to courtroom interrogations. The politicians are interrogated on behalf of the relatively powerless armchair electorate in order to expose evidence of duplicity and to make public hidden schemes and self-serving motives — in order to 'keep the bastards honest'. The interviewers act as powerful investigators, standing in for 'us' against 'them'.

But there is another view. Political interviewers, especially those based in Canberra, can also be seen as locked into a collaborative relation, a relation of mutual dependency with politicians — over the heads of those whose interests they are supposed to serve. Derek Parker has gone so far as to call the Canberra Press Gallery 'courtesans'. He sees politicians as satisfying the media's 'appetite for news, for a constant stream of "summits" and symbols, readily digestible announcements and information and with a flood of invective against those they see as their enemies'.[14] On this view political interviewers provide politicians with a powerful electronic platform, all the more effective because of the display of public scrutiny which the interview format allows. The two major parties, both based in Canberra, both 'power elites', in the end have more in common with each other than with the public.

We would argue that both cooperation and contestation characterise the media–politics relationship. They are always in tension, with cooperation more evident in some contexts, competition more evident in others, such as television interviews. But even here, a qualification is needed.

If the political interview is a contest, it may be a peculiar type — one in which there can be more than one (even more than two) 'winners'. We will now try to show this by looking in more detail at the interview between Paul Lyneham and (former) Australian Opposition Leader Andrew Peacock, first discerning the 'stages' through which the adversarial interview moves, then examining the kinds of questions (and answers) which linguistically realise each stage. In the final section of this chapter we will return in more detail to the two views briefly sketched above.

We see the adversarial interview as consisting of the following 'stages': (a) greeting, (b) soliciting opinion, (c) checking, (d) challenging, (e) entrapment, and (f) release.

GREETING

Not every kind of interview shows interviewers and interviewees greeting each other. Studio interviews with politicians, however, invariably do. The interviewer begins by playing the role of host, and the interviewee is, therefore, a guest. It follows that etiquette must be observed and the guest thanked before and after the interview. Before the contest begins, the contestants must verbally shake hands, as equals, or almost equals, for while political interviewers use the more deferential honorific ('Prime Minister...', 'Mr Peacock...', etc), political interviewees tend to use the interviewer's first name ('Paul . . .'), especially when they are trying to assert themselves.

Thus the interview begins on a cooperative note, establishing itself as 'fair play', a sportsman-like contest, and establishing the relation between interviewer and interviewee as one in which the interviewer is a courteous host and the interviewee a guest willing to play by the rules of the game. These rules, however, are those of the 'home team', and when the interviewee is not willing to play by the interviewer's rules, the interviewer will inform the audience of this. Negotiation might then have to take place before the contest can begin, as in this *60 Minutes* interview between Richard Carleton and the then Federal Treasurer Paul Keating:

> *Mr Keating, thank you very much for coming to the studios tonight. I'd just like to point out to the viewers the strictures under which this discussion is being recorded this evening. In twenty-one years of interviewing Mr Keating, since he first came into Parliament back in 1969, he has never imposed conditions on his television appearances with me. He has tonight. The Treasurer has insisted that every word he utters at this recording session is in fact broadcast, that is to say, his words have not been edited in any way.*

Carleton then asks his first question, but Keating interrupts, and the following exchange ensues:

KEATING: Richard, let me take that point up. I did this interview tonight on the basis that it would be like a live interview. If I do Jana Wendt live it goes live. I want the public to see what's actually said and not

	to find either your questions or my answers on the cutting room floor.
CARLETON:	*You imposed the condition . . .*
KEATING:	I'm giving the public a break you aren't prepared to give them.
CARLETON:	*In twenty-one years you've never imposed . . .*
KEATING:	Very picky, dear boy, very picky.

SOLICITING OPINION

In the interview with Peacock, Lyneham does not immediately attack. The first question, following the greeting, is a relatively 'easy', innocent one, allowing Peacock to settle into the interview. He is asked to react to the issue of the day (interest rates) in a way that gives him the freedom to state his views the way he wants to (*'What do you think of Paul Keating's attempt to cap mortgage rates at 17 per cent?'*). Such cooperative solicitations return towards the end of the interview. They extend the courtesy of the greeting and farewell, the tone of cooperativeness that brackets the actual contest. But they also provide the interviewer with statements he may subsequently challenge, with rope to hang the interviewee by, as in the case of the question about mortgage rates. Lyneham immediately uses this to suggest that 'home buyers' (note the appeal to the public again) might actually like what Peacock's political opponent has proposed.

Not all interviews begin with open questions of this kind. Some interviewers launch straight into challenges. Others cite a previous statement of the interviewee, rather than allowing him or her to formulate anew, as in this interview with Peacock by Jana Wendt, also recorded in March 1989:

> *You said last month that your Government would bring about a massive fall in interest rates. Do you stand by that claim?*

But the strategy of starting with an open question is a recognised one. In a videotape on the techniques of interviewing produced for the Australian Film and Television School, ABC reporter and interviewer Stuart Littlemore says that he often begins his interviews with a 'nothing question', to put the interviewee at ease. Such a question, he adds, can always be edited out if it does not yield a relevant or interesting answer.

CHECKING

Following the soliciting of opinion (if there is any), the contest begins in earnest. Many interviewers first prepare the ground for their later challenges by checking the relevant facts and figures ('Is that correct?', 'Got a date yet?') and the interviewee's previous statements about the issue at hand ('Do you stand by that claim?', 'Is that still the go?'). The checking of a previous statement is typically preceded by the interviewer's recapitulation of that statement, and the question itself will be brief, requiring only confirmation (or denial):

> *Now, in June, after your Federal Council in Sydney, you said to me in an interview that you would get to this two-tier system within the first term . . . of your Government. Is that still the case?*

Checking often amounts to a test — a test of the interviewee's knowledge and skill (the pace is rapid and interviewees must have all the facts and figures at their fingertips), of the consistency of their statements and 'promises' (they must never be seen to contradict themselves, or to renege on a 'promise') and the degree to which they have their plans and policies worked out. Checking also commits interviewees to positions from which they cannot easily retreat without being seen to contradict themselves, and these positions can be used by the interviewer as a springboard for later challenges.

CHALLENGES

One element never absent from the adversarial political interview is the *challenge*. Having established the facts, having committed the interviewee to a position, the interviewer will move onto the offensive, confronting the interviewee with statements which, implicitly or explicitly, contradict or weaken his or her position and require interviewees to defend themselves. The interviewer often backs such statements with an appeal to the authority of 'the polls', 'the public', and of 'what a lot of people are saying', or to that of the press:

> *And last month's poll that said 70 per cent of coalition voters didn't have a clear understanding of your economic position?*

At other times the interviewer used the interviewee's own statements, or statements by members of his or her own party, to contradict statements made in the interview:

> *Your industry spokesman, John Howard, has said that the prospects of a significant fall in interest rates are, to quote him, 'zilch'. Is he wrong?*

Whatever the method used, challenges always formulate objections to the interviewee's positions as stated in the interview. They always involve a 'but' or, slightly stronger, a 'but surely'. They always force the interviewee into a defensive position. The interviewee is always the batsman, never the bowler.

ENTRAPMENT

From the interviewer's point of view, a series of challenges ideally culminates in *entrapment*, in a statement with which interviewees can neither agree nor disagree without contradicting themselves or otherwise damaging or weakening their position. It is a kind of verbal checkmate. Paul Lyneham attempts such an entrapment with this question:

> *If you believe in market forces, Mr Peacock, and as a conservative you presumably do, the market is not buying what you are selling.*

Lyneham assumes that Peacock cannot argue against 'market forces' without contradicting his basic political beliefs. But neither can he agree with the proposition that 'the market is not buying what he is selling' without admitting defeat. Once led into such a trap, interviewees will flounder ('Well, ah, I'll, you know . . .') and struggle to get out. If they are experienced enough they will have developed counter-strategies to delay or avoid entrapment. In this example, for instance, Peacock gains a few more moves by substituting 'polls' for 'market forces', and the authority of the 'polls' he can question somewhat more easily than that of 'market forces' ('there are polls and polls and polls. We seem to have more polls than you and I have breakfasts').

But in the end he is forced into an admission of weakness ('Yeah, ah, that was worrying. I have to admit that to you'), and once this has happened, the interviewer will move on to the next issue, and start a new sequence of checks, challenges and entrapments.

Release

Lyneham challenges Peacock on every issue he raises in the interview — every issue, that is, except the last one. The final question in political interviews often deals with electoral victory prospects or 'leadership' ambitions and contests, and the Lyneham–Peacock interview is no exception:

> *And you're definitely going to be Prime Minister by this time next year?*

Lyneham could easily have challenged Peacock on this question. He could easily have punctured Peacock's display of confident optimism ('I would think earlier than that'), so securing his final 'victory' in the verbal contest. But he doesn't do so. He lets the interviewee go. He lets him have the final word. In the end, the contest has no 'winner' — perhaps because it is a story to be continued until defeat occurs in another arena, in an election or a 'leadership battle'. However many points he may have lost in the course of the interview, Peacock is allowed to exit as confidently and smilingly as he walked in. And however combative in tone the interview may have been, it ends as courteously and cooperatively as it began.

As we have already indicated, not all of these 'stages' appear in every adversarial interview: 'greeting', 'challenge' and 'release' are always present, 'soliciting opinion', 'checking' and 'entrapment' may be left out. Moreover, an interview may deal with a number of issues in succession, as in the Lyneham–Peacock interview, which deals with four issues: interest rates, tax scales, fringe benefits tax and the pilots' dispute. For each of these issues the sequence 'soliciting opinion' – 'checking' – 'challenging' – 'entrapment' is repeated, and in each case the interviewer can choose whether or not to open with 'soliciting opinion' and/or 'checking', and whether or not to attempt to 'entrap' the interviewee. In linguistic terminology, the structure is recursive (it can be repeated any number of times) and the elements are optional. And, also following the practice of linguists (for example, Halliday and Hasan)[15] the generic structure of adversarial political interviews can be summarised in a formula in which carets ^ stand for 'is followed by', round brackets for 'optional stage', and square brackets ($[...]^n$) for recursive stages or sequences of stages:

> Greeting ^ [(Soliciting Opinion) ^ (Checking) ^ Challenging Entrapment)]n ^ Release

The recursivity of the structure and the optionality of some of the stages are of obvious advantage for the timing of the interview. The interviewer can arrange the issues he or she wants to discuss in order of importance, in order of 'news value'. The least important and last of the issues can be left out if time runs out, or be dealt with more briefly, through an abbreviated version of the recursive part of the structure, for instance through a 'challenge' only. Moreover, each stage can consist of one or several questions, with the exception of 'greeting' and 'release'. This does not mean that the interview peters out towards the end, for the final question is always an important one — as we saw, the political cliffhanger of electoral victory and leadership ambitions and contests is a clear favourite.

The structure is realised, of course, through a very rapidly flowing exchange, involving knowing smiles and various tactics of evasion and charm: the interview is also a form of public entertainment in which politicians must appear to be competent or better according to the groundrules of the TV program. They cannot appear to 'lose', especially by being ungracious and petulant, for this would violate their status as guests. But they cannot appear to 'win' either, for that might threaten the status of the host who must, along with his or her program, remain for the succeeding nights' entertainment.

It is also quite a predictable and formulaic structure. This does not mean, of course, that the political interview isn't a difficult game to play well, both for the interviewer and the interviewee. But where Caroline Jones fashioned a new genre out of existing ones, Paul Lyneham is a skilled player in a game the rules of which are not of his own making, but have developed in the complex historical process we have tried to sketch in the introduction to this chapter.

It should finally be mentioned that the adversarial political interview is not the only genre of political interview, or at least not the only kind of interview with politicians. Politicians are also occasionally interviewed in celebratory, rather than adversarial, ways — addressed, not as opponents in a debate, but as protective father figures, as 'celebrities' (see Chapter 5), as 'ordinary family men' (or women), even as 'sports heroes', as in the following extract from a Channel 9 1990 pre-election interview between Mike Gibson and Prime Minister Bob Hawke:

GIBSON: *Couple of days to go, how do you feel?*
HAWKE: I feel good, Mike, I feel well, I feel relaxed. Not cocky or complacent — I believe I've given it my best shot and I hope I've done what the people want me to do.

GIBSON: *Lot more relaxed than you seemed to be when you kicked off.*
HAWKE: Well, I was relaxed at the beginning. I remember that people tried to run a story about the fact that I complained about a whole lot of microphones on a podium as though that was some real issue. They just misunderstood me completely. I was very relaxed and joking with the people about that.
GIBSON: *These last minute polls, any butterflies for you?*

The deferential interview has not disappeared altogether, but it is a different kind of deference now: deference towards the symbolic values represented by politicians' TV image rather than deference towards politicians as holders of high office. Which genre is adopted, how much interviews rely on 'personalities' (both presenters and guests), and to what extent they canvass soft, human interest issues and use populist–consumerist rather than politically investigative approaches, depend on the networks' projection of what their audiences need and want, and on the context of other programs in which the current affairs programs in question are placed.

Each network's early evening current affairs program has its own style and agenda. Each is a sub-genre of current affairs programming, for each seeks to hold the audience attracted to the evening news through to the 'soaps', dramas and comedy programs that follow. Their levels of formality, their news selection values and their reliance on celebrity or controversial journalists to identify their style of entertainment signify to the audience the personality of the channel or network, and quite literally link news to entertainment in various brands of 'infotainment'.

QUESTIONS AND ANSWERS IN THE ADVERSARIAL INTERVIEW

Each stage of the genre outlined in the previous section is realised through the interviewer's questions. However, Lyneham's questions are unlike those found in other media interviews, or in informal conversation. They are far more demanding than the open-ended requests for information we normally call questions. Rather than asking for information, they propose information themselves, and then require the interviewee to demonstrate his ability to deal with that information. By far the most information provided in the interview comes from the interviewer, down to very specific information, such as Lyneham's '28 per cent approval rating' and '70 per cent of coalition voters' (information which cannot be denied, only deflected by the interviewee), and the power to set the agenda of the interview is also entirely in the interviewer's hands. The interviewee can only respond to the interviewer's moves.

Such elements (issues, facts, personalities) as are introduced in the interviewee's answers are ignored in the next question, except when they serve to introduce a new (challenging) piece of information that can move the interview back to the interviewer's agenda. Consider, for example, the following extract:

LYNEHAM: *Mr Peacock, thanks for joining us. What do you think of Paul Keating's attempt to cap mortgage rates at 17 per cent?*

PEACOCK: Well, it really is just playing with the system . . . and therefore there's more available, but, eh, it is in essence a cosmetic job. What Australians want are real reductions in interest rates, not tampering in a cosmetic way like this.

LYNEHAM: *Could be popular with home-buyers though, couldn't it?*

PEACOCK: Well, it's hardly going to reduce their interest rates. It's certainly going to have the effect of pegging them at the moment, but while the Government continues with a one-dimensional policy of just high interest rates, they're not going to have people tiptoeing through the tulips with joy.

LYNEHAM: *Do you think it could send out the wrong signals and put a bit more heat back into the economy?*

PEACOCK: Well, it's an easing of policy, of course, so, er, to that extent it will have that effect. The Government's been squeezing money supply and therefore forcing interest rates up. And this, of course, is a slight turn in the other direction.

The key topic introduced by Lyneham, 'Paul Keating's attempt to cap mortgage rates', is referred back to in every question and every answer of the extract, by means of the pronoun 'it'. When, in the second question, Lyneham introduces a new element, 'home-buyers', this element, too, is picked up by Peacock in his answer ('their'). And the same applies to yet another element introduced by Lyneham, 'the wrong signals' and 'a bit more heat in the economy': in his answer, Peacock refers to it as 'that effect'. But none of the elements introduced by Peacock ('the system', 'more money', 'a cosmetic job', 'their interest rates', 'the Government', etc.) is picked up in this way by Lyneham. The references introduced by Lyneham tie the questions and answers together into a meaningful whole, forming the threads that hold the discursive tapestry together. Those introduced by Peacock are left dangling. This is graphically demonstrated below (with omission of some of the references introduced by Peacock) in a form of analysis known as 'lexical cohesion' or 'lexical chain' analysis.[16]

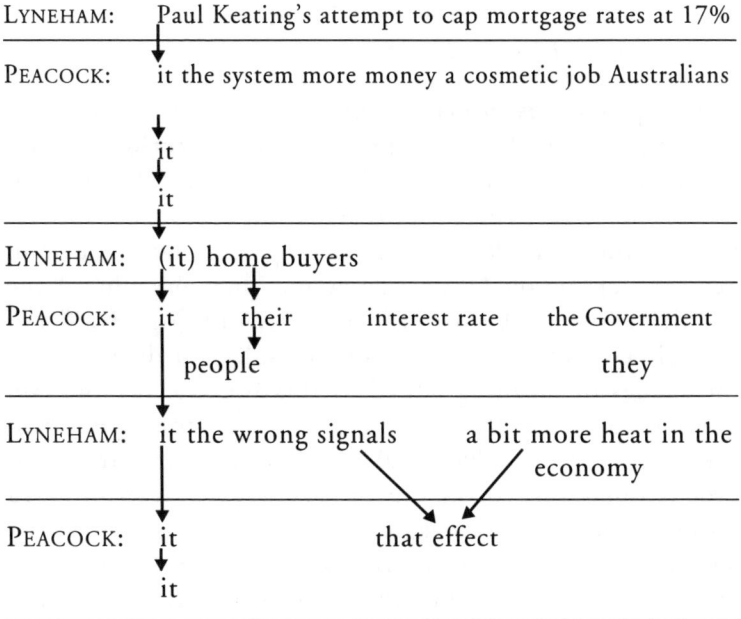

This contrasts with the more reactive approach of Caroline Jones, who, as we saw in the previous chapter, always takes care to tie in her questions with the interviewee's preceding answers by referring back to elements from those answers.

SOLICITING OPINION — QUESTIONS

In addition to controlling the agenda (which continually returns to the question of Peacock's popularity and the outcome of the election), the interviewer also controls the pace and tone of the exchange. His challenges are short, barbed and specific, yet his manner of delivery is sharp and ironic, implying complicity with the interviewee. The game which unfolds relies on pace and tone to involve the audience in a question continually at issue, yet never asked: how well will Peacock play the interview game? Hence the relatively open question which begins the interview is really only a 'warm-up', establishing the cooperation necessary for the game to begin:

> *What do you think of Paul Keating's attempt to cap mortgage rates at 17 per cent?*

The question is formally similar to what, in the previous chapter, we called a 'question inviting reflection': it is a WH-question, using the WH-word 'what'; it has second person address ('you') coupled with a 'cognitive mental process' verb ('think'); and it has a 'process noun', a noun denoting an action ('attempt') as the 'phenomenon' of the cognitive verb. The difference in terminology (inviting reflection versus soliciting opinion) reflects a difference in the shades of meaning added to this function by the two different contexts, the context of the 'revelatory' genre and the context of the 'adversarial' genre: in each case the question is open and leaves the interviewee relatively free to respond. Indeed, Peacock is invited to take a shot at his political opponent, and so given an advantage at the beginning of the interview. But where this open type of question plays a central role in the revelatory genre, its role in the adversarial genre is marginal. And that means that interviewees in the revelatory genre are given more power, more freedom to respond, than interviewees in the adversarial genre.

Some of the polar questions in the Lyneham–Peacock interview also serve to solicit opinion, for instance:

> *Do you approve of Justice Maddern's intervention in the pilots' dispute?*
>
> *Do you think it [Keating's attempt to cap mortgage rates] could send out the wrong signals and put a bit more heat back into the economy?*

These questions, too, are cooperative. They do not require the interviewee to be on the defensive. Peacock can answer them in the knowledge that they will not be challenged, either because both 'yes' and 'no' are likely to be acceptable to the interviewer, or because the answer he prefers is likely also to be the answer preferred by the interviewer. The issues involved are, as yet, issues on which interviewer and interviewee agree.

CHECKING QUESTIONS

Checking involves a less cooperative use of polar questions. In this stage, interviewers seek to pin down interviewees on specifics such as dates and policies, and on statements they have made on other occasions. Interviewees must either agree or risk being exposed as poor strategists, or as contradicting themselves, their party, or the record.

When polar questions are used for checking, interviewers are testing whether interviewees have worked out their policies and strategies. Negative answers will make the interviewee seem indecisive or, at best, non-committal. Another way of doing this is by means of WH-questions in which the WH-word seeks circumstantial information — the 'when', 'how much', etc. of information which is provided by the interviewer and not in question:

> *Got a date yet?*

> *Is the two-tier system still very much on your agenda?*

In another common form of checking, interviewers recapitulate or quote earlier statements by the interviewee, and then use formulaic polar questions such as 'Is that still the case?', 'Do you stand by that claim?' etc. to test the interviewee's consistency. Negative answers will make interviewees seem to contradict themselves, or to renege on a promise.

> *You also said in your speech in reply to the budget, 'We will ensure that the top rate for individuals is not higher than the company tax rate'. That still the go?*

In checking, interviewers prepare the ground for their later challenges and entrapments. The issues involved are no longer issues on which interviewer and interviewee agree. They are the issues under dispute, the issues on which the interviewer is likely to attack the interviewee, and the interviewee knows this. But the attack itself is held back, the challenge delayed. Before attacking, the interviewer seeks to commit the interviewee to an agreement with the premises of later challenges, with the facts and arguments that will later be used to support challenges. In this way interviewees can be trapped with their own words, challenged with arguments to which they have themselves agreed a moment earlier: checking is the first stage of a 'Socratic' questioning strategy in which, to quote W. Labov and D. Fanshell, 'as the interviewee answers each question, the possible arguments that he can use to disagree with the ultimate point are eliminated'.[17]

Experienced interviewees are aware of this, and may try to avoid being trapped into agreeing with premises that will cut the ground from under their feet, as in this March 1990 interview between Jana Wendt and Peacock on Channel 9's *A Current Affair* (the replies are shortened):

WENDT: *You said last month that your Government would bring about a massive fall in interest rates. Do you stand by that claim?*

PEACOCK: I've been saying consistently throughout the election campaign that we'd bring about significant, substantial and sustainable reductions in interest rates.

WENDT: *Can I stop you there. Your word was 'massive'. It's a grand term. It means 'huge'. Do you stand by that?*

PEACOCK: Well, what I've been saying throughout the campaign as you know is 'significant and substantial reductions' and the reason for that is that we have an anti-inflation policy.

WENDT: *All right, so you're telling me that you have a reasonable hope of bringing down interest rates, because you're going to bring in policies that bring about the conditions . . .*

PEACOCK: Oh no, significantly more than that.

WENDT: *I don't want to pin you down . . .*

PEACOCK: No, of course you don't, but the reality is, by cutting down expenditure we are reducing demand at the government level by boosting productivity. By way of labour market reform, by way of privatisation, by way of contracting out services from the Government to the private sector we make our attack on inflation as well as on our debt problem.

WENDT: *All right, Mr Peacock, I know, and, with respect, we have all heard that during the campaign. [She reads demonstratively from her notes.] 'Massive fall in interest rates under a Peacock Government.' Yes or no?*

PEACOCK: Yes, well, I've said to you, 'significant and substantial'.

WENDT: *We are playing word games, aren't we?*

PEACOCK: Well, I'm not. I'm not. You're playing games with words, if you don't mind me saying so.

CHALLENGING QUESTIONS

Checking the facts and the interviewee's knowledge of, and facility with them, merges into more challenging moves. These centre on the interviewer's ability to object, to contradict, and to confront the politician, acting as a devil's advocate. In a study of therapeutic interviews, Labov and Fanshell give the following formal definition of the challenge: 'a challenge is a speech act that asserts or implies a state of affairs that, if true, would weaken a person's claim to be competent in filling the role associated with a valued status'.[18] This definition can be applied also to the adversarial political interview. Its function is to investigate whether the interviewed politicians are competent and honest enough to deserve the high status they occupy or seek to occupy. Its function is to 'keep the bastards honest'.

In the previous chapter we saw that even Caroline Jones' 'revelatory' interviews contain challenges — challenges which serve to establish whether her interviewees deserve the status of exemplary individual which their inclusion in the program accords them. But whereas challenges play a minor role in Jones' interview, and are mitigated by her tentative formulations and intonations, in adversarial political interviews they form the core element, the *raison d'être* of the genre and the bulk of the questions. And far from being mitigated, they are formulated in bold, confrontational ways, even though their impact may be softened by irony, obliging the interviewee to respond through smiling teeth. The political interview, after all, is also a game, and it often contains an element of a battle of wits: both Lyneham and Peacock come out with flowery expressions such as 'tiptoeing through the tulips with joy', 'more positions than the Kama Sutra', etc. Yet the status of the interviewee is at stake in a very real way in these interviews. A challenge allows only two kinds of response: admission or defence and, needless to say, admission must be avoided if the politician's 'claim to be competent in filling his role' is not to be weakened in the eyes of the viewing public.

Although we tend to call all the interviewer's contributions 'questions', most challenges are not in fact questions. Rather they are statements in which the interviewer offers information that could, if not adequately countered by the interviewee, weaken the interviewee's position.

Usually these statements incorporate adversative conjunctions such as 'but', '(al)though', 'on the other hand' (a variant is: 'Let me put this to you . . .') to indicate their nature as objections to the interviewee's position. The adversative aspect may be intensified by adverbs such as 'surely' ('but surely . . .'), and frequent use of vocatives ('Mr Peacock . . .') and a berating tone ('you *should* be streets ahead, surely . . .') may enhance the confronting nature of the challenge:

> *They all say the same thing, Mr Peacock.*
>
> *With 17 per cent interest rates you should be streets ahead, surely.*
>
> *Mr Peacock, the basic fact is that since you replaced John Howard there has not been any decisive swing towards the conservatives.*
>
> *On the other hand there are a lot of people who think the Opposition has had more positions on this than the Kama Sutra.*

At times the challenges almost become *accusations*, as in this quote from Jana Wendt's interview with Peacock. She has just 'checked' whether Peacock consulted his shadow cabinet on a certain issue, and established that he didn't:

> *Mr Peacock, why did you make a policy decision on the basis of ignorance?*

But she uses the *form* of the question here, so that the accusation remains, to some extent, implicit.

Challenges tend to have high modality. Interviewers sound confident of their facts and of their quotes. They appeal to 'the facts' ('the basic fact is . . .') and to the ultimate authority of 'the people', 'the voters', 'the polls', etc. to lend credence to their challenges. And the authority of 'the people' is not one politicians can afford to contradict: like the interviewer, the political interviewee must be seen to act in the interests of the people. Interviewees, in turn, also endeavour to sound confident and frequently use expressions of high modality, such as 'certainly', 'of course', 'in reality', etc. in their answers.

Negative reactions also signify the devil's advocate role, for example when Lyneham comments that capping interest rates 'could be popular with home-buyers, couldn't it?'. They may use the 'Yiddish rise–fall intonation', the meaning of which could be translated as 'If you think that, you're crazy'.[19] Jana Wendt uses it when incredulously repeating a phrase from an answer Peacock has just given:

> *PROSpects of significant FALLS in interest rates?*

However, such negative reactions are often posed in ways which allow the interviewee to extend the topic further. In these extensions, the interviewer draws out the consequences of an answer, or confronts it with a fact, thereby challenging the original answer but retaining cohesion and allowing the interview to flow like a vibrant conversation. Usually these take the form of a statement that is preceded by 'and' or 'also' (conjunctions which signify its nature as an extension) and use a rising, question-like intonation:

> *Also within your first term of government?* (Lyneham)

> *And interest rates must come down?* (Wendt)

> *And you feel comfortable saying that despite the situation*

> *with our overseas debt, despite what's happening with interest rates?* (Wendt)

ENTRAPMENT QUESTIONS

The interviewer's power is shown most clearly in those exchanges which seek to trap the interviewee in an answer which implies weakness, logical inconsistency or the admission of defeat. Of course, challenges also seek to reveal weakness, but they leave at least the possibility of a valid defence open, and generally can more easily be escaped by judicious verbal sidestepping. But the stereotyped image of politicians as untrustworthy is surely reinforced by the hedging and special pleading that entrapment makes necessary. Entrapment 'questions' are unanswerable challenges, statements with which interviewees can neither agree nor disagree without losing face, or questions to which they can neither say 'yes' nor 'no' without contradicting themselves. Entrapment questions seek to drive interviewees into a corner.

In one of its forms, entrapment is a challenge carefully prepared by a series of Socratic checks, as in this example, which immediately follows the extract, quoted earlier, in which Jana Wendt attempts to force Peacock to admit he has promised a 'massive fall in interest rates'. Having more or less succeeded, she now confronts him with a statement from another member of his party, former Federal Treasurer and Opposition Leader John Howard:

> *All right Mr Peacock, your industry spokesman, John Howard, has said that the prospects of a significant fall in interest rates are, to quote him, 'zilch'. Is he wrong?*

By itself, this question can be seen as a challenge. Peacock could, for example, attempt to modify the term 'significant' and so end up being able to promise, say, at least a 'substantial' fall in interest rates. But given that Wendt has more or less committed him to promising a 'massive' fall, he is trapped. He must either contradict Howard, with all the political consequences thereof, or agree with him and so renege on a promise made earlier in the interview. As it happens, the trap doesn't quite close. Peacock accuses Wendt of quoting out of context:

PEACOCK: *Well, he was talking about under Labor. That's exactly the point.*
WENDT: I don't believe he was.
PEACOCK: *Well, yes, he was. He made a very clear explanation of that.*

Here is another example, from a *7.30 Report* interview between Paul Lyneham and Peacock's successor, Shadow Treasurer John Hewson. Again, the entrapment question is carefully prepared by a series of Socratic checks:

> *But to get your savings you've also included public debt interest relief, so you must have taken that money from your asset sales, given it to the bankers in Zurich or Rome or wherever to get the relief on the interest. So you can't have given it to them and still have it in your surplus at the same time.*

Entrapment can also take the form of a 'logical argument' that proves that the interviewee's position (or assumed position) is untenable. We have already quoted an example:

> *If you believe in market forces, Mr Peacock, and as a conservative you presumably do, the market is not buying what you're selling.*

By leaving the interviewee with no simple way of replying, entrapment shows that the interviewer is the better prepared, and has the greater control over the interview. However, as we have seen in Chapter 1, the illusion that interviews are as spontaneous as conversations, plus the requirement that guests do not upstage their media hosts, work against interviewees when they are successfully entrapped. The audience will not remember what they say, but may recall their general competence and 'mediagenic' presentation — or absence thereof. Hence interviewees must play the game, even when trapped. The best they can do is to exhibit grace under pressure. At least they can then be seen as fulfilling the requirements of the current affairs program to be worthy of a prime-time seat opposite its political interviewer. The principal obligation on the guest is to play the game, even if (s)he cannot 'win'. ('The play's the thing/Wherein I'll catch the conscience of the King.')

Release Questions

Contrary to the cliché that sees political interviews as contests won or lost, we have suggested that they are games that have no final victors or vanquished. This is so principally because television (indeed all the modern mass media) has to continue to produce the genres of program in which interviews form such an important (dramatic, personalised) part. Politicians are 'talent' — they must live to be interviewed again and again, and not be given the coup de grace prematurely. So Paul Lyneham allows Andrew Peacock to fly out of the trap without inflicting mortal injury. He does this by returning to the tone of the cooperative opening of the interview, allowing the Leader of the Opposition to volunteer without challenge his own positive information and opinion in response to the (admittedly tongue-in-cheek):

> *And you're definitely going to be Prime Minister by this time next year?*

Despite his earlier discomfort, Peacock ends the interview strongly enough to sound like Lyneham's equal when their mutual thanks are exchanged. Other political interviewers do likewise: the interviewee is always allowed to have the final word, however much the sparks may have been flying a few minutes earlier.

The Political Interview as Television Spectacle

So far we have not dealt with the visual aspects of television interviews, with television as spectacle. In this section we will do so, focusing in turn on the studio setting of the interview, the camerawork, and the non-verbal 'performance' of interviewer and interviewee.

Setting

In the introduction to this chapter we noted how, in the early years of television, interviews tended to take place in the homes or offices of the politicians, where the interviewee was host and the interviewer guest, and where the setting left no doubt as to the exalted status of the interviewee: Macmillan, seated behind an antique prime ministerial desk, an ornate mantelpiece with a Victorian clock behind him; Alec Douglas-Home and Robin Day, seated in antique chairs, a sofa, bookcases and paintings in heavy gilded frames in the background (a large globe was a popular prop also: the Prime Minister could put his hand on it in a proprietorial gesture reminiscent of Holbein's *The Ambassadors*).

In the modern studio, on the other hand, the interviewer is host and the interviewee is the guest. The interview is set, not amidst the trappings of political power, but amidst the trappings of media power, in studios which imitate the layout and decoration styles of the courtroom, the boardroom, or the lavish executive office. These evoke connotations to fit the approach of the program: slick efficiency, impartial arbitration, hardheaded investigation, and so on.

Thus Jana Wendt, in her 1990 interviews with Prime Minister Hawke and Opposition Leader Peacock, is seated behind a large desk with a massive, shiny black top edged in chrome — a modern altar, almost. Behind her, half hidden by lace curtains, is a view of Sydney's skyline at dusk, seen from above as though from the top of a tall corporate tower. Her interviewees sit at the short end of the table, at a distance from the interviewer. They have much less room to move and no view behind them.

Steve Vizard, in his much more entertainment-oriented *Tonight Live with Steve Vizard*, also sits behind such a desk, an arched window in the background. The shape of this window reminds us of a cathedral, but behind it we see a quasi-abstract nocturnal cityscape, with a television tower and a pattern of windows suggesting tall buildings ablaze with light. His interviewees sit on straight-backed chairs and have no table or desk to lean on.

Richard Carleton interviews politicians in a completely black set. Spotlights pick out the interviewees, who sit on none too comfortable white plastic swivel-chairs, in an arrangement reminiscent of police or secret service interrogations in movies, a style first introduced in the British interview program *Face to Face* (1958–62), whose interviewer, John Freeman, appears to have been an ex-military intelligence officer with much experience of interrogation.[20]

These references to power, borrowed from various spheres, are mixed with another set of connotations that suggest theatricality. Interviews are, after all, entertainment, spectacle. There may be curtains, or a hint of curtains. Interviewer and interviewee may sit on an elevated stage, facing or half facing a real or imaginary audience. These theatrical connotations may be more or less emphasised, depending on the mix of information and entertainment that characterises the program.

The current affairs set, then, can be described in terms of four characteristics. First, it signifies the power of the media by borrowing, in stylised ways, symbols of power from other spheres: the corporate sphere, the judiciary, even the church. Second, it establishes *differences* in power between interviewer and interviewee. For instance, interviewer and interviewee may sit on the same kind of chair (which suggests equality, at least in this respect), but the interviewer's (or interviewee's) chair may be larger and more comfortable (the latter was the case at least sometimes in Mike Walsh's long-running *Mike Walsh Show* on Channel 10). Sometimes the interviewer is seated behind a desk while the interviewee is seated, more precariously, on a straight-backed chair, at some distance from the desk, while different props, connoting different degrees of power, may be seen in the background of shots of the interviewer and the interviewee. Third, theatrical connotations may be mixed to different degrees, signifying how much or how little 'entertainment' is blended with 'information'. Finally, the current affairs set has become increasingly stylised. It has moved away from the naturalistic sets found in the cinema and in television drama (sets complete with doors, mantelpieces, paintings on the wall, etc) towards increasingly artificial and abstract designs. It does not, for instance, try to recreate the lavishly decorated corporate office in the studio, it merely hints at it, and this makes it possible for current affairs sets to be at once courtroom and circus, assembly hall and corporate palace, theatre and office.

The set of the *7.30 Report* interview on which we have focused in this chapter takes this development a step further. It no longer refers to anything outside television itself. We see Lyneham sit in what appears to be a darkened cubicle. Behind him a grid of blue lines converges towards infinity in the black void. These lines are not a piece of set decoration, like the abstract Mondrian-like backdrops that were popular in 1960s current affairs and entertainment shows. They are ethereal, insubstantial vectors, a holographic chimera in the dark space. In front of Lyneham we see a small desk, and a monitor on which the (very small) image of the politician, or indeed any other image from anywhere in the world, can be summoned up. Thus the interviewer is alone, like an interstellar traveller in his space capsule, or a spider in a telecommunicational web. And the interviewee is an image-within-an-image — an image which can be switched on and off at will. A step further still from the real world of the naturalistic set? Perhaps. But that real world is in fact becoming increasingly similar to this set: a world of isolated people in front of consoles and monitors on which they can summon up images of what was once the real world, and has now become a vast bank of images.

CAMERAWORK

In face-to-face communication, the physical distance we keep from one another expresses the formality of the occasion and our relation to those with whom we are communicating. As Edmund Hall has shown in his study of 'proxemics', these interpersonal distances are fairly well-defined.[21] Only an intimate, 'close personal' relation allows us to come close enough to make it possible to 'hold or grasp the other person'. When discussing 'matters of personal involvement' with people we know well, we do so at 'far personal distance', a distance which 'extends from a point that is just outside easy touching distance to a point where two people can touch fingers if they extend their arms'. Beyond this range 'social distance' begins, the distance, says Hall, at which 'impersonal business' occurs. And social distance increases as the status difference between the people interacting increases. 'Public distance', finally, is the distance between people who 'are and are to remain strangers'.[22] Furniture arrangements ('fixed feature proxemics', Hall calls this) are based on these distances: the counters and desks that may separate people doing 'impersonal business' become larger as the people behind them grow in status relative to their visitors; a considerable gap separates the actors on a stage from their audiences, or the judges behind their benches from the accused. As we have seen, fixed feature proxemics also plays a significant role in the design of current affairs sets, representing the power relation between interviewers and their interviewees.

Greater than the distance between interviewers and interviewees is the distance between them and their audience: television is 'tele'-vision, 'far' vision. But however great this distance may be in reality, the camera can override it and show interviewer and interviewee 'close-up', as though they were acquaintances, friends, even intimates. The 'size of the frame' can create an *imaginary* relation between 'them', on the screen, and 'us', at home. In the Lyneham–Peacock interview, interviewer and interviewee are shown mostly in close shot, but the shots of Lyneham are a little wider than those of Peacock, and the shot of the anchorperson who introduces the interview is a 'medium close shot', still wider, still keeping us a little more at a respectful distance (the industry defines the close shot as a 'head and shoulders' shot, the medium close shot as 'cutting off the subject a little above the waist'). Thus 'size of frame' sets up a hierarchy of social distance and shows Lyneham and Peacock to be *almost* equal in status relative to the viewer, but not quite. Lyneham's status is just that little bit higher. This pattern is common in other current affairs programs.

In many interviews the close shots are alternated with wider 'two-shots', which show both interviewer and interviewee and serve to represent their relation to each other, rather than their relation to the audience. These shots may be 'medium shots' (which 'cut off the subject approximately at the knees'), 'medium long shots' (which show 'the full figure'), or 'long shots' (still wider than this) — sizes of frame which correspond to what, disregarding peripheral vision, one would see of the other person at, respectively, 'close social', 'far social' and 'public' distance. They are not taken from the same angle as the close shots. Close shots of the interviewer are taken from behind the (unseen) interviewee, so that the viewer sees him or her almost from the point of view of the interviewee.

Close shots of the interviewee are taken from behind the (unseen) interviewer, so that the viewer sees him or her more or less from the point of view of the interviewer. As the interviewee does most of the talking, the audience's imaginary point of view, their imaginary point of identification, is for most of the time that of the interviewer.

The angles of these close shots, then, are *cinematic* — angles in which the camera is, so to speak, 'in the middle of the action' and in which the viewer is invited to identify with the point of view of one of the participants in that 'action'. The angle of the two-shots, on the other hand, is theatrical. Here, viewers see the action from a more 'objective' vantage point, from the position of a spectator in the theatre. They are not imaginarily transported onto the stage and positioned amidst the actors. Not surprisingly, such shots are particularly common in programs that involve a studio audience.[23] In the *7.30 Report* this 'theatrical' element is absent. The only two-shot is an 'overshoulder' shot of the interviewer, showing the monitor with the politician's image. When Lyneham's guest is actually present in the studio, as in the interview with John Hewson we quoted earlier, there may be brief medium-close shots of the interviewer with the shoulder of the interviewee, out of focus, in the foreground

In two-shots, camera position also determines whether the interviewer will be on the left or on the right of the interviewee and vice versa. This, in turn, determines the 'eyeline', the question of whether the interviewer, in the two-shots as well as in the close shots, will look towards the right or towards the left. This compositional factor carries much significance. In our culture we read from left to right. What is placed on the left therefore has priority. But that is not all. What is placed on the left, and hence viewed or read (or heard)[24] first, is also what is treated as the 'given', as something already familiar to the viewer (or the reader or listener), as a taken-for-granted departure point for the message. What is placed on the right, and hence viewed or read last, is treated as the 'new', as something not yet familiar to the viewer or reader, something which must therefore be paid special attention. In speech, the 'new' receives the strongest emphasis: in 'You are IT', 'you' is 'given' and 'IT' is 'new'; in 'It is YOU', 'it' is 'given' and 'YOU' is 'new'. As argued elsewhere in more detail,[25] the 'given'–'new' distinction also applies to visual composition, or at least to visual compositions which make significant use of the horizontal dimension in distributing the elements of the composition across the pictorial space.

And if the distinction is applied to the composition of the two-shots in interviews, a clear pattern emerges. In the early interviews we discussed in the introduction to this chapter, politicians were positioned on the left, and interviewers, in their as yet unfamiliar role, were the 'new'. In today's interviews the interviewer is almost always treated as the 'given', as the viewer's familiar point of identification, political intermediary and 'honest broker of opinion'. Today, the image invites us to take the interviewer for granted and pay special attention to the politician's performance.

NON-VERBAL PERFORMANCE

It has been noted that speech between people who know each other intimately is not as verbally explicit as more formal speech, and relies more on intonation and non-verbal communication to get its meaning across.[26] At personal distance half a word suffices. A simple sentence like 'Pass me the butter', at breakfast, can have many meanings (from 'I love you' to 'I hate you'!), depending on the nuances of intonation and facial expression. If this is so, it perhaps explains why television, which brings politicians so close to us it is as though they were sitting with us at the breakfast table, causes so much emphasis to be placed on the 'performance' of politicians, on how they say things rather than on what they say.

In discussing non-verbal performance, it is again useful to compare the performance of interviewer and interviewee. As Cate Poynton has argued,[27] differences in power are manifested by a 'lack of reciprocity' in what each participant in the interaction can say and do. We have seen many instances of this already, some of them favouring the interviewee (for example, the forms of address — 'Mr Peacock . . .' versus 'Paul . . .'), some of them favouring the interviewer (for example, the presence or absence of a desk). In other cases there may in fact be reciprocity: the way political interviewers and their interviewees are dressed, for instance, is often strikingly similar. The ultimate balance of power is the result of many such linguistic and non-linguistic factors.

When watching an interview, we generally see the interviewer listen more often than the interviewee. This has consequences, especially for facial expressions and the meanings they can convey. During speech, non-verbal expression usually plays second fiddle to verbal expression: head nods and hand gestures 'underline' important words, or illustrate parts of speech (a sweeping hand movement on the phrase 'this whole thing'; a slight wagging of the head or wavy hand gesture on the word 'approximately', and so on). During listening, non-verbal expression, especially facial expression, takes on a more independent role and serves to give feedback, to show agreement or disagreement, doubt or approval, scepticism or sympathy. It follows that the interviewer has more opportunity, non-verbally, to comment than the interviewee on what the other is saying. And such 'comments' are certainly noted by the audience. The typical expression of listening interviewees, on the other hand, is one of concentration: after all, the questions are short and treacherous.

Interviewees have little time to prepare their answer. Interviewers can also more easily hold the gaze of the interviewee while they are speaking. This is so, not only because they have trained themselves to do so, but also because they have had more chance to prepare in advance, and more time to think of their next question during the interviewee's long answer. For speakers who must formulate on the run it is difficult to hold the gaze of the other person. In ordinary conversation we see speakers look down or away as they are concentrating on formulating their sentence, then look up, for feedback, towards the end of each sentence. Not doing this, holding the other person's gaze throughout, can be a sign of dominance. Looking away when someone holds one's gaze in this way can be interpreted as submissiveness, or shiftiness. In general, Peacock successfully reciprocates Lyneham's stare. Yet he cannot avoid looking away more often than Lyneham, whose gaze never once wavers. Indeed, as Lyneham closes in for a challenge or trap, his whole body moves forwards while he keeps staring at Peacock in what is really a rather threatening gesture.

Peacock is seen to smile a number of times, showing his good humour under the interrogatory assault. Lyneham, however, does not reciprocate his smiles. Ethologists tell us that the smile originated as a sign of appeasement, hence as a sign of fear. There is a fine line between the 'nervous smile' and the 'friendly smile', and no doubt the smile — that 'most important social bonding signal in the human gestural repertoire'[28] — is another potential minefield for the political interviewee. Bob Hawke, for instance, smiles quite broadly in photographs, but avoids smiling in interviews, unless it be as an immediate (ironic) reaction to a question. As politicians, political interviewees cannot afford to be too submissive. As guests, they cannot afford to be too assertive (Harold Wilson is said to have adopted his famous pipe to avoid making the forceful clenched fist gestures which were his habit). The political interviewee walks a non-verbal tightrope.

Television presents politics and politicians in unique ways. It gives the otherwise distant and shadowy people who populate the sphere of political power a precise visual presence. It does not 're-present' them, in the past, analytical sense of the word, but actually gives (makes a present of) them to the audience. It presents them, in the present tense, albeit mediated by the presenters who host the current affairs and news programs. Never, before television, had representative democracy been so characterised by such omni-present, omni-presented politicians. What TV presents is people — individuals framed in close-up, talking to other individuals similarly present. Every night ('Tonight', 'Today Tonight', 'This Day Tonight') the current affairs programs arrange for the peculiar one-to-many intimacy of the television interview. They have rendered formal two-party politics immediate, personal and understandable (as television, at least). They have moved debate from the parliamentary chambers to the studio cubicle, making the antagonists, not abstract political ideologies, but particular identifiable politicians and 'us', or at least our media representatives, the familiar current affairs interviewers. In effecting these changes, television may have altered our conception of politics itself.

Corporatist Governments and Non-Partisan Parties

The current affairs interviewers whose interviews with Australian politicians we have analysed in this chapter are all highly recognisable to their audiences and very familiar with their political guests. The interviewers and interviewees seemed to know each other, both in the sense of knowing about the other's politics and personalities in a professionally related sense, and in that each pair seemed to be continuing a dialogue which depended on knowing about each other's media skills and professional persona. Even the prime minister spoke in familiar not just formal ways to his interviewers, who reciprocated with questions which showed that they knew their guest well and were, in television terms, his equal. They showed off their expertise and addressed their interviewees in non-deferential, even aggressive, tones. They were securely on their 'home ground', in front of their own audience, while the politicians were guests, in foreign territory.

As we have already indicated, some commentators have seen the familiar, game-like publicity of the current affairs interview as evidence of a dangerous inter-dependence between politics and the media. They have argued that this renders the media uncritical and even sycophantic in relation to the government of the day, making politics simply a game of cynical publicity. This encourages alienation and apathy among citizens who have little option but to become mere spectators at the circus of television politics.[29] At the same time, since the mid 1970s, governments in Westminster-style democracies have become more and more 'corporatist', a style which fits easily into the increasingly technical and cynical discourses of political commentators and interviewers.

Derek Parker discusses what he sees as the natural attraction between the corporatist Australian Labor Government (1983–) and the new class of tertiary educated, cynical press gallery personnel who feed off it.[30] He cites the following definition of corporatism by David Held:

> Corporatist arrangements generally refer to 'tripartite' relations between organisations of employers, labour and the state, steered ultimately by the latter.
>
> In the corporatist account, the directive capacities of the state have increased, allowing it to construct a framework for economic and political affairs. In return for direct channels of bargaining with state officials — a 'representative monopoly' — leaders of key organised interests are expected to deliver support for agreed policies and, if necessary, keep their own members in line. The politics of negotiation has become systematised along stricter, more formal lines, although most of the discussion between parties takes place informally, behind closed doors and out of public view . . . Political participation becomes the preserve of organisational élites.[31]

Parker argues that 'corporatism is built on the idea of centralised agreement by a collective of élites', and sees the press gallery (which includes Paul Lyneham and other TV political experts) as a similar élite collective, attracted to '[f]igures of power engaged in conflict, making speeches, organising deals, announcing resolutions'. In short, a mediagenic government, dependent on TV and press for publicity while the media depend on it for the very stuff of their existence — press releases and interviews. On this argument, politics has become too close to the media, and the media are no longer able to remain critics, or at least providers of independent information and analysis.

Paradoxically, a second view of the contemporary media–politics relationship begins with the observation that the media are increasingly like a political party themselves, and, instead of being dependent on the mediagenic government and state apparatuses for favours, are continually attacking the incompetence, economic mismanagement and profligacy of all politicians and of the bureaucracy. James Curran goes so far as to argue that the media, in modern Western democracies, have become 'parties of non-partisanship': they claim to represent the public interest and act as rivals to politicians of all colours.[32] As they detach themselves from partisan support for one or other organised political party, so the lines between these parties are blurred and the media themselves appear as an independent voice — a populist or a sceptical voice 'of the people', opposed to the powerful state, the government of the day, and to politicians of all persuasions. Hence the media are *anti*-partisan rather than bi-partisan, and continually set themselves 'above' politics, which is seen as a cynical game. They claim to speak on behalf of everyone, attempting to legitimise their own professional detachment by sceptically attacking all élite party spokespersons and by acting as the watchdogs of society. Technical, especially economistic questions are one indication that the media professional is fulfilling this role on the audience's (his/her constituency's) behalf. As Curran sees this:

> The rise of broadcasting has further weakened the position of the political parties. The emergence of television as the principal medium of political communication has resulted in a shift away from consumption of a medium with a tradition of partisanship to a medium which is required to be politically balanced and impartial. This trend has been particularly pronounced during the last two decades. There has been a very rapid growth of public affairs coverage in TV, with a three-fold increase on BBC TV between 1962 and 1974. And while public affairs items in the press only obtained a below-average readership (both before and after the introduction of TV), TV news programmes have secured above-average audiences. More people have thus been exposed to more bi-partisan communications.
>
> The progressive detachment of the mass media from the party system has been confounded by the mutual rivalry between professional politicians and professional communicators. Both groups have competing claims to legitimacy: they both claim to represent the public and serve the public interest. This tension is reflected in media portrayals of party politics which are, at times, not so much bi-partisan as anti-partisan.[33]

We might see in these two opposed analyses — the media as corporatist handmaidens or as a non-partisan 'party' — the genuinely paradoxical nature of public political discourses in the late capitalist states such as Australia and the UK. The television current affairs program represents its viewers as *consumers* of party politics, but it is also dependent for its audience appeal on the spectacle of the complexities of the government-versus-opposition game. The result is a style of technical (economistic), familiar, yet adversarial interviewing which suggests that party politics is a cynical, confusing and alien sphere, but which at the same time reinforces the audience's identification with the program and its personalities as charismatic representatives of the ordinary armchair electorate. Television is deeply dependent on what it increasingly constructs as the charade of politics so that it can define its own legitimacy by *contrast*. Hence, the political interview is intensely dramatic but of little consequence to the spectators. The *intervention* of the television program may act to alienate the *public* from the very power with which it brings it into face-to-face contact.

An Interview with Paul Lyneham

PHILIP BELL: *Could you comment on what you thought of the analysis of the 'devil's advocate' or the 'keep-the-bastards-honest' role of the political interviewer, which was our focus in this chapter.*

PAUL LYNEHAM: Well I don't think going after information and being the devil's advocate are mutually exclusive ideas anyway. The balance varies depending on who you are interviewing and at what time and about what subject. For example you are very often going after information in an interview with a minister because ministers have information whereas opposition politicians very often only have opinions. So you may well find yourself doing a much more search-for-information type interview with the Prime Minister or a treasurer, or a senior cabinet minister simply because there have been developments to which the government has responded and you simply want that information. That is the primary thing and then any comment or analysis on that information can only come after you've first worked out where you're coming from.

BELL: *Do you see yourself as interviewing on behalf of any constituency?*

LYNEHAM: I suppose I would see myself as, if you like, the viewer's representative. My theory is that there are many people in the community who are interested in these issues but they have other lives to lead, other things to do and that, I suppose, I am employed on their behalf to keep an eye on one area of national importance, but basically to get the pollies to spell out what they're on about, and then the final judgment about the merits of what the pollies say is up to the viewer.

BELL: *Has the role of the interview changed in the time you've been a journalist?*

LYNEHAM: I don't think it's changed so much — I suppose if you were to look at say the difference between the way I do this job and the way that, for example, Richard Carleton did the job [Lyneham's predecessor, now with Australia's *60 Minutes*], I would argue that I inject myself as a personality less into the interview than, say, Richard would have. That's not in any way to condemn Richard's approach, it's just a question of style. This may flow out of the many years I spent working out of the News Department where, of course, any expression of opinion or injection of personality — you were one step away from being relocated to Longreach.

›	The interview, I think, remains important however because the politicians believe it is a valuable way of first hand getting across their message, even at the risk of being subjected to, at times, fairly robust questioning. And I think it will always be important. I don't think overall that the style of interview has changed so much except you are seeing now a blend — more of an infotainment blend. We're seeing the interview perhaps go more into the mainstream of television. But as for my line of work in a straight ABC current affairs program, I don't think it's changed very much at all.

BELL: *Do the politicians think that you have a lot more power than they have because of what they see as your more unmediated access to their constituents?*

LYNEHAM: They may think that. They think, I believe, that someone in my position is potentially fairly influential (as distinct from powerful), and we have had some occasions where some new ministers after the last re-shuffle, for example (after the last federal election), were actually a bit timid about coming on the program — accepting invitations to come on. And I think in one or two cases that was simply apprehension and I was almost starting to wonder whether the image of the hard, tough interview was actually starting to work against us in terms of some of these people, but that seems to have smoothed itself out.

BELL: *Do you agree that rather than being a contest, political interviews have become something of a game in which there are a set of moves which each party engages in?*

LYNEHAM: My first reaction was that your analysis is an outsider's analysis that seeks to codify and make neat theorems about something that is a great deal more random, spontaneous and haphazard in the real doing of it. For example, I agree with you entirely about the idea of the welcome and the politician being there as a guest, and so forth. The fact is that viewers, in this society, in this country, rightly expect a certain amount of civility and politeness in public discussion — particularly with figures who in many cases they hold in fairly high esteem. I don't think that being polite to a leading minister or shadow minister is anything other than normal social behaviour, quite frankly. As for what you call checking, or the idea of putting propositions to them, I think you underestimate the extent to which, in framing those early questions, you're not so much checking on their position as drawing the viewer into the argument. A lot of questions are deliberately framed to both kick the interview along and inform the viewer at the same time.

And, as for the 'release', I think you again make more of that than is in fact really the case because in the example you cite there is not so much letting Peacock off the hook, and everyone emerging smiling and good mates at the end; it's rather, I would have thought, adding a new element, a bit of a mischievous sting in the tail . . . You could call it acting as a 'kicker' at the end, pointing to something that we all know is going to be the subject of discussion in the future, almost a warning about things that we might be talking about next. And don't forget, you are constrained enormously in these situations by the elapse of real time. So you might well be saying in some of these situations: 'We didn't get on to this one today, but don't worry, it's still there and we will come back to it at the next opportunity'.

BELL: *It's true that we do see release perhaps slightly differently from the way you just described it because the interviewee has to live to fight another day, but we* use that word to contrast it with the possibility of actually destroying someone in terms of their credibility in that particular interview. The reason we call it a game rather than a contest is that we felt you couldn't actually be too powerful. Nevertheless, despite the civility and the courtesy, the flow is in your hands.

LYNEHAM: Yes, but I think you make it out to be a lot more planned than it is, too. The last thing you want to do in an interview is have a prepared list of questions. What I do is really just define areas of discussion which I note down and have in front of me and then try to, as much as possible, get into conversation or debate with the other person. So one of the pieces of advice I offer to young, would-be interviewers is that the best thing they can do is to learn to listen, and I suggest to them that people don't listen enough to each other's conversation. If you have too many prepared questions, you're not a listener then; you're just a parrot.

When you draw your charts of sequential ideas and so forth, the implication, I think, can be drawn that the whole thing is a great deal more consciously planned than it really is in fact. Because I am listening intently and trying to develop the ideas, to flush them out from the things they're saying, and I will only then go on to another pre-planned area when the possibilities of that area seem to have been exhausted.

BELL: *Again, you may have internalised; you may not consciously plan your moves, that may just be the way you act.*

LYNEHAM: Well, there's a lot of adrenalin pumping when you're in a television studio, particularly when you're live. But don't forget that about 80 per cent of my output would be pre-recorded, and I edit it. I will obviously tighten them up because I will want to cover a range of material. Often, for example, a senior politician will say 'Why not come down to my office? Bring a couple of camera teams down and do it in my office.' And we will always try to resist that. Bring them up into a studio, which is not their territory, and they're a great deal more on their toes. It's not so much that you put them off-guard, or they're at a disadvantage, which I think you might argue, it's just that it's not their cosy patch. I suppose you could say it's my cosy patch but then, it's not a terribly cosy thing anyway. I don't know that it's anyone's cosy patch — a television studio — particularly not live-to-air.

BELL: *Is there pressure on you from outside, from your producers and so on, to be 'balanced'?*

LYNEHAM: The general rule that I apply is to seek to put to all parties the hardest and most robust line of questioning that their opponents, were they there, would put to them. And it seems to me that if that's applied at all times, then you can't go wrong. Now, you will always go wrong to the extent that half the people watching are going to think you're a bastard because they all vote for this bloke or his party, or her party. So you're inevitably on a hiding to nothing — the better you do your job the more some people watching are going to think you're a dreadful person, and biased, particularly if, in a live situation, you have five or six areas to discuss in five or six minutes. When you start to see their eyes glaze and you can hear yesterday's press release coming through the lips, you jump them and move the interview along. But then you are that 'rude young person' on the ABC who always interrupts those nice politicians.

BELL: *We canvass two different views of the relationship between politics and the media. Do you ever wonder*

	about the possible changes imposed on politics by the media?
LYNEHAM:	The outsider's view of a monolithic press gallery is absolute nonsense. The extent that television has become a de facto opposition against politicians and politics in general, I think, can be easily overplayed, because the bottom line is always policy and ideas. We are in the marketplace of ideas and policy development, and you can overstate the idea of anti-political cynicism that the media might have, because we are challenging them to justify themselves in ways that they are not challenged in parliamentary debate. Question time is a set up. There is really no other toe-to-toe discussion unless you get them together in a television studio. I don't think we're out to tell the people of Australia that politicians are all empty and crass and the situation is hopeless and ought to be the cause of great despair, because what is the alternative to a parliamentary political process?
BELL:	*You might be called sceptical without being called cynical. There's an important difference, there. To be sceptical is to put everything to question, not to see it all as having no value.*
LYNEHAM:	I think you're right. I can at times feel great cynicism . . . but that's different from damning the entire process. At the same time, the intimacy, the wealth of material coming across about politicians as individuals and the intimacy television especially gives, demands that they have a presence as people. It's not a Hollywood-style charisma contest, but they must be able to be credible and convincing individuals. There are many variations of the product, but no longer can you hope to hold a national constituency without having some sort of defined image of yourself out there in the marketplace.

BELL: *Do you want to add anything?*

LYNEHAM: I wouldn't overdo the extent to which press gallery journalists are seen as collaborators of politicians. Sure it's a potentially cosy relationship — we're all part of the same community in a very odd building, and it's an odd community . . . but to see us as too cosily ensconced with each other would be to underestimate the intense competition between journalists and between politicians, and to underestimate the enormous egos that are often at play on both sides.

The other thing I would say is that you might be in danger of being a bit armchair about our role, and underestimating a lot of the daily pressures, the extent to which sometimes you're simply flying by the seat of your pants . . . Sure, patterns can develop, but this is a very reactive, often fast-moving business and I would suggest to you, apart from anything else, that what you might see as patterns developing can be much more random and personal style rather than any consensus, however implied, about how interviews are done.

5

Aspel and Co: The Talkshow Interview

Michael Aspel interviews Norman Tebbit, on *Aspel and Co*. (This interview was part of a program on which the actor John Cleese and the singer Julio Iglesias also appeared.)

MICHAEL ASPEL: *Thank you, John, that was a good one. Now a couple of years ago, in a Radio One poll to find the funniest man in Britain, John Cleese was the winner. But my next guest picked up a few votes too along with Michael Fish and Neil Kinnock. But he is a man who has held high office and his undeniable skill as a political tactician has impressed even his enemies. He is the Right Honourable Norman Tebbit, MP.*
[*Tebbit enters*]
Now next Tuesday, 11 October, you'll be returning to the same Brighton Hotel where you were bombed exactly four years ago. Er, and is your wife Margaret going with you?

NORMAN TEBBIT:	Yes indeed, yes.
ASPEL:	*Did she need to be persuaded to do that?*
TEBBIT:	No, no, not at all. It's what we would expect to do. The conference is there this year. We go to the conference. Last year we went to Blackpool, now imagine that! You know I . . . so now we're ready for Brighton.
ASPEL:	*How, how is your wife now?*
TEBBIT:	She's in pretty good shape, in good spirits, good enough to come out with me this evening. She said she wanted to see some fella called . . . [*turns to Cleese, inaudible exchange*]. Aspel? A. . . Aspel?
JOHN CLEESE:	Oh Aspel, yes.
TEBBIT:	Aspel. Terribly sorry.
ASPEL:	*. . . trying to say Iglesias. I understand*
TEBBIT:	Oh we know about him, yes.
ASPEL:	*Thank you. I did notice having . . . seen her this evening before that there is an improvement, isn't there, in your wife's er . . . movements.*
TEBBIT:	Yes she, em . . . she has had some improvement. She . . . oh, I think it's about a year ago now, she found she could manage a champagne glass. Fortunately we've got teacups now, because it really was getting slightly [*inaudible*].
ASPEL:	*She didn't mind how she felt after that. Now, forgive me for harping on about this but it's still in everyone's mind, this experience you went through. Do you actually remember everything that happened that night?*
TEBBIT:	Yes, yes indeed. Em . . . it, it was not one of our best nights you know, quite clearly. And I've spoken to the manager of the hotel about it. It was . . . er . . . three or four hours waiting for the room service. He's promised that it won't happen again.

ASPEL: *What . . . Yes. What were you thinking about during all those hours waiting for rescue? Was your mind quite clear?*

TEBBIT: To the best of my belief. Em, to be serious one wonders under circumstances like that what the hell is going on — you don't know whether the whole hotel was down, I didn't know whether I was the surviving member of the cabinet, or, or what. No idea at all. And in some ways that's the . . . the worst of it. Know you're just there in total darkness, em, wondering what the hell has happened and how long it's going to be before anyone is going to find you. It's, er, very uncomfortable.

ASPEL: *And holding your wife's hand obviously was of a great help.*

TEBBIT: That's right. And then eventually the very welcome horny hand of Fred the Fireman who . . . I . . . I don't think I've ever held on to a man's hand quite so strongly as I held on to his when it got to me.

ASPEL: *Yeah. You've escaped death more than once of course. I mean you were a pilot and you were in a very narrow scrape. What happened?*

TEBBIT: Oh that was a . . . not untypical flying accident, em, when, for reasons which we've never quite sorted out . . . You know the airforce blames me and I blame the aeroplane, and everybody blamed everybody, so to speak. Em, I failed to take off one morning . . . er . . . on an air exercise and my number two just took off, you know you're supposed to stay in formation with him, and I spoke to him about it afterwards, and I said 'What sort of chap are you, deserting me at a moment like this?' — and, em, I went off the end of the runway and the aeroplane came apart and it was all sort of rather uncomfortable for a while. But em, you know, it's one of those things, I guess we get used to facing death if we use the M1 or the M25 terribly often, don't we all of us?

ASPEL: *Has it, has it, both of these experiences and others perhaps had a lasting effect then on your attitude to life?*

TEBBIT: Yes, to be serious I think they have. I think that I concluded from that first escapade that really I was fortunate to have survived and therefore every day is a bonus.

ASPEL: *Mmm.*

TEBBIT: And if you look on life like that, em, even the bad days are good days. You know, even if it's an awful day well, it's still a great day because it's a day which you might well not have had. And I think it gives you a good attitude towards life.

ASPEL: *Now you've got an autobiography and I'm going to read a bit of this — hence the bins here. And you talk about flying and you described it almost as if it's a love scene. Now John, er, listen to this, unless you've read it already, er, it's about flying and it says, em 'It was sheer animal thrill, the physical exertion of handling the last RAF fighter without powered controls, the numbing, bruising ride on a bumpy day, the sweat of excitement and the heat of the atmospheric friction as the two jets smashed the aircraft through the resisting air, all combined with the spur of competition and the thrill of danger' . . . Wow that's passionate stuff there.*

TEBBIT: It was great fun at the time too.

CLEESE: [*inaudible*] that kind of excitement about. You see, if you're a total physical coward like me, you can hardly believe that anybody does that voluntarily.

TEBBIT: Well I don't know — I don't think it's any more difficult actually, than stripping off in front of the cameras.

CLEESE: [*laughs*]

TEBBIT: It depends what you go in for.

CLEESE: That's as brave as I get.

ASPEL: *And what you do Norman doesn't hurt other people as well...*
    [Cleese and Tebbit laugh]
ASPEL: *These escapades, I mean, zooming motor bikes and, I think, pranging the CO's car as well and...*
TEBBIT: *That was not a good idea, I can tell you that.*
ASPEL: *No, reckless, er, boozy parties, I mean does this imply that you were, are, or were or are, reckless, even perhaps irresponsible?*
TEBBIT: *Well, now I'm a very sober, staid middle-aged chap. Em, but er... I think anybody that doesn't sometimes have just a little irresponsible outburst when they're young is never going to grow up.*
ASPEL: *John, have you, have you, well I was going to say, have you ever been reckless, but of course, we've seen the evidence.*
CLEESE: *[laughs]*
ASPEL: *Have you ever...*
TEBBIT: *Not all of it actually; it was very discreet.*
CLEESE: *No, I never have, I've always been, er, you know, highly introverted and, er, the idea is instead of going mountaineering or riding a motor cycle very fast, er, I mean it is quite clearly insane to me and I'm going to leave it to other people in their diminishing numbers.*
TEBBIT: *I ne... I never rode my motor-bike very fast. It wouldn't go very fast.*
CLEESE: *[laughs]*
TEBBIT: *... politicians are often victims of plots. It happened to me at a very young age and er... I was persuaded that I could ride my motorcycle upstairs. What I didn't know was that my friends — and I use the expression loosely — had loosened the clips on the stair carpet so that as I was about half-way up, I was conscious of having to use more and more throttle to stay where I was before the inevitable and awful moment when motorcycle*

	and I and stair carpet all finished up at the bottom of the stairs
ASPEL:	*Three brushes with death. Though you've both been involved [inaudible] with projecting and er politicians on television, em, do you feel that humour is a very useful weapon, er . . .*
TEBBIT:	Yes, you have to be very careful about humour in politics though, because you can very easily be misunderstood. And em, you know, sometimes people don't like politicians to make jokes, and er you have to do it very carefully.
CLEESE:	It's a shame politicians don't use humour more. I mean people are constantly telling me: Oh he's funny. I mean, you have this reputation — he's very funny, but he doesn't show it a great deal in public and I, I'm very curious why you don't.
TEBBIT:	*Well I think sometimes one is afraid, because a lot of jokes, em, there's some element of which, which may offend somebody in some way. Now you can get away with a joke about people who are old or people who are young or people who are bald or . . .*
CLEESE:	[*laughs*]. . . Laughing at ourselves . . .
TEBBIT:	. . . people who are lame, or something like that. Yes that's right. Em, but when a politician does, you know . . .
CLEESE:	Yes, it's true
TEBBIT:	. . . you get the sort of ninety-four indignant letters very very easily indeed, and if it's ninety-four, you're lucky, you know. Em, so one has to be very careful.
CLEESE:	But it's very persuasive isn't it, I mean if I can make a point and make you smile or laugh at my point, you take the point.
TEBBIT:	Mmm.
CLEESE:	You've agreed with me by smiling or laughing with me.
ASPEL:	*Yes.*

TEBBIT:	The other way [*inaudible*] in the House of Commons...
CLEESE:	Yeah
TEBBIT:	Where, of course, if you're in a corner of some sort, the easiest to defuse it; the easiest way to escape...
CLEESE:	Hmm...
TEBBIT:	... is with a joke. And equally if somebody, em, gets a good joke at your expense in the House of Commons, the best thing to do is really enjoy it, stand there, and laugh, you know, seething within but you laugh.
CLEESE:	[*laughs*]
TEBBIT:	And you keep laughing for long enough to give you time to think about how you'll come back at it.
ASPEL:	*Yeah, some of the jokes are very high order, er, I must say, but do you mind the other, I mean the, the 'Chinkford Skinhead' and the and the way you're presented on...*
TEBBIT:	[*laughs*] I come from Chinkford and just look [*gesticulates toward head*]. I haven't had the transplant, what can I do about it?
ASPEL:	*And* Spitting Image, *the sort of death's head look? You don't mind too much?*
TEBBIT:	No not particularly. I'm er... I think the puppets in *Spitting Image*, em, are very clever indeed. I think the jokes are puerile, the script is puerile. It's a great pity the script is not up to the standard of the puppets. But I'd rather have my puppet than if I'd been eh, David Steele, having his puppet...
ASPEL:	[*inaudible*]
TEBBIT:	That's right. I mean [*inaudible*] absolutely awful. It must have been really destructive.
ASPEL:	*Does er Mrs Thatcher enjoy a laugh?*
TEBBIT:	Yes. Yes she does indeed. Em...
CLEESE:	[*inaudible*]
TEBBIT:	You see how effective it is, don't you [*laughs*] yes, but er, but of course it's even more difficult for a

|ASPEL:|woman em in politics to er . . . to get the laughs, to have a joke because, em, so many jokes in fact have some sort of connotation which is just slightly off colour, now you and I get away with it — just, he [*points to Cleese*] gets away with it all the time, er, but, er, for a woman it's very much more difficult, much more difficult. I remember one occasion . . . probably be put in gaol for this because I think it's a Cabinet secret that I'm revealing, em, when we were having a discussion and em . . . it wasn't a Cabinet so it's all right, I hope, em, and er, somebody said 'well that's all very well' though it was the Prime Minister herself, said 'That's all very well, we're talking about it from our point of view but, but, what do normal people think about this?' And she turned around to George Younger and she said 'George, you're normal, what do you think?' And of course everybody laughed and there was this pause before she said 'Oh, men . . .'|

ASPEL: *Is she lovely when angry?*

TEBBIT: Ha! Depends whether you're in the firing line or not [*laughs*]. If it's one of your friends, well it is lovely [*laughs*].

ASPEL: *Because your life is dominated by two Margarets isn't it? Em, are they in any way similar?*

TEBBIT: Not really, no, not really. Em, I think it's very inconvenient because er, you know, I didn't have to think what I was saying, you know, I could just say 'Yes Margaret' very easily — it didn't matter whether I was at home or at work. Then I tried to do what I wanted to anyway [*laughs*].

ASPEL: *In the book you, em, you talk about your wife's depression which er [inaudible] had time in hospital. It's a very, very personal story, did you feel a need to tell it?*

TEBBIT: Well, we talked it over a lot and, em, as I think most people know, I've always kept my family out of the limelight, public life, and er, I think for most politicians that's probably a wise thing to do, but we came to the conclusion that it was right to refer to those times because so many people face that problem, and lots of people in this country, any country, have faced problems with mental illness, and it seems these days you can talk about almost anything else: you can talk about people having cancer, you can talk about them having AIDS, you can talk about them having almost anything, and everybody talks about it quite normally, and then you mention mental illness and it's as though something awful has happened, and people want to move away. And I don't think that helps anybody who has suffered any form of depression or mental illness, and it certainly doesn't help their families in coping with it. So we felt, em, both of us, that perhaps it would help other people, em, particularly their families, to know that people do get better. Because, you know, there's an awful feeling that if somebody is mentally ill, well, they're going to be ill all their lives, and it's simply not true.

ASPEL: *This led of course to you being both mother and father for a while. It gave you insights, no doubt, into the terrible stresses of being a mother.*

TEBBIT: Mmm, mmm, yes, in every way, in every way. I . . . how our young son survived, I don't know, but I can remember picking him up saying 'Go to bloody sleep!' [*laughs*].

ASPEL: *So, I mean, people who do go . . .*

TEBBIT: Very effective actually, he did.

ASPEL: *. . . three months at a time [laughs] . . . And did you become a good cook?*

TEBBIT: [*laughs*] Oh, I've always been a reasonably good cook, em, and er, you know, wasn't terribly good cook then, didn't have very much time. Er, you know, you watch Floyd, and you realize how it's done, you know, little sort of drink now and again . . . goes . . . goes very well.

ASPEL:	*Chef's nips I think they call it. Of course gluttony is one of your hobbies, John, you're very interested in all that.*
CLEESE:	Yes, I've given up sloth. I don't have the time for it but I can [*inaudible*].
ASPEL:	*Are you ambitious, Norman? Are you still hoping for ultimate office?*
TEBBIT:	I doubt if it will happen. I, I'm only four years or so younger than the Prime Minister and, em, I think she'll last a heck of a long time yet. Actually women, I think, really last longer than men . . .
ASPEL:	*That's true.*
TEBBIT:	And so . . .
WOMAN:	Hear hear . . . [*in audience*]
TEBBIT:	Thank you very much. And so I suspect that, em, er, I'll be drawing my old age pension before she retires and I hope that's the way it is. I, I'd like to see her go on for a long time yet.

The Exceptional and the Ordinary

The archetypal interviewee is Peter Ustinov. The ideal time of broadcast is Saturday night 'late' — 9.30 or later, after dinner, when witty and amusing conversation is *de rigueur*. The perfect host is amiable and professional, at ease with his (it *is* usually *his*) famous guests, yet at one with his audience of ordinary people. He is something of a celebrity himself, yet never upstages the personalities with whom he converses on our behalf. The colourful set reminds viewers of the theatre or the music hall and includes a live audience, looking up expectantly and applauding as the guest enters, after an effusive introduction by the host. These facts tell us something about the curious genre of the 'chat show', where recognisable people who like talking, talk to people who like to talk — about showbusiness, success, adventures, serendipitous events, people they have known.

As a genre the chat show probably has its principal origins in American radio, where interviews were heard as broadcast extensions of the fan magazine, *Profile of the 'Stars'*. Programs like *Forty-Five Minutes in Hollywood* (1934) and *Hollywood Star Theatre* (1938) included interviews with screen stars interspersed with lavish publicity build-up and aural 'excerpts' from movies about to be released (recreated by anonymous radio actors). They were not yet 'chat' shows, as the interviews were pre-written and unashamedly controlled by the Hollywood publicity machine.[1] But they paved the way for programs in which the interviews became more adlibbed and chatty, and the questions more personal. The guests of a 1937 NBC program included not only movie stars but also authors of recently published books and celebrities such as Mrs Roosevelt, who 'came to chat about life in the White House, and revealed such homey details as the Emperor Haile Selassie having to take his shoes off after a public occasion and wiggling his toes in blessed relief'.[2] Presenter Mary Margaret McBride (her name was also the title of the program) 'played the unknowledgeable one, asking questions that seemed naive, but were not', which meant that her guests often 'told more of themselves than they had ever meant to'.[3] The characteristics of the modern chat show began to emerge in radio programs of this kind. But it was only through television, with its even greater sense of being 'live' and its ability to suggest the togetherness and warmth of the music hall or the circus, that the genre came into its own and, in its various modes (talk only; talk and 'variety'; talk, variety and satire), became a major television format, creating its own international stars, such as Johnny Carson in the U.S. and David Frost and Michael Parkinson in Britain.

Perhaps the talking celebrity show is a latter-day version of the fan-magazine biography of the early years of the movies. Perhaps it is an electronic soirée or dinner-party enjoyed only voyeuristically. When Michael Aspel asks the actor Patricia Hodge if she believes in 'love at first sight' he is making conversation on behalf of an audience which recognises her face and name but which will never be able to be more intimate with her than this sort of question allows.

After-dinner talk of sex, 'relationships', the quirky side of public life, not-too-formal politics, entertainment and sport has been made public through the round-table or lounge-chair chat show since the 1960s. In Australia and Britain, evening programs hosted by men, featuring the famous and those aspiring to celebrity status (with or without portfolio) have paraded anecdote and opinion to their audiences since Bob Sanders (*People*, on ABC television from the late 1950s) and David Frost moved talk away from 'topics' and onto the talkers themselves. Michael Parkinson's British celebrities were exported to Australia in the 1970s and he followed in the flesh to produce for both the ABC and, later, commercial television, a series of very popular talkshows. The genial host, given to a combination of fan-like inquisitiveness and celebrity quick-wittedness, brought the genre to the popularity level on which (during the late '80s) its successor (in Australia, at least), Michael Aspel's *Aspel and Co.*, built its own following on the ABC. Entertaining self-disclosure by the famous is no longer the province of the letter or diary, but is given the immediacy and realism of spontaneous (if orchestrated) conversation in the audience's living room.

The televisual distinction between the interview and the talk or chat (in a *show*) suggests important differences between political interviews and revelatory, 'in-depth' interviews on the one hand, and 'talk show', conversational interviews on the other. To anticipate a theme of this chapter, we could say that the talkshow involves the talker in a *performance* of his/her cultural role or status, albeit a performance marked as 'real' or revealing in ways that invite audience members to see the celebrity as like themselves. Hence, the talker is not allowed to be too objectively a political expert nor too reflectively an actor or sportsman/woman (for that might turn the talk into an interview of another kind), but is invited to be subjectively *inexpert* about the things that might befall the star and the audience alike. As we shall see, the celebrity is not exemplary of the traditional virtues, and therefore famous, but is instead a model for transitory audience identification with the spectacle of, the stylish performance of, the role of being extraordinary or famous. But he or she must also be prepared to be revealed as a real person like the spectator. Interviewees must obliquely, through 'chat', show their non-celebrity humanity.

To introduce the talkshow, we should perhaps begin with those who do most of the talking: the guests. Who are they? What is it that makes them eligible to appear on talkshows? The answers to these questions can be summarised as follows: to be a guest on a talkshow, one must have *news value, entertainment value* and *symbolic value* —not necessarily all of these to the same degree (one or other value may be dominant in a particular case), yet all of them to some degree.

NEWS VALUE
To have news value, a guest must have accomplished something in the public domain that (a) can be claimed to be *successful*, and to have a wide 'mass' appeal; (b) is *recent*, or at least linked to a recent event (it can be the birthday of a well-known actress, for example); and (c) can be linked to one of the *fields* which, in the world of the mass media, make up the spectrum of human life (comparable with the 'sections' of the newspaper: politics, business, science, education, showbusiness, sports, the arts, etc.) Not all fields of human endeavour are in the public eye, not all achievements are celebrated in the media as individual achievements.

In the talkshow, pride of place is given to showbusiness and the arts (insofar as they can be said to have a wide appeal), because of their entertainment value: the most typical talkshow guest is the actor or actress who has starred in a recent movie, the pop star who is about to go on a world tour or the author who has just won a prestigious prize. But occasionally other fields spawn a celebrity — the scientist who has made a breakthrough discovery, say, in a field of medicine that is much in the public eye (organ transplantation, birth control, AIDS research), or the politician whose recently revealed leadership ambitions have made her or him an object of intense media interest. Provided always they also have entertainment value (are good 'talent' in the jargon of the television producers).

Whenever possible the audience is given a glimpse of the guest's achievement: a clip of the footballer's sensational goal in a recent match; the performance of a love song by the just-married pop star; the reading of a passage from the prize-winning novel.

There is, of course, a thin line between news value (the value of the guest for the program) and public relations or publicity value (the value of the program for the guest). The guests' achievements may be imminent rather than recent (the pop star about to go on tour), their successes hoped for rather than already achieved (the movie *about* to be released). Indeed, these successes may in part be brought about by the guests' appearances on talkshows. But in such cases the guests must already have *celebrity value*, and celebrity value is a form of news value too.[4] If they only have *potential* celebrity value, and are yet to be made into celebrities (in part by appearing on talkshows), they must be able to claim an actual recent success in an appropriate field — they must have been celebrated in the news media.

Entertainment Value

A talkshow is not a news show or a current affairs show, however closely related these genres may be through sharing the same news values, very similar formats, or even the same personnel (Michael Aspel was a newsreader before he became a talkshow host, for instance). Talkshow guests must not only have news value, but also *entertainment value*. Licensed to show off, they are obliged to be good talkers or story-tellers, witty and amusing, whether or not they are professional entertainers. Norman Tebbit, for instance, the guest in the interview which forms the centrepiece of this chapter, is a Conservative politician, but he also has entertainment value, and Aspel introduces him, somewhat ironically, as someone who 'picked up a few votes' in a Radio One poll to find the funniest man in Britain. Talkshows are always displays of the activity of talking which allow the audience to listen to the forms, the games, of conversation as a mode of revealing something about the participants and their milieu.

When the guests lack entertainment value, the presenter will have to provide it, and this changes the balance of power, the role division between host and guest. *In Aspel and Co.* and similar programs, the host willingly plays the 'straight man' and allows himself to become the butt of the guest's jokes, as in this exchange from the Tebbit interview (John Cleese is one of the other guests on the program):

ASPEL: *How, how is your wife now?*
TEBBIT: She's in pretty good shape, in good spirits, good enough to come out with me this evening. She said she wanted to see some fellow called [*turns to Cleese, inaudible exchange*] Aspel? A . . . Aspel . . .
CLEESE: Oh Aspel, yes.
TEBBIT: Aspel. Terribly sorry.

In the populist talkshows of, for instance, Morton Daly in the U.S., or Steve Vizard in Australia, the host frequently becomes the 'funny man' and the guest is the butt of his jokes. Daly, for instance, pours out his vitriolic wit over avant-garde artists, environmentalists, vegetarians and anyone else considered eccentric or deviant. Vizard embarrasses female guests with sexual innuendo, to roars of laughter from his studio audience. In such programs host and audience affirm common values opposite to those of the guests, while in programs like *Aspel and Co.*, host, guest and audience are assumed to share the same values (even when social taboos or rules are broken) in a cheerful, upbeat format meant to give everyone a sense of participation in the enjoyable conversation.

SYMBOLIC VALUE

News value and entertainment value alone do not make the ideal talkshow guest. Ideally, the talkshow visitor must be related, not just to a recognisable field such as showbusiness, art, or politics, but also to a discourse about that field, shared, supposedly, by guest, host and audience, and embodied in the person of the guest. As Richard Dyer has said, 'stars' are 'real people' who 'actually embody their image and the values associated with them', at once exemplary individuals and ordinary mortals like us. In the person of the star: 'A range of associations and values are drawn together to form a unique symbolic cluster, whose uniqueness and actuality are affirmed and legitimated by the fact that the performer is uncopiable and irreproducible'.[5]

In his book *Heavenly Bodies* (1987), Dyer elaborates this idea in relation to Marilyn Monroe, Paul Robeson and Judy Garland, stars who, he argues, personalise discourses of sexuality, ethnicity and sexual identity respectively. In the same way other stars could embody in their person and biography what politics, sport or science are essentially about. Just as the gods of antiquity were gods of (about) something (gods of war, of love, of wisdom, etc.) so the demi-gods from the pantheon of celebrities are also demi-gods of (about) something. And just as the symbolic value of the ancient gods was expressed through entertaining stories, so the symbolic value of the modern demi-gods is conveyed through biographical anecdotes. Indeed, we might speculate that one of the deeply buried ancestors of the talkshow revelation is the tale of the exemplary life, the life of the chivalric hero or of the saint or, conversely, of the rogue or trickster who exhibits excess and is licensed to violate society's taboos, at least in his (again, it is usually *his*) talk. Comedians like John Cleese, Dudley Moore and others are frequent guests on talkshows like *Aspel and Co.*, and their role is somewhat different from that of other guests.

In the television talkshow these demi-gods become ordinary mortals, people like us. Dyer has linked the 'gods to mortals' trajectory of the fallen star to the *talking* film in which 'their voices made them as real as the audience watching them', [6] and he cites Edgar Morin's analysis of the de-divination of (cinema's) stars. As television is an essentially domestic medium, emphasising the voice more than the spectacle, his discussion of Morin is highly relevant to the talkshow:

> The cinema was a 'plebeian spectacle' at first, drawing on the melodrama and penny-dreadful, characterised by magic, extraordinary adventures, sudden reversals, the sacrificial death of the hero, violent emotions, etc. 'Realism, psychologism, 'happy end' and humour reveal precisely the bourgeois transformation of this imagination' (p. 16). Chance and occult possession are replaced by psychological motivation. Bourgeois individualism cannot take the death of the hero, hence the insistence on the happy end. So stars become more usual in appearance, more 'psychologically' credible in personality, more individuated in image. The star does not cease to be special, but now combines 'the exceptional with the ordinary, the ideal with the everyday'.[7]

For the modern middle-class television audience, fictional heroes and heroines cannot, by themselves, qualify as exemplary, as positive (or negative) role models. Behind the fictional character there must be an actual character with consistent, meaningful characteristics, and this actual character must be compatible with the fictional character, the 'image'. Hence the thirst for biographies which on every page assure us that we are taken 'behind the scenes', 'beneath the surface', or 'beyond the image' to where the truth resides.[8] It is in the service of this need for biography, for the revelation of the private truth behind the public image, that the talkshow operates. The host seeks to elicit from his guests, not just the actual 'behind the scenes' character, but also the assurance that this character is compatible with the guest's public image. An author has invented a character who rebels against his father — did he, himself, in his own life, rebel against his father? An actress has played the role of a working-class woman — did she herself ever work in a factory (or, acceptable substitute, spend arduous months 'researching' the role in an actual factory)?

Take the appearance of actress Cheri Lunghi in *Aspel and Co*. Her recent starring role in the television series *The Manageress* constituted her news value. Her entertainment value was assured by her experience of playing the role of not playing a role (of 'being herself'), her wit and her beauty. Her symbolic value derived, potentially, from the theme of 'her' series: she played the manageress of a football club, in stories turning around her character's difficulty in being accepted in a man's world, despite her obvious competence. But in the talkshow this theme had to be given a biographical foundation. So Aspel first asked her whether she grew up amongst men. Alas, this turned out not to be the case. She grew up amongst women. Aspel therefore resorted to asking her to enlarge on her experiences during the shooting of the series. Was it difficult to be the only woman in the cast? One way or another her role in the series had to be anchored in her own, real experiences.

The symbolic value of some guests is, of course, well-established — their private life and 'behind the scenes' character already public knowledge. In other cases the guests are comparatively unknown and their symbolic value has to be constructed and elaborated in the course of the interview. In either case, if all goes well, the ordinary mortal is transformed into an exemplary person, and the exemplary person into an ordinary mortal — without any conflict between the two, for the exemplary person must be an ordinary mortal to have a recognisable, real embodiment.

The guest, then, has news value, entertainment value and symbolic value — and it is precisely this *mixture* of values that defines their role. Caroline Jones' guests, too, are exemplary. They, too, have symbolic value. But they need not, as Caroline Jones herself has said, also exhibit entertainment value. Current affairs interviewees must have news value and they may also signify symbolic value, but they need not have entertainment value. It is only in the talkshow that these three factors converge.

THE HOST

We have discussed the guest; but what of the host, and the studio audience? What roles do they fulfil in the talkshow game?

In programs like *Aspel and Co.*, the host is on the one hand the equal of his guests, urbane and witty, more at ease with the famous than the audience could ever be. He knows their gossip and the sorts of experiences that befall them. He shares their social networks. And often he lets the audience know that he has interviewed or 'worked with them' before. In some way he even has more power than the guests, for he alone can address the audience directly — when he introduces the guests, and in little asides, occasional gestures of complicity with the audience, played directly to camera. He is also in control of the final, edited program, orchestrating the interviews, making sure they have a beginning, a middle and an end, despite the appearance of spontaneity. And, unlike the guests, he is a regular in our living rooms, seen throughout the program every week or even several times a week, a mediator between the audience and the famous.

On the other hand, he is not himself a celebrity in the sense that his guests are. Though a 'personality', he is a personality only of television itself, while his guests are actors, writers, sports persons, etc. His biography is not usually part of the program's appeal and meaning (as is the case, for example, with Caroline Jones). Like the audience, he must be an audience for his guests' jokes, their anecdotes and their revelations, and he must never upstage them. In this, too, he is more at one with the audience, more like them than his guests can ever be. (There are talkshows in which the presenter is also a celebrity, someone who has made her or his name outside television — in comedy, or popular music, for instance — someone who is more than a professional presenter, and whose biography and 'image' form part of the program's appeal. In this chapter, however, we confine ourselves to the kind of talkshow represented by *Aspel and Co.*)

THE STUDIO AUDIENCE
The presence of the studio audience also sets the talkshow apart from the current affairs show, or from programs such as Caroline Jones' *The Search for Meaning*. It provides feedback (laughter, applause), a sense of something actually happening, an impression of a 'live', impromptu, unscripted event. It creates an atmosphere of a community enclosing that event, a sense of the ritual, like that of the theatre or the circus, where social taboos and rules can be broken with impunity, and where one goes to have 'a good time' and to 'escape' from the dreariness of everyday life — the notion of 'escape' still plays an important role in the thinking of television programmers.[9]

The Conversational Interview

Three (sometimes two) guests are invited to share the televisual loungeroom-cum-theatre stage of Aspel's program. The first is usually a showbusiness personality — an actor or actress or a comedian. The second may be from some other sphere of public life — sports, politics or literature, for instance. Such guests, though not showbusiness personalities themselves, are therefore always in the company of showbusiness people and, literally and figuratively, equated with them. They are interviewed in a 'showbusiness' frame and made to fill the same kind of role — of 'idol' or 'star' or 'role model' — as the other guests. The third guest tends to be a performer again, usually a singer, so that the show can end with a live performance on an entertaining, upbeat to be a performer again, usually a singer, so that the show can end with a live performance on an entertaining, upbeat note. Norman Tebbit, in the program on which we are focusing in this chapter, is preceded by comedian John Cleese and followed by singer Julio Iglesias.

One by one, these guests enter, and those who have already been interviewed may join the conversation with the next guest, either spontaneously or prompted by Aspel, so that the first interview, during which no other guests are present, is most like an interview and least like a conversation. In the interview itself we can discern the following stages:

INTRODUCTION

The guest is introduced before he makes his entrance:

> *Thank you, John. That was a good one. Now a couple of years ago, in a Radio One poll to find the funniest man in Britain, John Cleese was the winner. But my next guest picked up a few votes too, along with Michael Fish and Neil Kinnock. But he is a man who has held high office and his undeniable skill as a political tactician has impressed even his enemies. He is the Right Honourable Norman Tebbit, MP.*

Tebbit then enters, to applause from the audience, and sits down next to Cleese and opposite Aspel.

However much the talkshow may be intended to be 'conversational', this is not how conversations are initiated. It comes directly out of an entertainment tradition and is a low-key variation of the MC's well-worn 'And now . . . we present . . . the greatest . . .', followed climactically by the name of the star. It also explicitly lists Tebbit's qualifications for being on the show: he has celebrity value ('has held high office') and entertainment value (he 'picked up a few votes' in 'the funniest man in Britain' contest). Tebbit's news value will be revealed later in the interview (he has just published an autobiography), although his symbolic value is, of course, not made explicit, but elaborated by the interview as a whole. Thus the introduction claims for the guest in advance the status of celebrity in a way only television can — it is now up to the guest to show that he or she can live up to it, be successful talkshow 'talent' who can be asked to appear again, in later shows or in other, similar shows.

We might note also what the introduction does *not* mention — Tebbit's party-political affiliation and his precise executive roles as a politician. When Aspel praises his guest (he calls him 'skilled' and 'impressive'), his praise relates not to moral or politically partisan values, in the way Caroline Jones might praise her interviewees, but to Tebbit's popularity, success and entertainment value. His role as a politician is only of secondary importance (and his party affiliation is carefully suppressed in the interests of audience consensus around the individual's talent).

Confession

The opening of a talkshow interview forms its most 'interview-like' part. Ideally it elicits a confessional narrative, a first person story of dangers countered, adversity or illness overcome or challenges met, just as in Caroline Jones' interviews. However, rather than the revelatory quality, it is the entertaining quality, the drama of the confession which matters most here. Often the audience knows the story already, but that does not matter in talkshows. The pleasure of the story lies, to a large extent, in getting it 'from the horse's mouth' and in the entertaining way in which it is told.

The Tebbit interview contains no fewer than three such stories. First there is the story of Tebbit's wife's depression, a trauma which Tebbit has overcome by 'being both mother and father for a while' and by writing about it in his autobiography, in order to 'help families cope with mental illness'. Then there is the story of the Brighton Hotel bombing in which Tebbit, through humorous understatement, displays his heroic sang-froid. And finally there is the story of a narrow escape from death, another piece of heroism.

Such stories form an important part of the interview and, if they are not forthcoming spontaneously, the presenter, who already knows them, takes an active role in eliciting them, for instance by asking *information questions* like *How, how is your wife now?* Or by means of what is perhaps the most quintessential talkshow question, the *'this-is-your-life' question*, which is in fact not a question but a second-person statement that sums up an event in the guest's life, and thereby also displays the host's intimate familiarity with the guest's exemplary life story. The example below combines the two methods, but the 'this-is-your-life' question can also appear on its own:

> *You've escaped death more than once of course. I mean you were a pilot and you were in a very narrow scrape. What happened?*

In the first section of the interview, then, the host asks the questions, revealing nothing of him- or herself, and the guest answers them. The guest is required to bare all, but, as is often the case, struggles to keep at least some private matters private. In this interview Tebbit uses his wit to deflect the more personal questions directed at him.

Aspel tries to ensure that the confession has at least the semblance of another form of talk, a form of talk in which the participants are on a more equal footing, that is, conversation. He tries to ensure that the beginning of the interview gives the impression, not of an interrogation, but of a casual exchange, such as a meeting of two acquaintances who have not seen each other for some time. He achieves this in two interrelated ways: by displaying his familiarity with the interviewee, showing how much he knows about her or him already; and by *checking*, that is, by asking the brief, simple WH-questions ('How's the family?') and polar questions ('Still living in Eastwood?') which, when dealing with private life in the context of a meeting between friends or acquaintances, serve to catch up with the latest news and are not usually meant to elicit more than brief, summary answers. (As we have seen, checking has a different function in the political interview, where it serves to establish the facts that will later be used as agreed-upon premises for the interviewer's challenges.)

The opening question of the interview combines the two methods:

Is your wife Margaret going with you?

Here Aspel shows that he knows Tebbit is married, knows the name of his wife, and knows also that she has been ill and therefore might or might not be well enough to accompany Tebbit in public. He also shows that he does *not* know how well she is right now, and so must 'check up' on this. Note that he does not ask 'Is Margaret coming?', for that would distance him from the audience by implying that he is on intimate terms with Tebbit (which the audience is not) rather than that he just knows a lot about him (which the audience, supposedly, does). Hence the fusion between the language of the public whose curiosity follows the lives of celebrities from a distance ('Is his wife going with him?') and the language of the chance meeting between acquaintances ('Is Margaret coming?').

The structure of the exchange, meanwhile, remains that of an interview, despite the conversational surface. The relation between interviewer and interviewee remains unequal. Tebbit cannot, for instance, ask Aspel how *his* wife is faring. However, the need for a conversational surface puts the interviewer at a disadvantage. He cannot be too direct. He cannot appear too inquisitive. It must all seem to happen spontaneously and without direction. Perhaps this is why interviewers who are perfectly sharp and quickwitted in, say, political interviews, often appear less articulate, even a little clumsy (charmingly clumsy, of course) when hosting talkshows — better to seem a little clumsy than to upstage or intimidate the guest.

Although some talkshow interviews open with 'innocent' checking questions, delaying the start of the confessional narrative for a few moments of more or less free-flowing interchange, Aspel's opening questions are only apparently 'checking' questions. On a deeper level they are 'questions inviting confession'. Their indirectness gives them a conversational flavour but makes them less effective in achieving the purpose of eliciting a story, for they cannot oblige Tebbit to tell the story of his wife's depression. They can only fish for the story in more oblique ways in the hope, perhaps, that Tebbit will volunteer the narrative at the mere mention of Margaret's name. But he does not take the bait:

ASPEL: *. . . is your wife Margaret going with you?*
TEBBIT: Yes indeed, yes.
ASPEL: *Did she need to be persuaded to do that?*
TEBBIT: No, no, not at all. It's what we would expect to do. The conference is there this year. We go to the conference. Last year we went to Blackpool, now imagine that? You know, I . . . so now we're ready for Brighton.
ASPEL: *How, how is your wife now?*
TEBBIT: She's in pretty good shape, in good spirits, good enough to come out with me this evening. She said she wanted to see some fellow called [*turns to Cleese . . .*] Aspel? A . . . Aspel?

One is reminded of Milan Kundera's fictional (radio) talk-show in *Immortality*, in which the interviewee defends himself with anger, rather than with humour as Tebbit does, and in which the friendly masks are dropped to reveal that interviewer and interviewee have quite different interests at heart:

> Bernard's familiar voice sounded from the transistor radio lying by their heads; he was conversing with an actor whose film was about to have its premiere. The actor raised his voice and woke them from their light sleep:
>
> 'I came to speak to you about films and not about my son.'
>
> 'Don't worry, we'll get to films too,' Bernard's voice was saying. 'But first there are some questions about recent events. I've heard it said that you yourself played a role in your son's affair.'

'When you invited me to come here, you explicitly stated that you wanted to talk to me about films. So let's discuss films and not my private life.'

'You are a public figure and I'm asking you about things that interest the public. I'm only doing my job as a journalist.'

'I'm ready to answer your questions dealing with films.'

'As you wish. But our listeners will wonder why you refused to answer.'[10]

In a similar vein Aspel justifies his 'harping on' with an appeal to the demands of his role as a professional who must satisfy the desires of his audience: 'Forgive me for harping on about this, but it is still in everyone's mind, this experience you went through'. He pleads in vain, however. Only towards the end of the interview does Aspel finally get the story which he had, no doubt, hoped would lead the interview. Even then, it takes the form of a reflection (on the need for open public discussion of mental illness) rather than a personalised confession. When Aspel attempts to goad Tebbit back to the realm of personal revelation ('*This led of course to you being both mother and father for a while*') Tebbit again retreats behind the shield of his wit, relating how he would pick up his son, saying 'Go to bloody sleep', and then laughing: 'Very effective actually, he did.'

However, once an interviewee is launched into a confession, as Tebbit was when telling the story of the hotel bombing and the story of his earlier 'scrape with death', there is no need for such *subterranean* struggle for control over the direction of the interview. The role of the host changes. He becomes a sympathetic listener who helps to ensure that none of the key moments of the drama will be overlooked. Aspel does this, for instance, by means of what, in Chapter 3, we called extensions.

> *And holding your wife's hand obviously was of a great help.*

And he does it also by means of information questions that probe into Tebbit's thoughts and feelings at the time of the drama, to inject a dramatic element of emotion into the story:

> *What were you thinking about during all those hours waiting for rescue? Was your mind quite clear?*

REFLECTION

However much the talkshow may be oriented towards entertainment, it has its serious moments also. Like the confession of the revelatory interview, the talks how confession must be followed, where possible, by a *reflection* stage. Like the revelatory interview, the talkshow interview must reflect attitudes to life and make the anecdotally presented celebrity an exemplary person whose example can indeed be emulated by the viewer. The only difference, perhaps, is that the talkshow reflection is shorter and receives less emphasis than the reflection in the revelatory genre, which, as we saw in Chapter 3, may well take up a third of the interview. In the example below, Aspel explicitly invites the reflection and Tebbit obliges, signalling the change in mood by prefacing his answer with 'to be serious':

ASPEL: [*Have*] *both of these experiences and other(s) perhaps had a lasting effect then on your attitude to life?*

TEBBIT: Yes, to be serious I think they have. I think that I concluded from that first escapade that really I was fortunate to have survived and therefore every day is a bonus.

Aspel approves of this reflection with a 'Mmmm', thus encouraging Tebbit to elaborate:

TEBBIT: And if you look on life like that, em, even the bad days are good days. You know, even if it's an awful day well, it's still a great day because it's a day which you might well not have had. And I think it gives you a good attitude to life.

A story, whether in an interview or elsewhere, can never just be a story. It must also contain, in the words of Walter Benjamin, 'openly or covertly, something useful. The usefulness may, in one case, consist in a moral; in another, in some practical advice; in a third, in a proverb or maxim. In every case the storyteller is a man who has counsel for his readers.'[11]

TALENTS DISPLAYED

Following the reflection, Aspel reads a passage from Tebbit's autobiography. As mentioned earlier, each talkshow guest has a recent 'work' to his or her credit, whether a movie role or a prize-winning novel, a hit song or a sensational sports achievement, and this 'work' will be displayed one way or another in the course of the talkshow appearance — and praised by the host:

> *Now you've got an autobiography, and I'm going to read a bit of this . . . And you talk about flying and you described it almost as if it's a love scene. Now John, er, listen to this, unless you've read it already, er, it's about flying and it says, em, 'It was sheer animal thrill, the physical exertion of handling the last RAF fighter without powered controls, the numbing, bruising ride on a bumpy day, the sweat of excitement and the heat of the atmospheric friction as the two jets smashed the aircraft through the resisting air, all combined with the spur of competition and the thrill of danger'. Wow, that's passionate stuff there.*

CHALLENGES

Far from taking an adversarial role, like the political interviewer, the talkshow host constantly agrees with his guests. He compliments them, praises them, flatters them. To the excerpt from Tebbit's autobiography, Aspel reacts with a 'Wow, that's passionate stuff'; to his opinions, with a 'Yes' or a 'That is true' or an appreciative 'Mmmm'; to his jokes with laughter and praise. And yet the interview also contains a few challenges. Whether they play a minor role, as in Caroline Jones' interviews, or a major role, as in the adversarial political interview, interviews are not, it seems, interviews unless the interviewers challenge their interviewees at least a little. They cannot take the powerless stance of the awestruck fan or the admiring disciple, but must assert their independence as professionals whose allegiance is in the first place to the public, the audience. They must be seen to serve the interests of the public before they serve those of the guests who might see the interview as a platform for advertising, self-publicity or proselytisation. This, for all their differences, is what all media interview genres have in common.

Aspel challenges Tebbit twice. His first challenge is a direct *accusation question*, the kind of question that only just stops short of being a full-blown *accusation* because of its interrogative mood. In this example, the force of the challenge is mitigated by the past tense and the (deliberate?) clumsiness:

> *These escapades, I mean, zooming motorbikes and, I think, pranging the CO's car as well, and . . . reckless, er, boozy parties, I mean, does this imply that you were, are, or were or are, reckless, even perhaps irresponsible?*

Tebbit of course sidesteps this accusation easily by excusing the excesses of his youth: 'anybody that doesn't sometimes have just a little irresponsible outburst when they're young is never going to grow up'. But, spurred on by Aspel (*'John . . . have you ever been reckless?'*), this does lead to a spar between Tebbit and Cleese in which the latter sides with Aspel's challenge and declares the pursuit of danger 'insane'.

The second challenge is more oblique. Aspel invites Tebbit to react to the slights and accusations of his critics and opponents, passing on an insult ('You look like a skinhead') made by others, and asking Tebbit for a reaction:

> *Do you mind the other, I mean, the, the 'Chinkford Skinhead', and the way you're presented on . . .*

An opportunity for the seasoned politician to show he can take a good joke: 'I think the puppets are very clever indeed'.

DISCUSSION

Almost all Aspel's questions invite narrative. Tebbit is asked to characterise people — himself (*'Have you ever been reckless?'*, *'Are you ambitious?'*) as well as others (*'Is she lovely when angry?'*), and to narrate events that have befallen him (*'What happened?'*) and his reactions to those events (*'What were you thinking during all those hours?'*). The two exceptions are (a) questions inviting reflection and (b) a question which seeks, not narrative but opinion, probing Tebbit's reaction to a more abstract proposition:

> *Do you feel that humour is a very useful weapon?*

Tebbit, clearly more interested in debating issues than in self revelation, immediately warms up to this *opinion question* and launches into a discussion with Cleese.

GOSSIP

Gossip is an important element of the talkshow genre. It shows that the powerful and talented share the motives of the audience, and it humanises and ironises the players on the public stage at least in a limited way. Aspel solicits it through *curiosity questions*, pointed polar questions that invite Tebbit to reveal behind-the-scenes insights into Mrs Thatcher, as evidence of his privileged access to the corridors of power:

> *Does Mrs Thatcher enjoy a laugh?*

Needless to say, Tebbit happily obliges ('I'll probably be put in jail for this, because I think it's a Cabinet secret . . .')

Conversational Interludes

Aspel's challenges, opinion questions and curiosity questions trigger conversational interludes in which the interviewing mode makes way for interchanges between Cleese and Tebbit, during which Aspel sits back and lets the conversation flow, without attempting to control its structure and without trying to steer it in a particular direction. Questions and answers make space for statements and counterstatements as Cleese and Tebbit reveal themselves equally and spontaneously interrupt each other in a freeflowing give and take, all to the delight of the audience.

Yet these interludes are triggered by, and take their character from, definite moves by Aspel. A challenge triggers the spar in which Cleese and Tebbit take opposite viewpoints — Tebbit that of the thrillseeker who thinks that the pursuit of danger is 'great fun', Cleese that of the self-confessed coward who thinks it is 'insane'. An opinion question triggers the *discussion* in which Cleese and Tebbit, rather than exploring their differences, seek common ground in humour (remember that Aspel, already in his introduction, nominated a sense of humour, or at least, 'being funny', as the quality common to the two guests). A curiosity question, finally, triggers gossip.

It is as if it does not matter which *kinds* of interlude are included, nor in which order they appear, so long as the interview does contain these islands of freeflowing talk, and so long as they display something of the generic richness of talk (again: sparring, joking, gossiping, debating, etc.) and pick up some of the key themes of the interview in the process — here the theme of the hero facing danger, the theme of humour, and the theme of Mrs Thatcher whose role, as we will see, will not remain restricted to that of a target for gossip

Coda

The final question of the interview is the only overtly political question Tebbit, the politician, is asked. As it happens, it is almost exactly the same question that concluded Paul Lyneham's interview with Andrew Peacock — the 'leadership' question. But here, in the context of the non-political talkshow, the question is psychologised, framed in terms of Tebbit's personality:

> *Are you ambitious, Norman? Are you still hoping for ultimate office?*

In reply, Tebbit affirms strong loyalty to Mrs Thatcher, who, he says, is hardly older than him and will 'last a heck of a long time yet'. This echoes his earlier affirmations of loyalty to his wife — and remember that it was Aspel who introduced the theme of 'the two Margarets in your life', and asked Tebbit '*are they in any way similar?*'

It is clear, then, that the conclusion of this 'non-political' interview in fact allows Tebbit to display some deeply political attitudes, and to declare some deeply political alliances, albeit in the context of anecdote, humour and gossip. And it is clear also that the audience, by the time the interview concludes, will have pieced together what Tebbit, the celebrity, symbolises, what makes up the moral fibre of the conservative politician. Hence it knows also what it is celebrating this celebrity for in the festive Saturday night setting of the program: the heroism of the fearless warrior who can make sacrifices and shoulder responsibilities, but also the humility of the ordinary man, who puts his young son to bed, looks after his wife when she is ill, and takes life's adversities with a sense of humour. If such an exemplary person is also fiercely loyal, in private as in public life, who are we not to follow his example?

In conclusion, the shape of the talkshow interview emerges as follows: an introduction in which the host praises the guest and creates a sense of excitement and anticipation about her or his appearance on the show; the entrance of the guest, to applause of the audience, followed by a greeting and, perhaps, a few lines of 'catching up'; an anecdote or anecdotes in which the guest tells of, preferably, dramatic events in her or his life; reflection on what the guest has learned from her or his experiences; the display of a 'work' which can now be seen or heard in the light of its author's life story; conversational interludes in which, after quite a structured beginning, the interview is loosened up, and in which jokes, gossip, opinions and so on are exchanged in a free-flowing conversation; and a coda in which the interviewer takes charge again and draws the themes of the interview together.

Of course, not every interview displays all of these elements and any of the elements, except the introduction and the coda, may be repeated a number of times. The conversational interview is by nature more difficult to structure, and hence somewhat less predictable than, say, the political interview. In the Tebbit interview, for instance, a second reflection and conversational interlude follow the first conversational interlude. We have seen talkshow appearances which lack both confession and reflection, and do not go much further than gossip about the famous actors and directors an actor or actress guest has worked with, or only just bearable banter about the number of nude scenes an actress has appeared in. If the guest is articulate and lively, such interviews can still be entertaining. Ideally, however, the talkshow interview mixes all three strands: entertainment and performance; drama and revelation; and the pleasures of witty conversation. Summarised in the kind of formula we have used also in earlier chapters, the conversational interview, in its basic form, looks like this:

Introduction ^ [(Confession) ^ (Reflection) ^ Display Conversational interlude] ^ Coda ^

The Real and the Role

The talkshow celebrity must be an interesting talker — about him/her*self*, but not in the 'deep' psychological sense that is revealed (or created) through the revelatory interview. Rather, the self is revealed through stories, jokes and aphoristic observations related to the *role(s)* that make the talker famous. We might say that the answer to 'what are talkshows about' is that they are about celebrities who are *revealed as similar to their audience* through their way of talking about their roles (as sports, show-biz or cultural celebrities), but who are also *enviable* (glamorous, wealthy, publicly known) because of their roles. But they are not only asked to show how they have developed or triumphed through telling a narrativised biography, as Caroline Jones' subjects are, they are asked also or instead to demonstrate an ironic distance from their own ordinary selves when caught by the extraordinary contingencies of the roles which famous politicians or actors must play (on the edge of danger; breaking symbolic taboos related to sex or money; particularly embarrassing incidents).

What is revealed is not so much the 'real' or 'deep' personality behind the mask of the celebrity. It is, rather, the fascination of the role of the celebrity, both for the person who speaks about his/her own celebrity-induced experiences and for the slightly wide-eyed interviewer and audience. Hence the confessional anecdotes and gossip are about *situations* in which the already-famous *find* themselves. They are revealed through their 'anecjokes', to be as surprised or embarrassed by what befalls them as the non-celebrity audience might be. The interviewer invites them to see their roles as burdening them with experiences which are not of their own making (just as the audience's early-evening talk about what happened at work might also reveal). So we could say that the 'field' of the talkshow interview is talk itself, in the sense that it involves the display of witty anecdotes about being a celebrity. It does not so much reveal the real celebrity as reveal the reality of being a celebrity, a reality which is only or principally produced by the very mode of talking elicited by the television interview. Of course the visible presence of the talker is a necessary condition for this celebrity-as-talker to be acceptably *real* for the audience. But the celebrity status is already established *before* the interview which is, perhaps, why so little depth or history needs to be investigated. It is not the truth of the individual's biography that is being tested, but whether the individual is truly a celebrity. This is done through talk — through *how* (s)he talks as much as by *what* is talked about.

Celebrities are not just famous people. Intellectuals and scientists, bishops and professors, however famous, will not easily be recruited to the format of the talkshow unless they can amusingly relate the contingencies that they have stumbled across despite, or because of, their fame. Celebrities must have a history of being *celebrated* through the public media of the day: their lives have been constructed as exciting, glamorous, wealthy or powerful — they have been *successful* within fields given media publicity sufficient to make their names and roles famous. The talkshow trades on this; the celebrity trades on the talkshow trading on this. Hence the symbolic value of the interviewees is centred on success as celebrity, the latter based on values which some commentators have criticised as indicative of an increasingly 'narcissistic culture'[12] — one in which 'nothing succeeds like the appearance of success'. Here audience identification with the successful depends on these models being incorporated into the audience's own self image, not as traditionally was true of the hero, esteemed principally for his virtues or accomplishments. Christopher Lasch characterises this process of narcissistic identification with the celebrity in the following general terms:

> The narcissist cannot identify with someone else without seeing the other as an extension of himself, without obliterating the other's identity. A narcissistic society worships celebrity rather than fame and substitutes spectacle for the older forms of theatre, which encouraged identification and emulation precisely because they carefully preserved a certain distance between the audience and the actors, the hero worshipper and the hero.[13]

Nevertheless, it is possible to recognise in *Aspel and Co.* elements of identifications which are more traditional — these involve the audience valuing the skills and wit of the celebrity (hence their engagement with the guests' repartee) and the guests' other virtues (for example, Tebbit's personal drama and its pathos). The English talkshow we have discussed seems less an excuse for Lasch's narcissistic identification than do the American examples he perhaps had in mind, and more of an invitation to a nostalgic identification with the virtues exhibited by the famous in either deliberately or inadvertently *resisting* their own celebrity status in certain respects (Julio Iglesias' struggle to speak fluent English; Norman Tebbit's domestic duties).

The genre of the talkshow, therefore, is built on complex tensions between *revealing* and *masking* the *real* person and/or their role; audience admiration of publicly revealed virtues and narcissistic identification with media-glamorised personas; being extraordinary and being revealed as ordinary; role and circumstance; the licence to violate norms or taboos and the conventional inhibitions of society; audience envy and audience empathy; and public significance and superficial publicity.

Talkshows are neither linguistically nor socially univocal. They actively negotiate with their audiences the degree to which their products (celebrities) are allowed to remain 'real' or become 'commodities'. Norman Tebbit, John Cleese and Julio Iglesias are all, in different ways, both revealed *and* concealed through the ways they talk to Michael Aspel and to each other.

Television and Talk in the Nineties

Talkshow interviews reveal some more general features of television as it had evolved in Britain and Australia by the end of the 1980s. First, they underline the verbal, interactive (that is, audience-medium) relationships which have persisted through a decade of increasingly spectacular, 'spatial' cinematic and video representations. Second, they indicate how interviews themselves have become a performance medium — celebrities are judged on their ability to be interviewed, their capacity to be amusing and sincere, ironic yet deep. Third, television reveals itself to be dependent on its audience which remains *present* (in the studio and, metonymically, beyond) and remains an *audience of listeners*, not a group of spectators, and therefore is involved in the tempo and temporal dimensions of the conversational genres in which it participates vicariously.

Finally, one might speculate that the importance of talk, through the survival of the talkshow, consolidates the move towards a domestication or banalisation of the gods or stars of pre-television showbusiness. Or perhaps it reveals the tenacity of a genre of program which is deliberately old-fashioned, not yet 'post'-modern, and which therefore may be in the process of decline or marginalisation as talk which was once trusted as revealing the real behind the mask of celebrity comes itself to be seen as just another mode of signification, an end in itself — a show of talk.

The faint nostalgia of the talkshow format seems to suggest this: talking about one's craft (as actor, sportsman, artist etc.), talking about one's fate, talking as performance and talking about one's 'self' are increasingly unfashionable or unreliable indications of celebrity. What is 'real' and what is role are increasingly difficult to distinguish in the celebrity's behaviour. In the decade of Michael Jackson and Madonna, the assumptions which the audience brought to self-revelatory interviews necessarily changed to meet the newer concept of celebrity itself. Aspel's company may well be taken over by postmodern events in which biographical depth and the exemplary narrative which reveals the celebrity have no place. What makes the talkshow interviews appear old-fashioned is their assumption that conversational question-and-answer exchanges have as their purpose the revelation of an exemplary truth. A Madonna could not be interviewed on this assumption: when truth becomes 'truth' there is no role for the talkshow interviewer and the genre will radically change.

An interview with Michael Aspel

THEO VAN LEEUWEN: *The reason for wanting to talk to you is that we would like your comments on what we have written — what we've got right, what we've got wrong, what we've left out...*

MICHAEL ASPEL: Well, apart from being flattered that you should have thought it worth doing, it is actually a shrewd and accurate assessment. It is just what I think we are trying to do. What you said about the first interview for instance, that was very perceptive, when you said the first interview is most like an interview. That is true, because they are not sharing it with anyone. The conversation hasn't yet started. But ironically the most famous entities in showbiz get the last spot, the top of the bill as it were, to keep the audience waiting, and they get less time because they come on last. It is a funny thing that. Somebody who is quite unknown comes on first and is there the whole way through.

VAN LEEUWEN: *One thing we wrote about was the question of how you select your guests, what qualifications they need to be eligible to come on the show.*

ASPEL: Well, as you said, they either need to be currently of interest, through some film or publication or whatever, or they need to have such a status that they are constantly invited and would be top of the list in any series. And politicians, we haven't done them lately, but they are there not because of their achievements or affiliations, but because of their status. I mean, Thatcher came on and there was not a word of political interview in it. Not a word. It was simply meant to be a portrait of someone in office. And as not many people are aware, a chat show is a much much more difficult thing to do that a political interview. In the political interview you've got every excuse to go straight for the jugular and demand to be told. You have a right to know on behalf of the rest of the nation. But in a chat show you can't attack them the same way, because you have no right to do so. That's what happened when we had to tackle Norman Tebbit about his wife, as you pointed out. You couldn't be too direct and brutal about it, you had to sidle in. People want to know, and there are ways of suggesting something and not implying that you are actually probing or getting too prurient or whatever; there are techniques for getting them to say it without them realising that they have been asked.

The other thing with guests is, film stars, it seems to me they are soon to be replaced by television executives. They can get more press coverage than anybody else. I suppose people will be interested in knowing what Greg Dyke thinks. What I think one gets less and less ready to do is what we did in the old days, well, in the in between years, say in the Parkinson days, when someone would come on stoned and sprawl himself around the set. Nowadays we keep away from that. I have a stick mike now that we are doing the show live, a stick mike on the table, so that if somebody comes on like that I just get up and go into the audience and start talking to them. That's the theory anyway. I haven't done it yet.

And the other thing is who the audiences like to see, certainly the audiences in the studio. I found to my surprise that they like domestic stars best, people they can feel comfortable with. Someone like Dustin Hoffman will come on the show and get an enthusiastic response from the audience, and he will give you a good interview. But when you have someone like David Jason, who is a domestic star, they will become ecstatic. They'll love it, and that's a very important thing. They love someone who is British and who has just failed to win any championship whatsoever. They love it to death.

And regular guests are good of course. You have the luxury of knowing that you don't have to do any homework and can just have an easy chat. But the whole thing is insane, isn't it? How on earth can you expect to have an intimate conversation with somebody when in our case you're in a theatre in the round? People are sitting on all sides and you're expected to talk quietly and reveal your private thoughts.

VAN LEEUWEN: *When your guests start talking to each other, when the show seems to loosen up in a free-flowing conversation, do you still try to control the proceedings or do you allow things to take their own course?*

ASPEL: A bit of both. I always say, when we have a commercial break, to somebody who has just done his or her spot, please don't think that's the end of it, we would like you to stay on and come in whenever you want to, or even ask them questions. But I don't want it to drift away from me completely, or else I would become a cipher there. I have to be able, as you pointed out, to bring them round to what we wanted to talk about, or even just to wrap the thing up with a question of interest to them all. But yes, I like them to come in in their own way, and ideally to abandon questions and let it happen.

VAN LEEUWEN: *You have prepared questions?*

ASPEL: Yes, the thing about prepared questions is, as you may be aware, because I'm sure you do a lot of lecturing, is that the mind sometimes goes bland, so an aide-mémoire is invaluable, even if it is just a word on an autocue, to remind you of an area that you wanted to talk about.

VAN LEEUWEN: *Indeed, I have some in front of me right now.*

ASPEL: You know, the other thing is, in America hosts are almost all entertainers. Although, as you pointed out, I have been a newscaster, I have also been a radio actor, I have been a DJ and I have been a high-class dilettante I suppose you might call it, but the Americans are geographically in the right place and the guests become their chums. They just call in on their way home from work. So they don't need to go in for the biographical stuff and the settling down on 'This is who you are, and this is who I am'. They just say 'Hello George, how is it going? What's happened since I last saw you?' A friend of mine, oddly enough another entertainer, said that he liked my show because I didn't try to take too much of the limelight. He said his ideal chat show host would be somebody you didn't remember seeing afterwards. Well, naturally I couldn't quite go along with that. You have to have some status. Otherwise you're not even the catalyser.

VAN LEEUWEN: *So do you have some sort of theme in mind with each guest?*

ASPEL: Well, there's usually something. We try to find something that is not too well known, some unknown offbeat aspect. Something that will give a ripple of surprise in the audience and flatter the guest that one should have come to know so much more about. You will get one of the old stars and they trot out something you've read a thousand times. But if your research is thorough enough something worth mentioning will pop up, even if it just gets a raised eyebrow and nothing else from them, it will steer us away from the predictable. And humour of course, humour is a most important part of the mix. But you can't prepare for it. I had a producer once who used to slap me on the back as I went out and called anxiously 'Don't for-

	get the one-liners'. Well, you can't go out there with one-liners prepared. You just go out there and see what will happen. You don't have it prepared word for word, or even idea for idea. It hopefully comes out at the moment.
VAN LEEUWEN:	*When the show really works, what is it that makes it work?*
ASPEL:	Well, either they're quite simply much more responsive and forthcoming than you would have dared hope, or they are unexpectedly lively, or even outrageous. We had Sir Robin Day on the show, and I said at first, I don't think this is a good idea, we've had him before, and he doesn't understand at all what we're doing, he will alienate the other guests. But it worked, even if he tried to make a fool of me. I don't mind that, as long as there is a bit of unexpected fun there, something that people say: 'Did you see that?' Even if they misunderstand it, and say 'My God, I felt sorry for you the other night. So-and-so gave you such a hard time.' What they don't realise is that I am delighted that I had a hard time, because it made it worth watching.
VAN LEEUWEN:	*And when it doesn't work?*
ASPEL:	What makes a show not work is that it's simply boring. I had a guest, an American actress, and I had just done what we call a settler, a remark to make them settle in their seat. She seized on some story and it just went on and on, I think nine minutes. Every time I said 'Yes, but . . .' she closed her eyes as if to say 'I'm not finished yet' and went on. It is deadly. It kills the atmosphere and the audience's affection for her. Luckily it was a recorded show, so I was able to edit. But it did ruin the atmosphere.
VAN LEEUWEN:	*What did you think about the last section of our chapter?*

ASPEL: You made the point that the chat show is a dying genre. It's been a very long time dying. It's a very protracted farewell. You make the point about there being more spectacular television and so on, but I think maybe there is more of a place for relaxed programs than there might have been before.

VAN LEEUWEN: *So you're going on with it?*

ASPEL: I shall go on with it for as long as I'm asked, although inevitably things run their course. In the case of the Carson show, it goes beyond the time that people think, have we had enough of it. But I have been doing this for ten years now, although it has been an occasional thing. It's not forty weeks of the year, or every Saturday night, it's just a run of about twelve, fourteen programs. The trouble with that is, you get in some kind of gear, you find you're running quite well, and it's time to say goodbye, see you another time. Not terribly satisfying, and the brickbats make you wonder sometimes if it's worth it. People love to hate it.

VAN LEEUWEN: *You get much critique?*

ASPEL: Yes, the criticism is that chat shows are simply there to plug the book or film. Well, there is of course a great deal of that, but I don't mind that. I am interested in their film; I am interested in their book; so I want to talk about that, and if you can then use that to get on to something else, that's fine. The job has been done. You make the point of the show being the equivalent of a fan magazine, the old style fan magazine, which is quite true, the only difference being that in the old days the stars played the game. They knew what was expected of them and they were prepared to turn up and do it. They spoke admittedly in well-prepared and rehearsed anecdotes, and there wasn't much revelation. But nowadays the stars have got hold of this very useful phrase which their representatives trot out, they say 'He is a very private person'. That means they are absolutely scared shitless of appearing as themselves, whatever that may be, and that is their get out, so it gets a bit desperate at times.

VAN LEEUWEN: *You want them to speak as themselves...*

ASPEL: I always try to, yes, although there may not be anybody there of course. I have only once made the mistake of confusing an actor with the part he played. It was my favourite television series, my favourite character. I perceived a lot of depth in this man and thought he would be a tremendous guest, but although he was a very erudite character who had achieved a great deal in many ways, he was full of incomprehensible Southern Californian stuff, and really, I didn't know what he was talking about. I'll never make that mistake again. But when you talked about non-celebrity humanity, I mean, that is really I think what we are after. The mask slipping, or hoping that it will. I think Madonna would be anathema to this sort of thing. I think if we had Madonna on the show it would be a lot more like a political interview. We would actually have every excuse for being firm and direct and challenging.

VAN LEEUWEN: *You would challenge more...*

ASPEL: Yes, because, like with a politician, you don't know whether there is any kind of truth in there at all, and so you have every right to demand to know what it is. I think so anyway.

6

Interviewing: The First Word Or The Last Word

Curiosity and Power in the Media Interview In the preceding chapters we have shown how interviews are structured by *sequences* of different kinds of question, how revelatory interviews move from questions inviting confession to questions inviting reflection and revelation, and adversarial interviews from questions seeking to check the facts to questions seeking to challenge or even entrap interviewees. At the same time a particular kind of question seems to be central in each interview genre. The chat show, for instance, may have its moments of revelation (Tebbit, who, after a narrow escape from death, learns to be grateful for every new day), but it is only in the revelatory interview that the revelation is the crucial element without which the interview cannot achieve closure and fulfil its purpose of 'finding' meaning for the audience. And although there is an element of challenge in all media interviews, it is only in the adversarial interview that the challenge becomes the one indispensable element without which the interview cannot achieve its aim of 'keeping the bastards honest'.

Such aims are, in many ways, achieved over the interviewees' heads, for they pertain, not to the interaction between interviewer and interviewee, but to the interaction between the media institution and its audience. It is on behalf of the audience that the politician's honesty is put to the test. It is for the audience's benefit that the 'real life' foundations of celebrity are revealed. From this follows the danger of interviews becoming routine and ritualised, techniques for eliciting answers which interviewers already had in mind, regardless of what their interviewees might have wanted to say, or for casting people in predetermined and stereotyped roles, regardless of how they might have wanted to present themselves. Interviews are not merely conversations. They are 'professionalised', institutionalised interactions, performed for a third party — the audience, the viewer, the reader. Interviewers who elicit confessions are not just a listening ear for the interviewee. They are also, even more importantly, functionaries charged with selecting interviewees who, one way or another, will make suitable vehicles for the meanings the program seeks to present to its audience.

Adversarial interviewers do not simply put their interviewees to the test in a true 'person to person' contest. Their role is in the first place that of the 'honest broker', and for this reason they must always show that they suspect (and continue to suspect) their interviewees. The honest and just politician would subvert the genre, and cause the interviewer to fail in his or her task. Similarly, celebrity interviewers do not just chat with their interviewees, they bring into play their notions of the interviewee's symbolic value. They cannot allow the interviewee's sensitivities to stand in the way of these notions becoming the main theme of the interview, even if this does not always take as extreme a form as in this excerpt from *A Current Affair* (Channel 9, Sydney), in which Mike Willesee Jr interviews Madonna:

WILLESEE:	*Sex dominates your thinking — does it still?*
MADONNA:	It's very dominant in most people's lives.
WILLESEE:	*And in yours?*
MADONNA:	Yes . . . mm . . .
WILLESEE:	*How long since you've had sex?*
MADONNA:	Mm . . . I don't think that's relevant. When is the last time you had sex?
WILLESEE:	*I don't think people want to know when I last had sex.*
MADONNA:	Oh, why do they want to know when I last had sex?
WILLESEE:	*Your image is very sex-oriented.*

Interviews are asymmetrical or unequal verbal exchanges. Each of the genres we have examined has its particular inequalities of power, reflected in the verbal and contextual features of the respective interaction. The most obvious evidence of this imbalance of power can be seen in the fact that the interviewer can ask questions of the interviewee, but the interviewee, however powerful a politician or celebrity he or she may be in other contexts, cannot ask similar questions of the professional interviewer. This is the case in the Madonna interview, where Willesee, like Aspel, invokes the audience ('what the people want to know') to justify his 'important' question. Madonna's resistance can be read as hypocrisy or conventionality, but her polite rejoinder is evidence of her lack of power in the situation. The visual representation of the interview confirms the inequality. Willesee, though very much Madonna's junior, sits, in his suit, facing towards the right hand side of the screen, framed in medium long shot. Madonna looks right to left, framed in a much tighter close-up. He is 'given', distant, fixed. She is 'new', closely scrutinised and reactive. The visual semiotics of the interview and the assumptions incorporated into the questions make Madonna the enigma, the object of investigation — she is put to the test, her 'truth' interrogated.

All this points to the power of questioning as a technique for exercising control over meaning. As a form of interaction questioning is, potentially, a social gift, an expression of interest in the other, for the question is an unfinished utterance, in need of completion by the other, a hand reached out to the other. But, as we discussed in Chapter 1, questions can conceal statements and 'unquestionable' assumptions, thus forcing answerers into agreement if they are to be seen to return the gift, to respond in a polite and cooperative manner. Questioning then becomes an exercise in control over meaning, rather than the collaborative production of meaning. It is an instrument of power rather than a way of initiating dialogue. Still, questioning also always retains its potential of reaching out to the other, of creating a bond with the other, and thereby, albeit vicariously, with the audience. Questions can, at least in principle, also be motivated by interest, by a desire to learn, by *curiosity*. This may seem like an obvious point to reach in discussing interviews, for why else would questions be asked by professional media interrogators? That it is not obvious reflects the fact that interviews are so frequently staged as conflictual dramatic performances or unmaskings on behalf of audiences whose fleeting curiosity must be aroused by the interview itself. So the questions arise: under what circumstances is more open curiosity questioning possible in the media? And what form might it take?

For most people the open, curious question is asked only in special circumstances — when we find ourselves in a strange place (a new job, a new city) for instance, and have to come to terms with it, or when we are enchanted by a new person in our lives, so that every detail about him or her interests us — in short, when we are strangers and would like to belong. The circumstances of some of the interviews we discussed in Chapter 2 are not unlike this. An ethnographic inspiration, a desire to learn about the other, took film-makers to places where they had not set foot before (as the lightweight 16 mm sync sound equipment and the fast film stocks needed for these documentary 'field trips' were not then available). They sought out their interviewees in their own territory, but they had no professionalised, institutionalised roles and interview routines to fall back on. At times they questioned clumsily, 'unprofessionally'.

We quoted from Edgar Morin's interview with Marilou, in *Chronique d'un Eté*: although the personal and intimate subject matter of this interview reminds one of the confession, Morin does not restrict himself to eliciting confessions and lending Marilou a sympathetic ear, as would the professional counsellor. He also contradicts and challenges her, asks her impossibly difficult questions about the meaning of life and piles questions on top of each other in a way which makes them, strictly speaking, almost impossible to answer:

> *But what do you mean by reality? Is it a job that interests you? Doing what you like? Or is it to live? A man you love? Not have affairs?*

But Morin's interest in Marilou and his concern for her are always evident, and there is no sense in which he seems to have any ulterior motive in mind, or seeks to make her a positive or negative exemplum. The clumsiness of his questions in the end serves only to diminish his power, to make himself linguistically smaller. Like Marilou, he is perplexed, searching for words and searching for meaning. Caroline Jones made the same point in our interview with her: 'I ask very rambling questions and you know why I do that: it leaves a lot of doors open'.

It is in search of this open 'curiosity' question, and of its conditions, that we now return to the 'experimental' interviews of the *cinéma vérité* and its offshoots which we discussed in Chapter 2. We begin with an excerpt from an interview by two French film-makers.

Marcel: An Interview by Godard

In the late 1970s, Jean-Luc Godard and Anne-Marie Miéville made two twelve-part television series — *Sur et Sous la Communication (Six Fois Deux)* (On and Under Communication [Six Times Two]) in 1976, and *France/Tour/Détour/Deux Enfants* (France/Tour/Detour/Two Children) in 1978. In his many previous films Godard had never used interviews. Now, turning to television, he extended his experiments with cinematic forms to televisual forms, the interview among them. Here is an edited version of one of the 'episodes' of *Six Fois Deux*, the interview with Marcel Raymond,[1] a factory worker who makes 8 mm nature films in his spare time. It takes place in Marcel's workroom. Godard and Miéville (she only asks three of the questions) are not in shot, although Godard's gesticulating hand occasionally intrudes into the frame. Marcel, about sixty years old, grizzled hair *en brosse*, is seen from behind, in an 'overshoulder', as he is splicing film and talking to Godard at the same time. For much of the interview Marcel's slides (flowers, lakes with sunlight reflecting off the rippled water, snow-covered hills glowing pink from the setting sun) are projected on the wall behind him in such a way that Marcel's shadow becomes part of the image and the image is projected on him also. Only towards the end, when Godard asks Marcel what he thought of the interview, does Marcel turn towards camera. The interview is intercut with images of Marcel at work in the factory (many of them frontal and close up) and of him walking through the green hills of the Jura, tripod on his shoulder, like van Gogh with his easel ('*Do you think of your work as being like a painting or like a novel?*' — '*More like a painting*'), or carefully setting up his camera to film a flower. There are also images from Marcel's films (rippling water, pure movement) and the occasional joke (an image of a flower, on its side, with the sound of something falling over). When Marcel tells Godard about his 'Four Seasons' project and his intention to use Vivaldi, the sound of the interview fades down to make place for Vivaldi's music, and towards the end of the film Godard uses Vivaldi again: an image of Marcel walking with his tripod is first accompanied by rough sync sound of Marcel whistling, then, in a sound jumpcut, by the full instrumental version. Our extracts can hardly do justice to his fifty-minute interview in which Godard and Marcel also discuss beauty, solitude, the filmic sequence as an imprisoning 'chain', and the difference between still photography and film: 'with film the water moves . . . it's alive . . . but I have less freedom because I have to choose where I'm going to, like a writer writing a book . . .'

GODARD: *What are you doing with that?*
MARCEL: I'm viewing.
GODARD: *What are you viewing?*
MARCEL: A film made on 1 August 1973.
GODARD: *And this is your workbench here?*
MARCEL: Yes.
GODARD: *When you've finished viewing what are you going to do?*
MARCEL: I'm going to edit.
GODARD: *What does that mean?*
MARCEL: I've got three reels to view on the same subject, all made on the 1 August, and I'm going to remove the bits which aren't up to scratch.
GODARD: *What do you mean by that?*
MARCEL: I'll take out all the frames which aren't properly focused and aren't good enough to project on the screen.
GODARD: *Do you mind if we watch you working?*
MARCEL: Not at all.
GODARD: *Do you think of what you're doing now as work or pleasure?*
MARCEL: No, this is a release from the work I do every day, the daily grind.
GODARD: *And what is your work?*
MARCEL: I'm a watchmaker and I've chosen this marvellous hobby of amateur film-making in Super 8.
GODARD: *What do you mean by amateur, amateur film-making?*

MARCEL: It's like the cinema, but you use cameras which are on sale everywhere.

GODARD: *In what way is this a release from your normal work? What do you do with your hands when you're working?*

MARCEL: I find this hobby a release from my normal work because I'm not doing the sort of close manual work I do in the factory.

GODARD: *Could you explain the difference to us?*

MARCEL: Well, in the factory you have to concentrate very hard on your work and you've always got this glass stuck in your eye. But here the work I'm doing is much simpler and less close because the image is in front of me. I think it's wonderful, I get a great deal out of it.

GODARD: *What did you do then?*

MARCEL: I made a cut.

GODARD: *What did you cut?*

MARCEL: I found a frame which was not up to standard, and I'm going to remove it from the film and stick the ends together again.

GODARD: *It's not very nice for the frame that's eliminated. How do you decide whether it should stay or go?*

MARCEL: It isn't clear. Everything that isn't clear has to be removed.

[...]

GODARD: *What are you looking at so closely now?*

MARCEL: I'm looking at the emulsion on the film, you see the inside part along the top, and the outside along the bottom.

GODARD: *I wonder if you'd mind thinking for a moment about the difference between this and the work you do at the factory, and other people like you too, and to the onlooker it doesn't seem all that different. I saw how you got your eye very close to your work, and your hands were doing very precise things. Have you been a watchmaker for a long time?*

MARCEL:	Yes, for twenty-five years. I married someone who was too. It's a fine trade. And the work is varied.
GODARD:	*But when you lean forward to get close to the film isn't it like when you lean forward to get close . . .*
MARCEL:	Yes, it reminds me of watchmaking. But as your eyes get weaker with age, I have to get closer with this horrible magnifying glass attached to my eye.
GODARD:	*If you weren't paid for your work would you conceive of it as a hobby? If, for example, things were the other way round and you were paid to make films about nature? Would you give up your work?*
MARCEL:	No, not for a moment.
GODARD:	*So then there must be something you like in it, mustn't there?*
MARCEL:	Yes. But it's difficult to explain. I'd like not to do it for money.
GODARD:	*Would you like to make films for money?*
MARCEL:	No, definitely not. In any case, my trade is what provides me with enough money to pursue my splendid hobby. [...]
GODARD:	*We'll let you work for a bit now . . . What's that picture, there on the wall?*
MARCEL:	It's a cutting from a plant which grows on Montendre at the beginning of Spring.
GODARD:	*I thought it was a bird.*
MARCEL:	It does look very like a bird. It's very small and very pretty, and for someone who loves nature it's only one of the subjects one can capture.
GODARD:	*When you wanted to film that plant, what was it that made you want to? To keep it for yourself or to be able to show it to other people?*
MARCEL:	First of all for myself, but also so that I could show it, to children especially. I had planned to do a series of spring subjects just when the buds were bursting, so as to show the spring awakening. And it was designed for use in schools. I've also done a

	series on mushrooms which I've shown to the Mycological Society. And they enjoyed it a great deal.
GODARD:	*And what's that little house there?*
MARCEL:	That little house is my chalet in Montendre. It's called Aurora. There you see it against a winter landscape. It's very pretty and quiet and peaceful. And that's where I'm going to begin the film on the four seasons. I shall have a splendid starting point for my film, and I think it will turn out very well. *[...]*
GODARD:	*There is something I don't really understand: why would you mind if we tried to pay you for your pictures? After all, if someone thinks they're beautiful and wouldn't know how to do it himself, surely it's only right that he should pay the craftsman?*
MARCEL:	It's not exactly that I'd mind, but I don't want to turn my work into a financial proposition. For instance, I gave the Swiss Chamber of Watchmakers a few photographs for a book they were putting together in English. And they automatically paid me, without me asking. It was their usual commission. But I don't do it for money.
GODARD:	*Do you sometimes work on other people's films?*
MARCEL:	Yes. This winter I worked on 450 metres of film for some friends who hadn't the time to do it themselves. I did the titles, viewed it, cut it, edited it, and delivered, more or less for free.
GODARD:	*Is that a good reel you're looking at now?*
MARCEL:	Very good. Not much to be cut.
GODARD:	*Do you just cut when the image is out of focus?*
MARCEL:	Or when the sequence isn't good.
GODARD:	*You don't ever cut because you find the sequence too long or too short?*
MARCEL:	Sometimes if it's too long.
GODARD:	*How do you decide if it's too long?*

MARCEL: If sequences are too long you can make them shorter.
GODARD: *Could you give me an example of when you had to cut because the sequence was too long?*
MARCEL: When I was filming at Zermat I made a sequence on the Alps which was much too long and I had to edit it.
GODARD: *What did it show?*
MARCEL: Too many of the Alps.
GODARD: *Too many mountains?*
MARCEL: Too many mountains. I cut about eight metres of film, which was quite a lot. But I've kept it here and one day I might decide to put it back again.
GODARD: *Have you found this interesting? We've been talking for an hour. Perhaps you've found it a bit boring.*
MARCEL: Not at all, not at all.
GODARD: *What do you think of what we've been doing?*
MARCEL: Splendid.
GODARD: *Were you frightened?*
MARCEL: Not at all.
GODARD: *But earlier on you . . .*
MARCEL: This morning I was a bit. But not now.
GODARD: *We were too, you know.*
MARCEL: No, you were relaxed.
GODARD: *Relaxed?*
MARCEL: Yes
GODARD: *Is there anything you'd like to say a few words about, or anything we ought to have talked about and haven't?*
MARCEL: No, I don't think so. Perhaps I could have explained a bit more about working in nature. Because on Monday you're going to ask me questions at the factory, is that right?
GODARD: *Oh no.*
MARCEL: Somewhere else?
GODARD: *Just a couple of shots.*
MARCEL: On Monday I'll be making gold fountain pens.

GODARD:	*Gold fountain pens. That's what you're working on at the moment, is it?*
MARCEL:	That's it. On Monday I'm going to do the mount specially for you. And the ring will go inside. So then you'll see it in gold and silver.
GODARD:	*So you're working for the novelists as a painter when you're making things to write with?*
MARCEL:	That's it.
GODARD:	*Could you tell us what your name is?*
MARCEL:	Marcel. Marcel Raymond.

THE FIRST AND LAST WORD

In his films, Godard has often used 'self-reflexive' devices, cinematic figures that serve to make the audience aware it is watching a film rather than a slice of real life: actors addressing the camera directly, intertitles commenting on the action, cameras or other items of film equipment visible in the shots. In his interviews, Godard is equally self-reflexive. He does not pretend that the interview is a spontaneous conversation, which could have taken place in the same way if the camera had not been present, but ensures that there is comment on the interview within the interview itself and that the audience will be aware of the interviewee's apprehensions about being interviewed, of his awareness of the inequalities between interviewer and interviewee, of his relief when the interview is over:

GODARD:	*Were you frightened?*
MARCEL:	Not at all.
GODARD:	*But earlier on you . . .*
MARCEL:	This morning I was a bit. But not now.
GODARD:	*We were too, you know.*
MARCEL:	No, you were relaxed.
GODARD:	*Relaxed?*
MARCEL:	Yes.

In the way he addresses his interviewee, Godard tries to diminish the inequality between him and Marcel. He asks him permission to watch ('*Do you mind if we watch you working?*), and his questions are polite, at times almost deferential ('*I wonder if you'd mind thinking for a moment...*') The tone of the interview is lightened by the occasional quirky, Godardian remark ('*It's not very nice for the frame that's eliminated*') and, as the fragment quoted above shows, the role division between interviewer and interviewee is not always strictly adhered to. It is not always Godard who asks the questions and Marcel who gives the answers, and such role reversals do not cause the interview to stagnate, as, for instance, in Mike Willesee Jr's interview with Madonna, but instead form a deliberate and integral part of it.

When 'ordinary' people are interviewed on television, they are usually asked for their attitudes or *opinions*: the television interviewer seeks them out to establish the temperature of public opinion, to find out what the 'people in the street' think about the issue at hand. If not, they are asked for their emotional reactions to situations or their own 'fate' — 'how do/did you feel' being the clichéd form of this enquiry. Godard, on the other hand, is in the first place interested in concrete, material issues, in what Marcel is doing:

What are you doing with that?

What are you looking at so closely now?

These are maximally open questions, questions that invite Marcel to speak freely about what he knows best. The question does not presuppose an answer. It may be difficult for him to answer 'why' questions about values and beliefs he takes for granted and may not be in the habit of formulating. It may be 'difficult to explain', for instance, why he does not want to 'do it for money', but about his skills as a watchmaker and film-maker, and about his love of nature, he can speak articulately and authoritatively. It is this kind of answer which Godard seeks from him. He treats Marcel with respect, as an 'expert' rather than an 'ordinary person'. In 'expert' interviews in the media, interviewers usually play a less intrusive role, and rarely challenge. And although Godard is a film-maker himself, and could therefore be said to know the answers to his questions already, his interest in Marcel's working methods is not just a strategy to make him talk. Godard has always questioned accepted conventions of film-making, challenged the rules of mainstream professional practice and explored other possibilities. His long series of questions about the length of shots, for instance, betrays a genuine curiosity about the thinking of the 'naive' film-maker, from whom there is, perhaps, something new to learn, some simple truth that might have evaded the sophisticated film director.

Just as concrete and open are his questions about the slides projected on the wall and the images from Marcel's films which are, from time to time, intercut with the interview. It is in this way that new lovers look at each other's old photograph albums: no detail about Marcel and his environment is considered insignificant. Everything holds interest. Everything is worth exploring. And the pictures do show the things Marcel holds dearest: his chalet in Montendre, a plant which grows there at the beginning of spring:

> *What's that picture, there on the wall?*

Sometimes Godard uses this kind of question to open up the interview again when it has narrowed down to what, in the end, are perhaps more Godard's preoccupations than Marcel's, as when, immediately after questioning Marcel about the difference between working for money and working for pleasure, he changes the subject abruptly and returns to a more concrete question:

> *Is that a good reel you're looking at now?*

Frequently he asks Marcel to elaborate further, again in the most open way possible:

> *What does that mean?*

> *Could you give an example . . .*

This too shows his interest in Marcel's way of working, his desire to understand, to get to know the other man. And he does not restrict himself to asking Marcel for descriptions of his way of working, he also asks him for *definitions* and *explanations* This kind of question is rare in interviews with 'ordinary people', and usually reserved for the 'expert':

> *What do you mean by amateur, amateur film-making?*
>
> *Could you explain the difference to us?*

Marcel happily takes on this role, switching from first person procedural narrative ('I take out the frame . . .'), to impersonal, generic exposition ('It's like the cinema, but you use cameras which are on sale everywhere'). Here, however, Godard's questions become, at times, less open, narrowing down the possible answers to alternatives determined in advance and informed, perhaps, more by Godard's own agenda than by what Marcel wants to talk about:

> *Do you think of what you're doing now as work or pleasure?*
>
> *When you wanted to film that plant, what was it that made you want to? To keep it for yourself or to be able to show it to other people?*

Marcel accepts the objective conditions of his life, the distinction between paid work and work done for pleasure, for instance, as given without 'understanding' them in the sense in which Godard seeks to understand them. What he wants to talk about is his love of nature, and his passion for film-making. What Godard wants him to do, on the other hand, is to take distance, to 'think for a moment' and to see that it is not his watchmaking itself which differs from his film-making, but the alienating conditions under which it is done. He wants him to realise that these conditions are the conditions of a capitalist economy, and that they apply, not just to Marcel's individual case, but generally, also to 'other people like you'. In this he *does* challenge Marcel, like any other media interviewer, however politely, and albeit through a very concrete image, that of the man 'getting his eyes close to his work' and of his 'hands doing very precise things'. The questions is in fact preceded by a montage of shots of Marcel at work in the factory and at work splicing his films, against a continuous, and apparently synchronous, soundtrack of 'industrial' noise:

> *I wonder if you'd mind thinking for a moment about the difference between this and the work you do at the factory, and other people like you too, and to the onlooker it doesn't seem all that different. I saw how you got your eye very close to your work, and your hand was doing very precise things...*

It is true that Godard refrains from spelling out his message. He does not 'entrap' Marcel. Nor does he elicit from him a telling revelation which will allow the audience dismissively to understand his 'real' personality (as in the other interviews we have analysed in detail). The conclusion of the interview remains tentative, an open question, a suggestion made by the contrasting images of Marcel in the factory and Marcel at work on his films, and of nature and gold fountain pens.

Nevertheless, Godard's unfeigned curiosity and interest in the naive film-maker does make way for a Socratic line of questioning in which Godard uses Marcel to lead his audience to the realisation that Marcel's hobby may provide him with an escape and a release from alienating labour, but it cannot provide him with true emancipation, or with any chance to make an impact upon the world.

Of his and Miéville's interviews Godard has said: 'In our questioning it looks as though we always want to have the last word, whereas it's the first word we want'.[2] In this instance Godard's 'first word' allows Marcel to be revealed in an affectionate portrait of the naive film-maker, which can make us see how articulate 'ordinary people' can be in television interviews if they are addressed in an open way, with respect and genuine interest. But the 'first word' makes way for the 'last word' when Marcel becomes the vehicle for the message Godard wants to get across, an 'example' of the alienated condition of workers in capitalist society.

It is not this message to which we object, but the fact that it estranges us from Marcel, just as we were coming close to him. Is there not a case to be made, a 'last word' to be said, also about the message *Marcel* wants to get across ('especially to children'), the message about people's alienation from nature? And should not a genuine 'ethnographic' enquiry, a genuine attempt to understand the other, allow us to understand it on Marcel's own terms? And is it not the case that, in asking Marcel whether he makes his films for himself or for an audience, Godard prevents Marcel from formulating a third possibility, the one which we would think is Marcel's crucial motivation — love for his subject matter? In saying that it is 'the first word we want', Godard has shown that he is aware of this, and his failure to limit himself to the 'first word' may have much to do with the difficult problems inherent in interviewing, and with the troublesome double nature of the question, as a tool for reaching understanding and as a technique of control.

It is here that Fallacci's interviews differ from those of Godard, and the key lies in her view that the interview is 'like a love affair'. Love is an attraction to the other in all his or her strangeness and difference. It does not need to lead to uncritical adulation, and can involve ambiguity, doubt, conflict, struggle, but it is always predicated on an unconditional interest in the other, in negotiating and resolving difference, in creating a bond that cannot be professionalised. It is always 'amateur', by definition. 'Using' others — objectivating them, turning them into positive or negative example — are antithetical to it. Therefore stereotypes cannot survive it: the macho bullfighter, for instance, becomes a complex individual, insecure about his lack of education yet enthralled by the vastness of the universe and eager to learn about it, naively sexist and violent yet unable to finish the killing his hand began. In Chapter 2 we showed how the deconstruction of stereotypes is realised by breaking the conventions of interviewing, how Fallaci challenges the celebrity, asks the politician to confess and the expert to reveal, and how she is always reactive, allowing the interview to lead her into unexplored and unexpected territory, instead of leading the interviewee gradually into revealing himself as the embodiment of a predetermined symbolic value or coaxing him into agreeing with a predetermined interpretation of events. For these reasons Fallaci is an exceptional interviewer. Despite her vehemence and deeply subjective approach, she is one of those rare people who never have 'pat' answers, and always remain capable of wonder, curiosity, interest — what she calls 'love'.

Her love, of course, is not indiscriminate. She falls for the famous — politicians, movie stars, famous authors, heroes. Godard, the Marxist artist/intellectual, on the other hand, falls for 'ordinary people' and interviews children, factory workers, peasants, housewives, prostitutes, the unemployed. And while Fallaci seeks to learn something about El Cordobes as a person, Godard, so long as he restricts himself to having the 'first word', seeks to learn from Marcel. In so doing, Godard treats him as an 'expert' from whom there is something to learn that might be of interest for his own purposes. Fallaci explores the emotive, Godard the intellectual side of the curiosity question. Between them, we can at least begin to sense something of the contours of this kind of question and something of the conditions or forms of interviewing that might help to bridge the distance that separates the questioner from their subjects.

Power and Publicity

Curiosity from the interviewer presupposes candour from the interviewee. Yet the sheer frequency of media interviews with 'celebrities' has made the latter adept at resisting the intrusive questioning of famous and anonymous interviewers alike. The interview has all too frequently become only a predicably staged confrontation, with dramatic conflict per se its principal aim. Such interviews suit the interests of those media institutions that rely on dramatic novelty which is of little audience interest for its particular content. On the other hand, 'personalities' and others seeking publicity also increasingly seek to control the form and agenda of interviews, to resist the power of the media institutions or to turn it to their own ends of self-promotion. Recent interviews with Madonna reveal some of the balances of power that are being renegotiated in media interviews.

Attempts to interview Madonna in the genres of television talkshows are revealing principally in the negative sense that they show how her constructed persona cannot be penetrated by the usual styles of questioning that we have discussed in earlier chapters. They show how 'curiosity' can become merely a pretext for voyeuristic or moralistic sensationalism.

Madonna's persona (or personae) is built on sexual and personal confession as a tactic for concealing private truths. Her 'life' is not revealed as exemplary, but is deliberately presented as an invitation to libertarian, arbitrary, non-moralistic adventure; her 'credibility' is self-consciously rendered ambiguous as a ploy to encourage media speculation. Against this impenetrable persona are opposed the questions of the curious (in more ways than one) media interviewers.

Not surprisingly, therefore, when Madonna was interviewed in an ostensibly talkshow format by Terry Wogan on English television (BBC-1), the host found the guest so elusive that his questions managed only to invite the star to explain her own stardom. Revelation through an anecdotally chatty conversational interview is not possible with Madonna. As Aspel commented in our interview with him: 'Like with a politician, you don't know whether there is any kind of truth in there at all'. Instead, Madonna became a commentator on her own phenomenon, answering questions about her own sincerity or credibility — questions which made Wogan sound naive and timid. He was unable to seek the 'real' Madonna beyond the public persona except by asking the 'post'-modern star to analyse herself. Madonna was addressed as too different from Wogan, as too bright a star (in the talkshow's terms), to allow her to be revealed as 'like us'. All the interviewer could do was to encourage Madonna to reassert her difference, despite Madonna's apparent frankness. For her, honesty was not of the inadvertent, 'natural', kind that reveals the subjectively true, ordinary person behind the mask (compared with Julio Iglesias on Aspel, above), but of an objective, evaluative kind. Wogan asked questions such as:

How much of [your film] is for real? ... Was there any point [when] you could forget the camera?

What are you trying to achieve on stage?

Is it all done with a sense of humour?

That's the problem, isn't it — people think you mean it most of the time, don't they? Do you mean everything you say?

Would you say that people are frightened of you?

Wogan asked about her 'success', 'power', 'suffering', 'hair colour', her recently released film (*In Bed With Madonna*), her 'regrets' and 'sense of humour'. Madonna was introduced as Cannes (film festival's) 'biggest star', but one of the first questions she was asked was: 'Correct me if I'm wrong ... you're a brunette aren't you?' This was followed up by 'So, has the change in hair colour in any way changed your personality?' Curiosity and candour are clearly a long way from this type of conversation.

Unlike the Aspel interview genre we have discussed, the Wogan interview lacked questions seeking what we called 'confession' and 'display' as well as 'conversational interludes'. It did include reflection — indeed, it was almost entirely centred on reflection. Madonna was repeatedly invited to reflect on herself, but not on her 'life' as an exemplary person, instead on her own star-hood or performance. It is, perhaps, this which makes this interview sound clumsy because the celebrity is explicitly called on to be her own analyst, not merely invited to reveal herself.

Modernism, with its emphasis on what is new and its psychological or subjectivist view of the social world, involved what Georg Simmel saw as cravings for excitement, changing impressions and relationships, and novel information ('the ephemeral, the fugitive and the contingent', in Baudelaire's terms[3]). Social critics such as Christopher Lasch have seen in the individualistic and consumerist values of modern capitalist societies a form of 'cultural narcissism' which is obsessed with appearance, immediate gratification, fame (including celebrity status) and is afraid of death but indifferent to the past.[4] Rapidly changing tastes, fashion and consumerist cravings for novelty in experiences and in relationships these critics interpret as compensations for the tensions of modern life in which traditional oral culture is declining.

The types of interviews analysed in this book — Jones' confessional revelations, Lyneham's adversarial confrontations and Aspel's conversations — all exhibit some features appropriate to what might be briefly characterised as cultural modernism. These include the objectification of the subjective; revelation of the truth of the individual's life as socially exemplary; credibility as a political virtue; the author (interviewer) as star and as the guarantor of truth; a focus on the individual; and the personalisation of history and of the social realm generally. Interviews have become a dominant public form for revealing what might be termed 'deep subjectivity', and they thereby constitute a thoroughly modernist, not merely modern, cultural form. Interviews were intended to reveal the *essence* of the social world through the truth of the individual in the recorded interaction between professional interlocutor and exemplary subject. But by the 1990s they have become increasingly formulaic, intended for publicity, predictable displays of the media's power or of a celebrity's enigma.

Ethics, Interviewing, and the Future

Interviews, as we have said before, are never neutral. They are always conducted from someone's perspective. In mainstream television the perspective is that of a powerful social institution hiding itself behind the mythical 'us' it has constructed for viewers to identify themselves with. In a Godard or a Fallaci interview it is the perspective of the unattached, marginal, and often oppositional artist/intellectual (who, as a member of the left-wing fraction of the white middle class, is of course not quite as unattached as he or she may think) whose work is usually only made available to like minds. Godard's television programs, for instance, were shown on France's second television channel in a late night 'art cinema' slot, rather than on prime time, as Godard, in turning to the mass medium of television, had hoped. Fallaci's interviews were originally published in upmarket magazines. This in no way diminishes their value. It is important that there should exist public spaces for such experiments, and it is worrying that these spaces at present seem to be contracting.

But if curiosity questioning is potentially of vital importance in fragmented and divided societies where people nevertheless have to learn to come to terms with each other, it should not, in the end, be practised only by the small artistic/intellectual élites which the dominant class allows to exist on its margins. Rouch and Morin, in *Chronique d'un Eté*, understood this. Towards the end of their film, they reversed roles, letting their interviewees (a Renault worker, a black African student, a Jewish woman scarred by her past) become interviewers in turn, ethnographers among well-to-do French tourists in St Tropez. They allowed a (limited) reversal of the power relationships which interviews usually express.

The idealised examples we have discussed in this chapter have all been published or broadcast in relatively marginal or minority media. We might hope that the increasingly ossified forms of mainstream media interviews will be given new life and movement by practices developed in contemporary minority media. This may not be a forlorn hope. Interviews, as we now know them, emerged from diverse, marginal sources — from *cinéma vérité* experiments, 1960s 'counter-cultural' new journalism, an emboldened television public affairs sector — and 'took over' some of the social roles of interrogations, confessions and political speech-making. Interviews continue to change.

From the marginal, curious, self-conscious interviews mentioned above, we can perhaps draw some hopeful conclusions. These are ethical (or political) conclusions, and each reflects our hope that, although interviews always involve people engaged in intense interactions within the context of institutionalised power, knowledge and insight will continue to emerge from these conversations.

First, interviews are not only phenomena of the mass media, and interviewing is too important to be restricted to institutionally established interviewers; we might all learn to be more curious about each other, all act at times as the questioner as well as the questioned. To paraphrase Caroline Jones' formulation, we should all sometimes be accompanists, sometimes soloists.

Second, interviews should become more open in the questions which they ask, aiming to learn about the 'otherness', difference and particularity of their subjects so that audiences might learn from the interaction instead of merely being distracted by the rhetorical form of celebrities' verbal jousting.

Third, interviewers need to exhibit good faith in entering into relationships with their interviewees if they hope to encourage genuine communication. That is, interviewers need to ask non-leading questions; to respond to, and follow up, answers; to allow interviewees to reveal their unexpected selves, opinions and values without fear of incredulity, cynicism and 'one-upmanship'.

We might summarise these conclusions by hoping that interviews should be more *amateur* and less *professional* —

technique should not be an end in itself. To learn *about* the other requires one to be reactive, exploring different avenues of questioning instead of reserving certain narrow kinds of prearranged questions for particular classes of people. To learn from an interview, as either interviewer or audience, requires open questions and genuine curiosity.

This is not asking for something radically new, for a utopian reversal of all values. It is merely a plea to keep alive a flame that has always burnt in the potential for the question to be the first, tentative word, the hand reached out. And if, in the few places where experiment and exploration can still take place — in schools and universities, perhaps, or in public radio stations — such attitudes are actively fostered, there is every reason to think that interviewing can once more become an art of the 'first word' rather than a mode of control over meaning in which the professional media star invariably has the last word.

Endnotes

1   QUESTIONS IN SOCIETY

1. S. Harris, paper presented at The Working Conference on Language in Education, Armidale, November 1985.
2. Ibid.
3. M. J. Christie, *Aboriginal Perspectives on Experience and Learning*, Deakin University Press, Geelong 1985, p. 26.
4. E. N. Goody, 'Towards a Theory of Questions', in E. N. Goody (ed.), *Questions and Politeness*, Cambridge University Press, Cambridge 1978, pp. 17 – 43.
5. C. Painter, *Learning the Mother Tongue*, Deakin University Press, Geelong 1985, p. 24.
6. Goody (ed.), *Questions and Politeness*, p. 23.
7. S. Blum-Kulka, 'The Dynamics of Political Interviews', *Text* 3(2), 1983, pp. 131 – 53.
8. C. Warren, *Modern News Reporting*, Harper and Row, New York 1959, p. 191.
9. E. Evans, Radio: — *A Guide to Broadcasting Techniques*, Barrie & Jenkins, London 1977, p. 35.
10. J. Herbert, *Techniques of Radio Journalism*, Edward Arnold, Melbourne 1976, p. 37.

11 S. W. Hyde, *Television and Radio Announcing*, Houghton Mifflin, Boston 1971, p. 222.
12 Evans, *Radio*, p. 35.
13 Goody (ed.), p. 24.
14 J. Huizinga, *Homo Ludens: A Study of Play Elements in Culture*, Tjeenk Willink, Haarlem 1986, Ch. 6.
15 J. Fiske, 'TV Quiz Shows and the Purchase of Cultural Capital', *Australian Journal of Screen Theory*, 13/14, 1983 pp. 5 – 20.
16 M. Foucault, *History of Sexuality*, Vol. 1, Pelican, Harmondsworth 1981, especially pp. 58 – 70.
17 K. V. Kumar, 'Holding the Middle Ground: The BBC, the Public and the Professional Broadcaster', in J. Curran, M Gurevitch and J. Woollacott (eds), *Mass Communication and Society*, Arnold, London 1977, p. 247.

2 A SHORT HISTORY OF THE MODERN MEDIA INTERVIEW

1 Quoted in D. Boorstin, *The Image*, Penguin, Harmondsworth, 1962, p. 27. See also T. van Leeuwen 'Levels of Formality in the Television Interview', *Australian Journal of Screen Theory*, 13/14, 1983, pp. 59 – 69.
2 See G. Boyce, J. Curran and P. Wingate (eds), *Newspaper History: From the Seventeenth Century to the Present*, Constable, London 1978, for detailed history of The British 'popular' press especially pp. 247–64.
3 G. Turnbull, 'Some Notes on the History of the Interview', *Journalism Quarterly*, 13, 1936, pp. 272 – 79.
4 Ibid.
5 Ibid.
6 M. Stephens, *A History of News: From the Drum to the Satellite*, Viking Press, New York 1988 pp. 242 – 43.
7 Ibid., p. 246.
8 Ibid., p. 243.
9 Boyce, *et al* (eds), p. 59.
10 Ibid., p. 60.
11 Quoted in Stephen Koss, *The Rise and Fall of the Political Press in Britain*, Fontana, London 1990, p. 343.
12 E. Barnouw, *A Tower of Babel: A History of Broadcasting in the United States from 1953*, Oxford University Press, New York, 1966, p.168.
13 S. Ewen, *Captains of Consciousness: Advertising and the Social Roots of Consumer Culture*, McGraw-Hill, New York 1976.
14 D. Cardiff, 'The Serious and the Popular: Aspects of the Evolution of Style in the Radio Talk 1928 – 1939', *Media, Culture and Society*, 2, 1989, p. 31.
15 Ibid., p. 32.

16 G. Leitner, 'BBC English and Deutsche Rundfunksprache: A Comparative and Historical Analysis of the Language of the Radio', *International Journal of the Sociology of Language*, 26, 1980, pp. 75 – 100.
17 Cardiff, 'The Serious and the Popular', p. 38.
18 Ibid.
19 L. Johnson, *The Unseen Voice: A Cultural Study of Early Australian Radio*, Routledge, London 1988, p.76.
20 Ibid.
21 Ibid.
22 K. Inglis, *This is the ABC: The Australian Broadcasting Commission, 1932 – 1983*, Melbourne University Press, Melbourne 1983, Ch. 5.
23 A. Ellis, *The Documentary Idea: A Critical History of English Language Documentary Film and Video*, Prentice-Hall, Englewood Cliffs 1989, p. 118.
24 T. Wolfe, 'The New Journalism', in T. Wolfe and E. W. Johnson (eds) *The New Journalism, with an Anthology*, Picador, London 1975, p. 66.
25 Ibid., pp. 66 – 67.
26 Ibid., p. 28.
27 Hunter S. Thompson, *The Great Shark Hunt: Strange Tales from a Strange Time*, Picador, London 1979, p. 599.
28 Ibid.
29 O. Fallaci, *The Egoists*, Tempo Books, New York 1969, p. viii.
30 Ibid., pp. ix – x.
31 Ibid., pp. 172 – 85.
32 S. Arico, 'Breaking the Ice: An In-depth Look at Oriana Fallaci's Interview Techniques', *Journalism Quarterly*, 63(3), 1986, p. 590.
33 It is notable that following the rise of 'new' journalism and the development of well–defined genres of television interview, the interviewer has become the author of his/her 'work': Hunter S. Thompson, Oriana Fallachi or David Frost gave their names to interviews with celebrities and the powerful as the interview became an important, recognisable media form. Instead of a 'television interview' or a 'political interview', the media came to speak of a 'David Frost interview' — the named interview is today the norm — for example, a Caroline Jones Interview; a Paul Lyneham Interview; or Carrie Fisher's Madonna Interview in *Rolling Stone*. (See later chapters in this book for discussion of these.)
34 D. Vaughan, *Television Documentary Usage*, British Film Institute, London 1976, p. 14.

3 CAROLINE JONES AND THE SEARCH FOR MEANING

1 C. Jones, *The Search For Meaning*, Vol. I, ABC/Collins, Sydney 1989, pp. 205 – 6.
2 Ibid., p. 208.

3   Ibid., p. 3.
4   Ibid., p. ix.
5   Ibid., p. xii. Jones' second volume of interviews (1990) and third (1992) are also published by ABC/Collins.
6   This concept of genre derives from work by Hasan, Halliday and Hasan, Martin, Rothery and others. See: M.A.K. Halliday and R. Hasan, *Language, Context and Text: Aspects of Language in a Social-Semiotic Perspective*, Deakin University Press, Geelong 1985; R. Hasan, 'Text in the Systemic–Functional Model', in W. Dressler (ed.), *Current Trends in Textlinguistics*, Walter de Gruyter, Berlin 1977; J. Martin, *English Text: System and Structure*, Benjamins, Amsterdam 1991; J. Rothery, 'The Development of Genres — Primary to Junior Secondary School', in *Children Writing: Studyguide*, Deakin University Press, Geelong 1984.
7   Jones, *The Search For Meaning*, Vol. I, p. 7.
8   M. A. K. Halliday, *Introduction to Functional Grammar*, Edward Arnold, London 1985, p. 130.
9   Ibid., pp. 106–11.
10 E. Evans, *Radio: A Guide to Broadcasting Techniques*, Barrie & Jenkins, London 1977, p. 38.
11 R. Nelson-Jones, *The Theory and Practice of Counselling Psychology*, Holt, Rinehart and Winston, New York 1982, p. 31.
12 See, for example, G. Collins, *Helping People Grow*, Vision House, Santa Anna, CA., 1980.
13 P. C. Vitz, *Psychology as Religion: The Cult of Self-Worship*, Eerdmans, Grand Rapids 1977, pp. 7, 91.
14 Collins, *Helping People Grow*, p. 323.
15 Vitz, *Psychology as Religion*, pp. 93, 95.
16 A. C. Zijderveld, *The Abstract Society*, Penguin, Harmondsworth 1974, p. 97.
17 Ibid., p. 96.
18 Ibid.
19 Ibid., pp. 101 – 2.
20 Ibid., p. 13.

4   POLITICAL INTERVIEWS

1   S. Duganis (producer), *Television and Number Ten, Part 1: In the Torture Chamber*, BBC Television documentary, 1986.
2   F. Wheen, *Television: A History*, Century Publications, London 1985, p. 72.
3   Ibid.
4   P. Beilby (ed.), *Australian TV: The First 25 Years*, Thomas Nelson, Melbourne 1981, p. 100.
5   S. Hall, *Turning On, Turning Off: Australian Television in the Eighties*, Cassell Australia, Sydney 1981, p. 20.
6   K. Inglis, *This is the ABC: The Australian Broadcasting Commission 1932–1983*, Melbourne University Press, Melbourne 1983, p. 269.

7   Ibid., p. 270.
8   T. H. White, *The Making of the President 1960*, quoted in E. Barnouw, *The Image Empire — A History of Broadcasting in the United States from 1953*, Oxford University Press, New York 1970, p. 169.
9   Duganis, *Television and Number Ten*, Part 1.
10   Ibid.
11   Quoted in K. Inglis, *This is the ABC*, p. 271.
12   K. Kumar, 'Holding the Middle Ground: The BBC, the Public and the Professional Broadcaster', in J. Curran, M. Gurevitch and J. Woollacott (eds), *Mass Communication and Society*, Edward Arnold, London 1977, p. 247.
13   P. Bell, K. Boehringer and S. Crofts, *Programmed Politics: A Study of Australian Television*, Sable Press, Sydney 1982, pp. 141 – 47.
14   D. Parker, *The Courtesans: The Press Gallery in the Hawke Era*, Allen and Unwin, Sydney 1991, Ch. 1.
15   M. A. K. Halliday and R. Hasan, *Language, Context and Text: Aspects of Language in a Social-Semiotic Perspective*, Deakin University Press, Geelong 1985.
16   See, for an elaboration of this method, J. Martin, *English Text: System and Structure*, Benjamins, Amsterdam 1991.
17   W. Labov and D. Fanshell, *Therapeutic Discourse: Psychotherapy as Conversation*, Academic Press, New York 1977, p. 102.
18   Ibid., p. 97.
19   See ibid., p. 91.
20   R. Kitts, personal communication. See Kitts' MA thesis, 'Make Believe', School of English and Linguistics, Macquarie University 1993.
21   E. Hall, *The Hidden Dimension*, Doubleday, New York 1966.
22   Ibid., pp. 100 – 20.
23   T. van Leeuwen, 'Proxemics of the Television Interview', *Australian Journal of Screen Theory*, 17/18, 1986, pp. 125 – 41.
24   M. A. K. Halliday, *An Introduction to Functional Grammar*, Edward Arnold, London 1985, discusses 'given–new' information structures. See also Kress and van Leeuwen, below.
25   G. Kress and T. van Leeuwen, *Reading Images*, Deakin University Press, Geelong 1990, pp. 102 – 15.
26   M. Joos, *The Five Clocks*, Harcourt, Brace & World, New York 1967.
27   C. Poynton, *Language and Gender: Making the Difference*, Deakin University Press, Geelong 1985.
28   D. Morris, *Manwatching: A Field Guide to Human Behaviour*, Jonathan Cape, London 1977, p. 259.
29   See, for example, Bell *et al.*, *Programmed Politics*, 1982.
30   Parker, *The Courtesans*.
31   D. Held, *Models of Democracy*, Polity Press, London 1989, p. 48.

32 J. Curran, 'Communication, Power and Social Order', in M. Gurevitch, T. Bennett, J. Curran and J. Woollacott (eds) *Culture, Society and the Media*, Methuen, London 1982, pp. 202 – 35.
33 Ibid., p. 215.

5 ASPEL AND CO.

1 E. Barnouw, *The Image Empire: A History of Broadcasting in the United States from 1953*, Oxford University Press, New York 1970, p. 104.
2 Ibid., p. 93.
3 Ibid.
4 J. Galtung and M. Ruge, 'Structuring and Selecting News', in S. Cohen and J. Young (eds) The *Manufacture of News: Deviance, Social Problems and the Mass Media*, Constable, London 1973, pp. 62 – 73.
5 R. Dyer, *Light Entertainment*, British Film Institute, London 1973, p. 30.
6 R. Dyer, *Stars*, British Film Institute, London 1979, p. 24.
7 Ibid., p. 25.
8 R. Dyer, *Heavenly Bodies: Filmstars and Society*, British Film Institute/Macmillan, London 1987, p. 11.
9 Dyer, *Light Entertainment*, pp. 9 – 12.
10 M. Kundera, *Immortality*, Faber and Faber, London 1991, p.138.
11 W. Benjamin, *Illuminations*, Fontana, London 1977, p. 86.
12 C. Lasch, *The Culture of Narcissism*, Abacus, New York 1980, p. 59.
13 Ibid.

6 INTERVIEWING: THE FIRST WORD OR THE LAST WORD?

1 We have used the English translation of Tom Milne and Gilbert Adair, by permission of the British Film Institute.
2 Quoted in C. Penley, *The Future of an Illusion: Film Feminism and Psychoanalysis*, Routledge, London, Ch. 6.
3 Beaudelaire is quoted in D. Fisby, 'Georg Simmel: First Sociologist of Modernity', *Theory, Culture and Society*, 2(3), 1985, pp. 49 – 66. See also, for discussion of modernism as a culture 'fragmented', D. Fisby, *Fragments of Modernity*, Cambridge 1985.
4 C. Lasch, *The Culture of Narcissism*, Abacus, New York 1980, p. xiii–xviii.

Name Index

Adams, Phillip 116
Ali, Mohammed 44-45
Apted, Michael 42
Arico, S.A. 54-55
Arnold, Mathew 34
Askin, Robert 133
Aspel, Michael 178-189, 191-221, 224, 240-242
Attlee, Clement 129

Balzac, Honoré 43
Baudelaire 242
Bell, Philip 170-177
Benitez, Manuel, *see* El Cordobes 47-59, 239
Benjamin, Walter 205
Bennett, James Gordon 29-30, 31, 32, 37
Blackman, Barbara 97
Bosanquet, Reginald 132
Bozic, Magda 123

Cairnes, Margot 60-104, 112, 116
Caldicott, Helen (Dr) 116

Cardiff, David 35-36
Carleton, Richard 132, 138-139, 159, 171
Carlson, Oliver 31
Carson, Johnny 188
Catmach, Jemmy 29
Charlton, Michael 132
Chataway, Christopher 132
Christie, M.J. 4
Churchill, Winston 130
Cleese, John 73, 178-187, 192, 194, 202, 206-208, 213
Cohen, Ian 122
Colby, William 55
Collins, G.R. 112
Connery, Sean 49
Curran, James 168-169

Daly, Morton 192
Day, Robin 131-132, 158, 219
Dickens, Charles 33, 43
Didion, Joan 43, 46
Douglas-Hume, Alec 133, 135, 158
Dyer, Richard 193-194

NAME INDEX

Dyke, Greg 216

Eden, Anthony 129
Einfield, Marcus 116
Einfield, Sid 24-25
El Cordobes (Manuel Benitez) 47-59, 239
Ellis, A. 40
Evans, Elwyn 11, 106

Fallaci, Oriana 47-56, 238-239, 243
Fanshell, D. 150, 152
Fellini, Federico 48
Fish, Michael 178, 198
Fiske, John 15
Foot, Michael 130, 135
Foucault, Michel 17
Freeman, John 159
Freud, Sigmund 112
Frost, David 134, 188

Gawler, Ian 123
Garland, Judy 193
Ghandi, Indira 54
Gibson, Mike 144-145
Gielgud, Maina 107
Godard, Jean-Luc 227-239, 243
Goddard, Trish 124
Goebbels, Joseph 36
Goody, E.N. 8, 13
Greeley, Horace 30

Hale, Clive 133
Hall, Edmund 161
Hall, Steele 133
Halliday, M.A.K. 99, 143
Harris, S. 4
Hasan, Ruquaia 143
Hawke, Bob 144-145, 158, 166
Held, David 167-168
Hewson, John (Dr) 125, 156, 163
Hilton, John 35-36
Hodge, Patricia 189
Hoffman, Dustin 216
Hollowes, Fred 122
Holt, Harold 133
Howard, John 126, 141, 155
Huizinga, Johan 14

Iglesias, Julio 178, 179, 198, 213, 241

Jackson, Michael 214
Jason, David 216
Johnson, Robert (Dr) 75

Jones, Caroline 43, 60-123, 144, 148, 152, 196-197, 199, 206, 211, 226, 242, 247

Keating, Paul 125, 128-129, 146-149
Kennedy, John 133
Kennedy, Ludovic 132
Kennedy, Robert 48
Kinnock, Neil 178, 198
Kissinger, Henry 54
Kumar, Krishan 20, 134, 136
Kundera, Milan 202-203

Labov, W. 150, 152
Lasch, Christopher 212, 242
Lindsay, Norman 84
Littlemore, Stuart 140
Lunghi, Cheri 195
Lyneham, Paul 124-177, 208

MacArthur, Douglas 62
McBride, Mary Margaret 188
McFadden, Bernarr 35
Macmillan, Harold 131, 133, 158
Maddern, Justice 128
Madonna 214, 221, 224-225, 240-241
Mailer, Norman 43, 48
Malinowski, B. 8
Marker, Chris 39
Marten, Maria 29
Martin, Allan 133
Maslow, Abraham 109
Mauss, M. 8
Maysles brothers 39
Menzies, Robert 133
Miéville, Anne-Marie 227, 237
Millikan, David 90
Monroe, Marilyn 193
Moore, Dudley 194
Morin, Edgar 39-40, 194, 226, 243

Nasser, President 131
Nelson-Jones, R. 109
Nguyen Van Thieu, General 55
Nixon, Richard 133

Parker, Derek 137, 167-168
Parkinson, Michael 188-189
Peach, Bill 132
Peacock, Andrew 124-177, 208
Pennebaker, Donn 39
Poynton, Cate 164

Raymond, Marcel 227-238

NAME INDEX

Rivkin, Rene 107, 117
Robeson, Paul 193
Rogers, Carl 109
Roosevelt, Franklin 36
Roosevelt, Mrs (E) 188
Rouch, Jean 39-40, 42, 56, 243

Sanders, Bob 189
Sanders, Kevin 132
Selassie, Haile (Emperor) 188
Shearer, Moira 132
Simmel, Georg 242
Skynner, Robin 73
Spinks, Leon 45
Stead, W.T. 34
Stephens, Mitchell 32-33
Stone, Gerald 132

Tebbit, Margaret 179, 201-202
Tebbit, Norman 178-189, 192, 198-210, 212-213, 216, 222
Thatcher, Margaret 184-185, 207-209, 215
Thompson, Hunter S. 43-47
Totaro, Paolo 110

Uren, Tom 122
Ustinov, Peter 187

Van Buren, Martin 29, 30
Van Leeuwen, Theo 116-123, 215-221
Vaughan, Dai 57-58
Vautier, Dorothy 37
Vitz, P.C. 112-113
Vizard, Steve 158, 192
Walden, Brian 135
Wallace, Mike 55
Walsh, Mike 159
Weber, Max 114
Wendt, Jana 139, 151-156, 158
Wheen, F. 131-132
Whitlam, Gough 133
Wilcox, Desmond 135
Willesee, Mike 132
Willesee, Mike, Jnr 224, 234
Wilson, Harold 133, 135, 166
Wiseman, Fred 39
Wogan, Terry 240-241
Wolfe, Tom 43-44, 46, 47

Young, Brigham 30
Younger, George 185

Zijderveld, A.C. 114-116
Zola, Emile 32

Subject Index

ABC 10, 38, 60,89–90, 107, 124, 130–132, 136, 140, 172, 175, 189
abstraction 98
accusation (question) 206–7, *see also* challenges
advance planning 10–13, 37, 120–121
adversarial genre 91, 129, 136–170, 205, 222
(The) Ambassadors (Holbein) 158
Aspel and Co 178–221
audience 12–13, 111, 197, 203, 209, 213, 222, 237, 245
Australian Film and Television School 140
Australian Labor Government (1983–) 167

BBC 11, 35–37, 130–132, 169, 240
British Stamp Abolition Committee 33
broadsheets (19th Century) 29

camerawork (TV studio) 160–164, 224–225
CBS 54
celebrity/ies 55, 187, 189–197 *passim*,
211–214, 223, 239, 241, 244–245
challenge(s) (speech acts) 55, 100, 108, 137, 141, 143, 150, 152–155, 200–201, 205–208, 222–223, 226, 235–236
Channel 7 132
Channel 9 132, 151–152
Channel 10 *Actionline* 24–26
charisma 114–116
chat shows, *see* talkshows
checking questions 137, 140–141, 143, 150,153, 200–201, 222
Chronique d'un été (1961) 39–42, 43, 226, 243
cinema 26, 39–43, 56–57, 161–170 *passim*, 174, 188, 194, 213, 225–226, 233, 235–237
cinema vérité 39–43, 56–57, 226, 244
City Extra 89
closure 101, 105, 108, 222
coda (to interview) 208–210
commercial media 21, 131
Compass 107
conceptual fusion 101–102

SUBJECT INDEX

confession(s) 3, 15–18, 20, 29, 38, 40, 55, 89–91, 95–103 *passim*, 108, 200–203, 208, 210, 211, 214, 222, 239, 243–245
connecting topics 102–103
content questions, *see* Wh– questions
conversation 56, 108, 146, 154, 156, 189, 193, 197–210 *passim*, 214–217; interview as 197–210 *passim*, 214, 217, 225, 233, 241, 244; *see also* talkshows, dialogue
corporatism 167–170 *passim*
counselling interviews 15, 17, 40, 92, 109–116 *passim*; Christian 112–115, *see also* confessions
cultural differences 3–16 *passim*, sub-cultures 46–47
curiosity (questions) 207–208, 222, 225–226, 239, 240–241, 243–4, *see also* Wh– questions
(A) Current Affair 132, 151–152, 224–225
current affairs *see* news

demands 7–8
devil's advocate 152–157 *passim*, 170, *see also* honest broker
dialogue(s) 21–22, 37, 94, 225
direct cinema, *see documentary*
distance (social) 161–164
display (of talent) 205, 208–210, 241
documentary 39–59, 92
ethnographic 42, 44, 225–226, 238, 243; scenarios 44, 47–59 *passim;* mannerism in 57–59

editing 23, 25–26, 54, 119–120, 161–170 *passim*, 174, 196, 224, 227–234 *passim*, 236
education 3–8, 13–15
elites 168
entertainment value 190, 191–193, 195–196, 198–199
entrapment 137, 141–143, 150, 155–157, 222, 237
ethnography 42, 44, 225–226, 238, 243
ethologisto 165
extensions 101, 204

face–to–face 159
feedback 106–107
field (of text) 19, 93, 211
films noirs 46
formality 11–13, 46
Forty–Five Minutes in Hollywood 188
Four Corners 89, 132

France/Tour Détour/Doux Enfants 227

generalisation 98–99
genre, documentary 35–59 *passim*; interview 91–108 *passim*, 113, 143–166 *passim*, 187–221 *passim*, 222–223; speech 37
gifts, questions as 8–9, 12–13
given–new structure 163, 224
gnosticism 115
gossip 207–208, 210–211
greeting 137–139, 143, 198–199, 209

Heavenly Bodies 193
Hollywood Star Theatre 188
honest broker 20–21, 23, 223
how – questions 103–104
humanism 110

Immortality 202
In Bed With Madonna 241
information questions 200, 204
interrogations 18–20, 92, 100, 200, 244
intertextuality 108–116
interviewer
honest broker role 20–23, 129–177; 'subjective' role, 39–59; 'objective' role 39–59; control by 8–13, 101–108, 110, 116–124, 130–166, 196, 201–210
interpellations 20–21
intonation 154
introductions, *see* greeting
invitation(s) (speech acts) 55, 97–101, 108
ITN 130–131

(Le) Joli Mai 39

Kevin Sanders Reports 132

lexical cohesion (chain) analysis 147–148

(The) Manageress 195
Meet the Press 132
(The) Mike Walsh Show 159
modernism 242–243
modality 105–106, 154
montage 237
(The) Moonstone (1868) 33
Mormon Church 30
moves (linguistic), *see* stages (of interviews)

narcissism (culture of) 212–213
Nationwide 136
new journalism (19th Century) 34

SUBJECT INDEX

new journalism (20th Century) 43–58 *passim*; 'gonzo' 44; scenes/scenarios 49, 58
New York Herald 29–31
New York Sun 31
New York Tribune 30
news 1, 13, 38–59 *passim*, 124–177, 196, 244
news value(s) 190–193, 195, 196
nominalisation 97–98, 108
non–verbal aspects of interviews 105–108, 110, 158, 160–166

objectivation 99, 108
open questions, *see* Wh– questions
opinion (questions) 137, 139–140, 143, 149, 234–235

Panorama 133
parliament 130–131, 167–170 *passim*
parties of non partisanship 168–170, 176
pastoral interview, *see* counselling interview
People 189
polar questions 149–150, 200
political interviews 1, 3, 13, 55, 58, 124–177, 189, 207, 208–10, 223
politics/politicians 32, 55, 58, 124–177 *passim*, 199–220 *passim*, 223–224, 239, 240, 244
postmodern(ism) 96, 214, 241
power (of interviewer) 8–13, 17–27, 101–108 *passim*, 224–226, 233
presidential election (US) 133
press gallery (Canberra) 137, 167–170 *passim*, 176
Profile of the 'Stars' 188
proxemics 161
psychiatric interview, *see* counselling interviews
psychotherapy, *see* counselling interviews

questions – types and functions of 1–27, 56, 91–108 *passim*, 145–158 *passim*, 197–210 *passim*
question–and–answer exchanges, *see* dialogue, questions, speech acts, stages
quiz shows 16

radical journalism (19th Century) 33–34
radio
    chatshows on 188; Europe 35–36; history of 35–38; interviews on, 60–124; 'voice' of 107–108, 121
reflection 92, 95, 97–101, 108, 149, 205, 209–210, 222, 243

release 137, 142–143, 173, *see also* 'coda'
revelation(s), *see* confession(s)
revelatory genre 91–97, 108, 149, 189, 204, 222, 237, 240

scenario 47–56 *passim*, 58
(The) Search for Meaning 43, 60–124, 197
self–actualisation 109–113 *passim*
self–reflexive cinema 233
settings 157–160
7:30 Report 124–129, 136, 156, 162
star(s), *see* celebrity value
Sixty Minutes 54–55, 171
social contexts (of interviews) 13–27
Socratic questioning 22, 150, 155–157, 237
Soviet Union 20
spectacle, TV as 157–160 *passim*, 212–213
speech acts 55, 92–108 *passim*, 137–145 *passim*, 197–210 *passim*
stages (of interviews) 93–108, 137–145 *passim*, 197–210 *passim*, 222
stars, *see* celebrity/ies
statement(s) 7–8, 104, 129, 141,150, 153–155, 225
Sur et Sous la Communication (Six Fois Deux) 227–239
symbolic value 190, 193–198 *passim*, 212, 223, 239

talkshows 178–221, 240
tape–recorders 39–40, 56
television 9–11, 15, 22–26, 121, 124–170 *passim*; documentary usage 55–59
testimony 56, 93, 95–96, 108
tests 13–15
That Was the Week that Was 134
theatre (settings) 159–
therapeutic interviews, *see* counselling interviews
35–Up 42–43
This Day Tonight 89, 132–133, 136, 166
This Week 133
Tonight Live with Steve Vizard 158
28–Up 42–43
21–Up 42–43
2BL 89

vox pops 36

Weekend World 135
wh– questions 6–8, 99–100, 148–149, 200, 234
why– questions 16, 234
Yeshiva 21